AN INSIDE IN

CW01472336

Perspectives of Autism and Bipolar Disorder

ALEXANDRA WEST

outskirts
press

DEDICATION

To my therapist, Tracey Rogers, PhD, thank you for your wisdom, patience and numerous unselfish acts of kindness and for always treating me with humanity and respect, regardless of my frame of mind. If not for your abounding care, guidance, and gentle pushes to get me out of my comfort zone, I would not have made peace with my mind and come out the other side. For this, I will be eternally grateful.

I also want to thank Beth Keller, PsyD, who was the director of the Partial Hospital Program in Boston where I was a patient several times. Beth was the "heavy" when I was unable to make good decisions for myself, and she let me borrow her sanity when mine was on cracked ice.

Most importantly, thank you to my parents for never, ever giving up on me, even when the educational and mental health systems did. No matter how severe my disabilities were, you refused to believe that my prognosis was "grave" and always said that I could succeed if I just put my mind to it.

And finally, to all those who came before me with their battles and all those who have yet to come, may my journey pave the way to make your own path gentler and kinder.

"Life is like a camera.
Just focus on what's important and capture the good times,
develop from the negatives and if things just don't work out,
take another shot."

- Ziad K. Abdelnour

TABLE OF CONTENTS

PROLOGUE

DURING THE COURSE of my life, I have gone on an unforgettable journey that wove in and out of a developmental disability called autism spectrum disorder (ASD) and a psychiatric illness called bipolar disorder with psychosis. I'm not like other people. I know that. But I also have an unquenchable thirst for understanding what makes me so different. I strive to understand what it's like to be "normal"—whatever that means.

So, at forty-nine years old, I decided to finish a manuscript that I started in my early twenties. My hope is that, by completing this book, others may benefit from my experiences. I also wanted to write this book because, as far as I know, there is no other memoir that chronicles the life of someone with both autism and bipolar disorder. When I was crawling out of what life handed me, I would have loved to have a book like this to serve as a guide.

My naturally obsessive nature, coupled with a relentless desire to understand why I am the way I am, has given me twenty-four years' worth of journals filled with copious notes detailing my experiences and perceptions. When writing this book, I relied heavily on these journals. I also went back and reviewed (sometimes on microfiche) all of my educational and psychiatric records. It is clear from my records that I exhibited autistic symptoms at least as early as kindergarten (I have no records from before that), and my first bipolar symptoms appeared around age ten (though I wasn't officially diagnosed until age nineteen). I also tracked down old therapists, psychiatric nurses, and former fellow-patients to gather maximum data. I was in my early twenties when I wrote the first draft of this book and am thankful that all of the institutions still had my records. Now, almost thirty years later, due to the passage of time, many of these records have been purged, but I still have the information from my first draft. I have done my best to tie all of this together to create a comprehensive narrative.

When I was growing up, the adults around me taught me various social skills and societal norms. I studiously memorized these, but to effectively apply these skills and norms, one must also understand the *intention* behind them. Understanding intention is gained through inference, an ability that, for me, was quite rocky. As part of my developmental disability, I had a very shaky "Theory of Mind," also known as "perspective-taking," which is a complex and sophisticated understanding of how to attribute mental states and emotions to other people and consequently alter one's behavior. For example, I may have exciting news to tell my friend, but if I arrive at her house and she is crying, I can now *infer* that something is upsetting her and that I need to put my own agenda on hold and take care of her. Growing up, I had a very poor grasp of inferential thinking. Fortunately, I learned this skill in my twenties. It took about three years of intense lessons from talented professionals to learn how to do this and another seven to solidify my proficiency. My Theory of Mind is also impaired when I'm manic or psychotic because in those moments, my agenda is the only one that matters and I'm unable to access the learned rules from my autism training. When manic, my thoughts dance and race so quickly that there is no room to pause and take a pulse on the situation.

Autism Spectrum Disorders (ASD) used to be defined as three distinct disorders of varying degrees of disability: autism, pervasive developmental disorder – not otherwise specified, and Asperger's syndrome. In 2015, they were combined into one category. ASD involves missing various social skills, including an impaired ability to read non-verbal cues and understand what others are thinking and feeling. If you lack these social skills, it makes interacting with people challenging and undesirable. All people with ASD have this in common; the spectrum in the name only refers to the degree to which it impacts them.

According to the National Institute of Health, approximately forty percent of people with ASD also have co-occurring anxiety disorders. Most people with ASD also tend to have "funky" sensory systems, meaning they are either ultra-sensitive or under-sensitive to stimuli. For example, brushing up against a person may feel like a slap for one person with ASD, whereas for another might not even notice the touch.

Language development also ranges from people who are non-verbal to those who are eloquent speakers. The primary issue with language for all people with ASD is pragmatics, or social language. Pragmatics is, in essence, everything relating to communication except for the literal words themselves. It involves the meaning and context of the spoken word. Depending upon a person's degree of ASD, they may lack the ability to read nonverbal cues or take turns in a conversation.

The last primary symptom of autism is perseverations, which are obsessions with specific limited topics, items, or activities. This symptom generally impacts most people on the autism spectrum; again, it's the *degree* that influences the person's life. Some people are all-consumed by their perseverations, whereas others have strong hobbies, but can maintain a conversation without defaulting to their preservative interest(s). For example, I know a young boy with autism who is obsessed with the show *The Office*. He spends most of his free time watching it on his phone and has very little interest in other subjects. His method of engaging with others is to start conversations or interject into existing ones by using one-liners from the show. While this was tolerable with his family, his peers soon grew tired of it and began to shun him. As for me, I've always had a few obsessive interests that have shifted over time, often for no rhyme or reason, and this is still true today. I can temporarily suspend my perseverations to engage with others by mentally hitting the *Pause* button on my thoughts and forcing myself to attend to what others are saying. But once the conversation is over, I generally always return to my obsessions. And this all happens very consciously.

The above autism symptoms are all present in me, though now to a milder and quieter degree. Unlike when I was younger, my autism may go undetected unless I'm really pushed out of my comfort zone.

Autism is considered a spectrum disorder because no two people present with the same constellation of symptoms. The spectrum is quite broad. Just because someone with autism is severely impacted in one area (say, social skills), it does not necessarily mean that they are severely affected in another area (say, language). There is also not a clear "formula" for outcomes. I've witnessed people who are considered "lower functioning" in early childhood grow out of their symptoms, and conversely, I've seen people who are "higher functioning" deteriorate in adolescences.

For boys, ASD can generally be detected between the ages of two and seven. However, it's not unheard of for them to be diagnosed in their teens. On the other hand, girls, especially less-severely impacted girls, tend to fly under the diagnostic radar for years. This is because girls with ASD often exhibit less-severe symptoms and display more social desire than boys. They often mask their symptoms by having "neurologically typical" interests, such as stuffed animals or collecting necklaces. When compared to boys with ASD, they may have fewer or less-dramatic public tantrums and make better eye contact. Again, this is an overgeneralization. As the saying goes, "If you've met one person with autism, you've met one person with autism." Yet it is a fact that girls are often diagnosed later than boys and are frequently misdiagnosed with depression, low self-esteem, or ADHD.

I am considered "higher functioning," which, prior to the 2015 reorganization of the three autism disorders into ASD, was called Asperger's syndrome. Asperger's wasn't even a diagnosis until 1994, though, and when I dug through my elementary-school files from the mid-1970s, I found what looked like a consultation note describing me as "withdrawn and difficult." The report concluded that I had "Childhood schizophrenia with autistic aloneness." Given the lack of diagnostic criteria at the time, I assume that working diagnosis was the best they could do. On my diagnostic journey, in 1995 I was eventually diagnosed with Asperger's syndrome.

I don't have difficulty speaking. My intelligence is intact, and currently with extensive teaching, my social skills enable me to "pass" for "normal." In general, I don't require much social interaction. At work, I have daily meetings that involve conversation, and I sometimes leave my office door ajar so that I feel I'm part of the camaraderie. Outside of work, I have a few friends and one best friend, Sharon, with whom I visit about every three-to-six weeks. This is about all I can tolerate, especially since work can be extremely draining.

Powerful interests continue to occupy my time, but I can branch out of my comfort zone when necessary. My sensory processing is still quite impaired. For example, I hate tags on clothing, don't appreciate even light touch, and have a disdain for wearing shoes and socks. In fact, I never wear socks, even in New England's winters as my feet feel like they are suffocating. My executive function skills (things like organizational skills, etc.) are quite impressive, though only with *considerable* amounts of effort, obsession, and rule-based logic. In other words, after twenty years of instruction, I can pull it off!

I was married, although this ended in divorce, like approximately fifty percent of all American marriages, and I gave birth to two amazing, kind, and sensitive children. It's not true that people on the autism spectrum can't fall in love, marry, or have kids. I identify with autism. It's a core part of who I am, but it doesn't feel like a "disorder." I think my kids would say that I'm quirky and odd, which makes for a unique relationship, but between my autism and my bipolar disorder, the latter is a much more significant hindrance in my life. Otherwise, we are just a typical divorced family.

The core symptomology of bipolar disorder is quite different from that of ASD and is often more disruptive. Bipolar disorder has two primary symptoms, mania and depression, which manifest in various ways and have different levels of intensity and dimension. While autism and bipolar are unique disorders, studies show that as many as twenty-seven percent of people with ASD also experience this specific comorbidly, meaning that they have symptoms of both that are significant enough to meet the diagnostic criteria for each disorder (Joshi, 2013). Additionally, as with ASD, 51.2 percent of people with bipolar disorder also have an anxiety disorder (Simon et al., 2004).

So, let's now dive in to bipolar disorder.

Imagine a piece of paper. The top represents overly ecstatic and purely thrilling elation (and for some, like me, the addition of psychosis). This is mania. The bottom represents deep, dark, cavernously despondent moods (and, for some, suicidality). This is depression. The middle of the page contains the average range of emotions that we all experience, such as normal levels of depression, happiness, sadness, anger, elation, etc. Everyone experiences changes in mood. This is normal. However, for those of us with bipolar disorder, we lack a boundary. We tiptoe, slide, jump, or leap into one of these extreme camps and struggle to find our way back. Normal moods become increasingly intense and problematic the further they drift from the center, and they can also last for an abnormally long time. So, it's not the emotion itself, but the degree to which the emotion is expressed and the extent to which it interferes with daily life that can cause problems.

Bipolar disorder involves having both manic (above the center) and depressive (below the center) periods or episodes. However, exactly what constitutes an "episode" is vague, and the duration of each episode is unique to each individual. One person may experience mild depression for three months, whereas another person's mania may require hospitalization lasting a few weeks or more. As with ASD, not everyone fits the exact medical profile of symptoms and degrees, which makes diagnosing challenging. It can take up to ten years to get an accurate diagnosis of bipolar disorder, especially for teens, whose symptoms may be misinterpreted as typical moodiness.

There are two main types of bipolar disorder: bipolar I and II. As a general rule, people with bipolar II have lengthier, stronger, and more stubborn depressive episodes and brief or rare spurts of slight mania.

Symptoms of depression for both bipolar I and II may include a feeling of hopelessness, a loss of energy or interest in activities, changes in sleeping or eating habits, and difficulty concentrating. It can even result in suicidality. Studies have shown that the rate of actually carrying out suicide is ten to thirty times higher in people with bipolar disorder than in those without a psychiatric diagnosis. When a person with bipolar II does experience slight mania (hypomania,) they usually remain lucid and reasonable at all times. Their energy is peppy, they can maintain social interactions, and they generally continue to work. Unfortunately, because these symptoms can sometimes appear to be nothing more than vague variances on "normal" emotions, diagnostically, people with bipolar II may fly under the radar and not receive the help they desperately need.

Bipolar I, on the other hand, involves intense and drastic oscillating mood instability that ranges from the despair of depression (similar to bipolar II symptoms) to the highest wired, vigorous, boundless energy of mania (or even agitation). Mania has its own continuum ranging from hypomania (or slight mania, where the person's mood is elevated, but their functioning is intact) to fully manic (where all aspects of introspection, functioning, and judgment are generally impaired).

I have bipolar I with psychosis. One of the first signs that I'm having a manic episode is that I will stop sleeping for days or weeks on end, yet will feel fine and not at all tired. In bed, I toss and turn to no avail, then concede and get up. When my hypomania (or very slight mania) slowly begins to ratchet up toward full mania, I have an ounce more control than before the episode started and, at this stage, ever-so-slight introspection, which helps coerce my mind into behaving when absolutely necessary. This is the sweet spot of mania that comes before I lose perspective and when I can still take pleasure in the jubilation I experience. At this stage, everything is easier: I can think clearly, and my ideas flow. My creative juices gush, my projects are satisfying, and I produce good-quality work. Additionally, several of my autistic traits vanish, my social desire increases as I flip through my contacts to see who I can call, and interacting with others is noticeably effortless.

If I could only stay in this hypomanic stage, life would be grand! However, that's not the way it works. Hypomania always slips into mania for me, and while the feeling is sensational, the ramifications of my actions, when viewed in hindsight, are disastrous.

When I'm manic, my mood is extremely elated and my thoughts race. It often feels like my mind is dancing so quickly that I can barely keep up; think of Jennifer Beals's legs in the movie *Flashdance*. Whatever idea enters my brain seems brilliant, important, and actionable, regardless of how absurd it might be. And I'll be sure to let everyone I come into contact with know of my ideas. My mouth is electrified, discharging sentences that may or may not be coherent to others. When a person is manic, their behavior and thoughts become less organized. For me, carrying out a coherent conversation is straining. Thoughts leap from my mouth, regardless of relevance or appropriateness; they are just simple non-sequiturs that must be discharged. Internally, I feel like I'm conquering every challenge with my brilliant ideas. There is a sense of being invincible, which can be dangerous. My thrashing, perpetual thoughts consist of illogical, crazy ideas; quick, harebrained schemes; and inventions that keep me in constant motion. I spend money wildly without forethought of consequence. In the moment, being manic feels terrific.

Only when I'm immensely manic or profoundly depressed do I also experience psychosis. For me, psychotic symptoms present as delusions (such as "I'm going to purchase the largest Whole Foods" or "I can control electricity with my mind"), paranoia ("my office is trying to poison me" or "a taxi company stole part of my brain"), and hallucinations (seeing and hearing stimuli that do not exist). When the psychotic symptoms emerge, they feel real and complicate my bipolar episode. When this psychosis is combined with the speed of mania, my brain metaphorically collapses in upon itself, making all rational thought nearly impossible.

Between my autism and bipolar disorder I struggled tremendously in school. Growing up, I did "hard time" in resource rooms and then special education programs. Cumulatively, I spent approximately six years of my life institutionalized. At the tender age of fifteen, during my first mental hospital stay, I was told that I would never live outside the institution's walls. In my chart, my prognosis read, "grave."

Over the years, by accident and through direct teaching, I have acquired some skills and abilities that the educational and medical professionals from my childhood never thought possible for me. These so-called experts condemned me with their low expectations, constantly telling me in a condensing tone, "You can't," "You won't," "It's not possible with your diagnoses..." But the fact is that I did and will continue to succeed.

Having a diagnosis doesn't mean that one's life or future are "grave." In my case, twenty-six years ago, I decided that I wanted to make a real difference in this world. No one should have to endure what I did. In school and in institutions, I was constantly told I was "bad," "weird," "disordered," or "retarded." Our society needed a different place, a place where people saw students' strengths and optimism for what they *could* do. I swore another kid would never live through what I did so I started an agency providing services to people with special needs. This eventually morphed into a special-education school called Ravenwood Day School for students between the ages of seven and twenty-two. We provide an intense therapeutic program delivered in a nurturing environment as well as comprehensive and challenging academics. Yes, you can have a disability *and* soak up academic rigor.

There is so much stigma surrounding developmental delays and even more shame with mental illness. Since my late twenties, I have been speaking publicly about my developmental delay. My goal has always been to break down an impenetrable wall of prejudice and to educate people by providing insights into my own thoughts. I say "my own" here to make it clear that all people are different. This is just my story, and others with similar diagnostic profiles may feel differently.

Despite my openness about my autism, until my early forties, I kept the mental illness component of my life entirely private (except when institutionalized.) Fear of stigma kept me hushed. After I left the world of institutions behind, I skirted by with very little medication and just quiet mood swings for years. Then, unexpectedly, I had a colossal manic episode with psychosis. There was no rhyme or reason to it. It just happened. I could no longer pretend that I wasn't ill, and I was no longer able to be appropriate as work. During this period, I was hospitalized four times and committed a few. The school almost slipped away. And, worst of all, the courts put restrictions on how often I could see my kids.

Finding my way out of autism involved detective work, and so would bipolar disorder. If I wanted to improve my life, I needed to take my medication consistently and don my red checkered sleuth hat, investigating the path to unvarying stability. It was difficult for me to reconcile the incongruence between my being the CEO of a successful company *and* psychotic simultaneously. I couldn't integrate these two facets of my life.

After I got through that psychotic crater and returned to a wider aperture of lucidity, I realized that if I wanted to be whole, I needed to begin addressing the mental illness part of my life. I did some research and found very few others with mental illness and autism, especially those with successful careers who "outed" themselves in the community. For this reason, I again picked up my notes for this book and decided to share my story. It represents my observations and reflections and offers insights into the inner workings of my mind through its varying degrees of lucidity.

Many people have asked how I managed to live for so long with such faulty logic, erratic sensory processing, poor social skills, mood swings, and intermittent psychosis. However, the world I live in is the only world I know. Only when I discovered, by accident, that others naturally have the ability to make educated guesses about what another person thinks and feels did I realize just how different my thinking was. It was also only when I was properly medicated for bipolar disorder that I understood what is considered normal energy and thinking patterns. Over time, after learning perspective-taking and consistently taking my medications, I was able to compare my thoughts to others' and articulate how my brain worked.

This book is the story of my life thus far. Part of it is a narrative detailing my experiences, but there are also aspects that I hope will educate people about both autism and bipolar disorder. I delve deep into how I learned the Theory of Mind (perspective-taking), executive functioning skills, how to regulate my sensory system and emotions, how to stabilize my mood swings, how to attack my psychoses, and ultimately come to terms with living with both autism and bipolar disorder. More importantly, I share insights into my emotional and cognitive states as my journey unfolded. Ultimately, I hope the reader will come away with an understanding and appreciation of the complexity and simplicity that emerges when autism and mental illness collide.

CHAPTER 1

RECLAIMING MY LIFE

ON SUNDAY, APRIL 10, 1994, I was twenty-four years old and by myself, on leave for the day from one of the numerous mental institutions I had been in and out of since adolescence.

To secure a leave pass, I had to check in with my psychiatrist once a week for less than five minutes so that he could ascertain my stability level. At my most recent check-in, my psychiatrist, Dr. Absher, had done most of the talking—as usual. He had gushed in his Midwestern accent, "Seems like you've stayed out of your room this week. Great job! I also see that you went to the Occupational Therapy group and made a collage. And, of course, you did your crossword puzzles. You're showing great improvements, Alex! I heard you want an eight-hour pass on Sunday. That's granted!"

I had simply nodded. In truth, I had been quite suicidal lately and feeling hopeless about my institutional living situation. However, there wasn't time for this to come out in my brief check-in. Without getting any further input from or gaining any insight into me, he signed my pass, which would allow me to leave the institution the following Sunday.

On Sunday, before leaving, I ruminated about how I would kill myself while on my day pass. I felt wax-like—emotionless and lifeless. I was dead inside. All I knew was that I had endured enough and wanted life to be over. In the hospital's parking lot, I sat in my car for several minutes, staring at the steering wheel. Suddenly, an eerie plan of high lethality came into my mind. I pulled out a cigarette and lit it with a pack of matches I had in the car. Then, I started the engine and drove away.

*This photo of "the just right spot" was taken years later when writing this book

I drove north from Pennsylvania on Interstate 81. Once I had crossed the New York state border, I stopped at a Mobil station, bought a bright-orange jug, and filled it with gasoline. Outside of Binghamton, I stumbled upon a novelty shop where I purchased a pair of metal handcuffs which added to my plan. Then, I turned onto Route 12 and continued my trek north, driving another twenty miles or so before exiting onto a narrow, winding country road.

The sun shone brightly as I drove, and I could feel its warmth beating through my windows, letting me know that the dark days of winter were finally over. I occasionally glanced out of the side window and noticed that tiny green leaves were starting to peek out on tree branches; a new season of life was beginning. In contrast, mine was about to end.

I soon located a densely wooded area that felt "just right"; I felt at peace almost as soon as I saw it. I turned off the road and drove into the woods on a wide dirt path until I reached a small clearing. I stopped the car. This was the place.

I had endured enough torture in this life, and now, here, I would end it.

My impulsive plan to commit suicide involved handcuffing myself to the steering wheel of my car, throwing the key out the window, pouring gasoline all over myself, and then lighting myself on fire. The handcuffs hadn't been part of my initial plan when I envisioned it in the hospital parking lot, but they were a lucky find that would now certainly ensure my demise.

This was not the first time that I had impulsively decided to commit suicide. When I was fourteen years old, I overdosed on Belladonna, a prescribed sedative, but was revived. I made a second attempt a year later while institutionalized, with the same result.

As I took the cold metal handcuffs out of the hard plastic container, my mind wandered. Memories of my life, mostly from the various mental institutions and "specialized programs" where I had felt tortured by frequent visits to "quiet rooms" and the use chemical and mechanical restraints, flashed through my consciousness. I wish I could say I felt something, but I was already dead inside.

I placed one of the cuffs on my right wrist. For some reason, I thought of the longing, hungry eyes of Fritz, the alley cat that my bunkmate had snuck into our room at Stonyfield Psychiatric Hospital when I was fifteen. He was always roaming the grounds.

As I placed the second cuff on the steering wheel, I recalled how, from when I was about four to about nine, my beloved grandmother often took me to what we fondly called "the stinky place" on Saturdays. This was a pet store in Brooklyn, New York, where a chunky, bald manager in red-and-black checkered pants stood outside, bellowing, "Live chicks being born every minute! Come inside and see!" For only one dollar, you could see the chicks and were given a baby bottle filled with milk to feed another set of animals: the caged monkeys. The sight of the thin monkeys trapped in cages, squawking, thrashing back and forth, and begging for someone to let them out had haunted me for years. A handwritten sign loomed over their cage: "Stand back. Monkeys can become violent without being provoked." Even as a child, I had thought, *If I were a wild animal trapped in this small cage, I'd be violent, too.*

Suddenly, I snapped. The depressive numbness that had engulfed my body for so long was instantly gone, and I could think straight for the first time in what felt like forever. It was jarring. I realized that these monkeys had become a metaphor for my own life. I had been institutionalized for so long that any shred of independence living and dignity I had once possessed was now long gone. My self-image had fused with the stark white institutional walls that I lived within, and by this point, my identity as a mental patient was quite prominent and deeply rooted. Having been locked up so young, I had little experience with life itself and little chance to forge my own identity. Frankly, it had never even occurred to me that I *could* leave the institution; it had become my way of life. Lured by colorful brochures and the appeal of professional help—not to mention the promise of a place to sleep and three meals a day—I had signed away my mind and my soul and had committed to a life of institutionalization. After years of walking miles within the sanitarium's sterile white hallways and working on my 1,328th crossword puzzle, it was now abundantly clear to me that if I were to succeed in life, I would need to find a different venue. Relying on these systems and professionals so completely would only perpetuate the institutionalized cycle I had been trapped in for years.

As I sat there in my car, with one wrist handcuffed to the steering wheel, I realized that I needed to break out of the hospital's cage, not end my life. I couldn't simply throw away my life without having at least attempted to succeed outside the institutional walls. For the first time in months, a glimmer of hope entered my heart.

I took the handcuffs off, threw them out the window, and drove back to the institution in Pennsylvania. I never told anyone what had nearly happened that day with the can of gasoline, the handcuffs, and the unlit match.

The next morning, I sat in the gloomy white-walled community room that smelled of feet. The TV was on, and my peers were spread across the room on the itchy, forest-green couches, apparently hungover from the previous evening's round of medications. I looked around and studied them. Walter's tan robe was wide open, and his jewels were hanging out. Sophia was mining her left nostril. And Curt, well, Curt just sat there, not talking. It's all he ever did.

I glanced over to the television, and my attention was

immediately hijacked by a news story that featured the Boston Common in Massachusetts. In stark contrast to my current surroundings, the Boston Common, a spectacular garden tucked away in the middle of the city, seemed to be brimming with life. Following my typical impulsive pattern, I arbitrarily decided that I would leave the hospital and make Boston my new home.

Soon after, during my three-minute Monday-morning check-in with Dr. Absher, I announced that after years of institutional living, I was leaving.

Dr. Absher had a grandfatherly look, complete with a shoulder length snow white beard and bright blue eyes. Now, those eyes creased in worry as he pleaded his case as to why I should stay and gently—and validly—poked holes in my weak, impulsive plan.

His best efforts at persuasion fell short, though, and not long after our meeting, I checked myself out of the institution. While I was not mentally prepared for the outside world, they could not legally detain me. I was neither suicidal (that they knew of) nor homicidal, and I independently showered each day. They could not keep me there against my will.

I packed up all my worldly possessions, which included my paint swatch collection from the local hardware store, a few sketch pads and pencils, my favorite pair of blue sneakers, my favorite thick gray hooded sweatshirt (which protected my ears from unwanted noise), and a few changes of clothes. When I appeared at the front desk to check myself out, the nurses rallied, pleading with me to stay. I refused to listen. They capitulated and handed over my discharge paperwork, the prescriptions for my various medications, my wallet, keys, and items from the sharps closet, such as my razor and nail clippers. With that, I walked out the door grinning from ear to ear. I was finally free.

As I sat in my red Volvo, which my parents had given me years earlier, I looked at the Rand McNally map I kept in my glove box and decided on a route to Boston. As I did so, the ramifications of my decision and poor planning grew increasingly evident. I was elated, yet terrified.

I needed an emotional check-in with the nursing staff, but I was now on my own. I hadn't yet filled my prescriptions and was now missing my twelve o'clock psychiatric meds. Even worse, there wasn't anyone to get them for me or remind me to take them. I also missed my parents. I spoke with them about once a week, so they were still unaware of my impulsive decision. If they had been aware, they likely would have contacted the institution to create a more robust discharge plan.

Still, while I *was* frazzled, I had been planning on killing myself just the day before, so I figured I had nothing to lose. I made an unyielding decision to stick to my plan and not go back inside.

I drove off.

My new life awaited.

CHAPTER 2

SPROUTING UP

I GREW UP in New York in the early 1970s as an only child. My dad, Jeffrey, was handsome and dapper and had a larger-than-life personality. He was a tall, had a thick head of wavy brown hair and emerald-green eyes, and was built like a football player. However, a middle-school football accident left him in a full-body cast for a year. His injuries didn't heal correctly, resulting in a permanent limp and limited mobility. However, his personality always overshadowed his limp, though, and it seemed like a non-issue.

My dad grew up in Forrest Hills, New York, where a posse of thorny neighborhood teens always trailed behind him. They sought out trouble of the mostly harmless variety, and my dad was the ring-leader for many schemes. One time, when my grandparents were out of town, he painted their newly polished hardwood floors white and then invited his friends over to hit golf balls into the giant fish tank. Unsurprisingly, it broke. Water and floundering fish were scattered about. Another time, when he was seventeen, my father paid the me-chanic who was working on my innocent nana's new car to replace the engine and soup it up so that hitting the ignition switch made it emit a roar of thunder. When my nana picked up her car, she was shocked, remarking, "Boy, this is peppy!" This powerful car earned the posse "cred" on the street where, on Thursday nights, the adoles-cents gorged themselves on countless White Castle burgers and raced their families' autos down Cross Bay Boulevard.

My grandparents, Helen and Ernie, were extremely poor and could only afford a cramped one-bedroom apartment. My dad slept in the living room. While he never complained about his circumstances, he knew early on that he would break the cycle of poverty. Despite barely graduating from high school and without a formal college education, he worked exceptionally hard and did eventually find his way to a better life. Ernie, his father, worked in a dental laboratory, which is where false teeth are made. My dad also got a job there after graduating, and he received some hands-on technical training. My grandfather took my dad under his wing and showed him the tricks of the trade.

In 1979, my dad was working as a salesman for the lab and had considerable contacts in the industry. However, his eyes were set on owning his own lab. His dream came true when two partners of an existing laboratory, Perfect Smile, which was located on Park Avenue South in New York City, let him transfer his contacts to them and taking him on as their salesman. My dad was able to buy his way in to being a partner in the company over many years. His dream finally came true.

This laboratory became his first business love, and he struck it rich. My dad was quite proud to employ hundreds of people from all walks of life. In addition to various businesspeople and craftsmen, he also hired underprivileged New York City street kids to teach them a trade. Among the regular employees, these kids were later known as "Run DMC" because their rapping echoed loudly throughout the workplace. This drove many people crazy, but my father saw something in those street kids. Each and every one eventually proved themselves, earning full-time employment.

Very proud of his accomplishments and inherently brilliant at business, my father had finally broken the cycle of poverty. He made Perfect Smile a colossal success.

One of Dad's favorite stories was of the day his high school guidance counselor, Mr. Trevor, told him he was a looser and that he would never make anything of himself. My father's tenacity ultimately proved him wrong. About ten years later, my dad pulled up at Forest Hills High School and dragged Mr. Trevor out to the parking lot to show him his brand-new, shiny, white Rolls Royce. "What do you think of me now?" he asked with a wide grin.

Throughout my childhood, everything was over-the-top, as my father always surrounded himself with excitement. Heavy partying was commonplace in the 1970s, and he certainly indulged! There were chartered jets with full bands flying to Canada for the weekend, food fights in the kitchen, a "winter party" in July with snowmaking machines in the back yard, dabbling in illegal substances… the list goes on. The fun never ended with my dad.

Because his business sense and tolerance for high-risk moves had been my dad's golden ticket out of poverty, he insisted on instilling these virtues in me. He passed down an excellent work ethic and strong business sense, both of which I embraced and took to heart.

Everything in life was a teachable moment with him. When I was about eight, I started watching Louis Rukeyser's *Wall Street Week* while snuggling with Dad in bed. I always looked forward to this ritual, even though I was too young to fully understand what the show was about. But it meant a lot to my dad, and that was enough for me.

In an effort to bond with my father, I spent hours as a child learning about various aspects of finance, such as the S&P, the bond market, and how to read the daily stock exchange. I loved watching the ticker tape declaring the rise and fall of stock prices; it was actually quite stimulating for me! As a child standing in Times Square watching the Times Building, I recall a plethora of lit up symbols and numbers scroll. This visual stimulation caused my mind to race and insides to jiggle with joy. This sensation felt phenomenal!

My dad and I shared other interests as well. On weekends, he often took me to LaGuardia Airport, which I loved, and we watched the planes take off and land. The noise from the planes was a low rumble that didn't offend my ears. He also loved to gamble, mostly at casinos and on horseraces, and we occasionally speculated at the

Belmont Stakes together. I always had my heart set on Saratoga Sunset for no other reason than her pretty name. When I was in high school, I decided to live up to my father's betting legacy and cut class one day to bet on the horses at Off-Track Betting on the east side of New York City. I was busted by our doorman, who spotted me cashing in my winning ticket. He tattled to my mother, and I got in a lot of trouble.

My dad's eccentricities as an adult extended to a love of electronics and gadgets. When I was growing up, it seemed like we had every imaginable device that required a battery or had a plug. In this regard, Dad and I were a match made in heaven. As a child, my nickname was "Little Jeff" or "Jefferina" because we were so much alike. I loved to emulate my father, and I spent hours in front of the mirror trying to talk like him, using the same prosody and cadence.

I was in awe of my father. He's a genuinely great man. That is why I regret not spending more time with him as a child. While his business was successful, he worked long hours and didn't prioritize attending my school activities, which was often heartbreaking for me. During the week, he was barely home while I was awake, and I spent countless weekends with his parents.

I wish I had spent more time with him.

I wish I knew him better.

My mother, Julie, was a brilliant, gorgeous woman with straight, shoulder-length blonde hair and a perfect body. She was naturally good at everything she tried; things just came effortlessly to her. She also had a quasi-photographic memory, and nothing she put her mind to was insurmountable. While she had a lot to be conceited about, she never put on airs and was always very genuine and down-to-earth. She balanced my father's eccentricities with some much-needed reality.

Growing up, my mother was quite studious and cultured. She had few friends, but was very close with those she did have. She grew up in Atlantic Beach, on Long Island, and spent the weekends jumping waves with her friends and hanging out at the malt shop.

Her parents, Calvin and Miriam, were very inspirational to her.

My grandfather Calvin died when I was only two years old, so I have no memories of him, but my mother speaks very highly of him. He always told my mother that she could be anything she wanted so long as she put her mind to it. He also taught her the value of money, gave her a solid business sense, and constantly provided her with positive feedback. When he died, my mother jumped right into learning and taking over his real estate business, which everyone was grateful for.

My grandmother Miriam was very strict and frugal, and while I respected her as my grandmother, I never felt like I was a priority in her life. She spent her days playing mahjong with her girlfriends and volunteering at the local hospital, which she did literally until the day she died. Miriam had been an adult during the Great Depression, and she never lost that scarcity mentality. She was exceptionally thrifty and could not tolerate waste. Whenever we went out to eat, she would shove the sugar and ketchup packets into her pocketbook. I often argued that this was technically stealing, but since she was my elder, I never won. While my mother did not inherit this frugal mind-set, it likely contributed to her down-to-earth nature.

When I was in elementary school, my mother worked at H&R Block as a tax preparer. As a gift, my father bought her a navy-blue Mercedes sedan one year. He thoughtfully parked it in the driveway with a giant yellow bow. Instead of being elated, she was upset at how showy it was. When she drove to work, she would park the car around the corner so that none of her colleagues would know about it. My mother never really cared about materialistic things.

Initially, she went to Queen's College as an education major but did not enjoy working with students, especially those who had disciplinary problems. When they slashed her tires after school one day, she left the field. Loving finance, she obtained a post-bachelor's degree as a Certified Financial Planner and spent the rest of her career teaching her clients about money, advising them, and preparing their taxes.

When I was in fourth grade, my mother bought me some stocks in Toys-R-Us and Mattel, which further piqued my interest in the stock market. After that, we sat at the kitchen table each morning with the financial section of the *New York Times* and charted the stocks' values. I loved spending time like this with my mom; she's a natural educator, and I learned so much from her.

Likely due to my odd behaviors, friends were scant when I was growing up. However, I was never without fun escapades that my mother planned for the two of us. We were avid ice skaters and frequented the chilly outdoor rink. I loved watching her gracefully glide across the ice or spin like a delicate ballerina. Her talents always surpassed mine, but I gained pleasure in just watching her achieve. On Thursday nights, my mother played in a bowling league, and she often hit strikes or spares. She taught me the craft when she took me bowling on the weekends. My favorite adventures, though, involved animals. We often visited the Bronx Zoo and could be found feeding ducks at our local library. Whatever the affair, she always made it fun and educational.

My mother had boundless energy and unfailingly wore bright red lipstick, which complimented her red-and-white checked Swiss Miss dress that frequently sprang from her wardrobe. At the deli where she bought me roast beef sandwiches with ketchup on a bulky roll and a Coke for lunch every day, the counter boys called her "flash." Everything she did, she did immensely fast and accurately. She would play board games with me, help me put together my Lego sets, and assist with my homework every day. She also harnessed her whirlwind energy to clean our house. I never once saw a dish sitting in the sink. Nothing was ever out of place. She seemed to always be bustling around. Even later in life, when she was going through chemo and radiation treatment for breast cancer, she never missed a step. Her boundless energy and ability to multitask continues to this day well in to her seventies.

My mother taught me that no matter how bad you have it, someone else has it worse and that I should be grateful for what I have. One of her favorite quotes was, "I felt bad that I had no shoes until I saw the man who had no feet." There was never any occasion where

I was given permission to feel bad for myself. Even now, as an adult, I try to avoid throwing myself pity parties, though I can now acknowledge when I'm entitled to feel badly.

My parents met when Mom was dating Dad's friend Ian. Ian arranged for Dad to join them on a double date with Mom's best friend, Candy. Dad was not wowed by Candy, but he took an immediate liking to Mom. However, she was his best friend's girlfriend and should have been off-limits.

For a week, Dad tried to get Mom out of his head by asking out other girls. When none of them agreed to go out on a date with him, he decided to call Mom. He asked her to go see the movie *West Side Story* with him. Given that Dad met her criteria—"he was taller than me and had a car"—she agreed.

It was a blustery winter night, and Dad's windshield wipers broke as he was driving her home. Due to the storm and the dangerous roads, he slept at her house. My grandfather took this opportunity to pummel Dad with questions. Dad lied, claiming to be a college student who also held down a job—in truth, while he did have a job, he did not attend college. My grandfather was very protective of Mom and was initially impressed by Dad. Of course, he eventually learned the truth!

Both of my parents are only children, so I don't have any real aunts, uncles, or cousins. I do, however, have an "Aunt" Meri who was part of my dad's Forrest Hill posse, and she has always played an active role in my life. She's sort of an obsessive-compulsive new age spirit. Meri never cared that I was ill. In fact, she provided me with an abundance of cards and books on healing long before I was diagnosed with bipolar disorder. She took lots of courses on spirituality and self-discovery from places like Kripalu and then imparted her newfound knowledge to me. And while she was warm and caring, she was also a lot of fun. My heart raced whenever we were together, since I knew that no matter what we did, it would be entertaining. Our adventures were as varied as going skiing, eating colossal bowls of ice cream, and riding down Park Avenue in the snow with the top down on Dad's car. She also taught me kindness and compassion by taking me to volunteer at the Special Olympics and other charities. To me, Meri is family. After all, emotional bonds are often more important than blood ties.

My mother learned this for herself as a young adult. One night, she was attending a family party when her cousin Jerry, the family clown, barreled over to her. Quite tipsy, he asked, "How do you feel about being adopted?"

Dumbfounded, she answered, "I'm not adopted."

But not long after that night, she spoke with her parents and learned that she was, in fact, adopted. They had simply never told her. She was shocked and upset.

I can't be certain, but it's possible that they waited so long to tell her the truth about her background because my grandmother Miriam was *exceptionally* concerned about appearances.

In September 1989, I was nineteen years old, had just been diagnosed with bipolar disorder, and was being hospitalized for the second time. I was manic. Out of control. Alone. And quite scared.

After speaking with my mother, who was very upset with me (as if my diagnosis were under my control), I called Miriam at the direction of my mother. My grandmother's voice was like an icicle over the phone. The only thing she had to say to me was, "I hope you will be out before Thanksgiving. After all, what would I tell the rest of the family?" *Click*. There was no compassion, just cold, hard orders.

I was twenty-nine and had a fully established educational consulting practice when Miriam passed away. When it was clear that she was on her deathbed, my mother called and asked me to come down from Boston to New York to see her one last time. I put on some nice clothes—including her favorite caramel blazer with brown leather elbow patches—because I knew that would make her happy and ran to the airport to catch the next flight to New York. The only thing Miriam had to say to me was, "That outfit needs a scarf. And what, no lipstick?" She passed the next day. While I admired her generosity in the volunteer work she did, that was all I could admire.

Strangely, Miriam's closest friend was her sister and polar oppo-site, Rachel. They always lived near each other on Long Island, often in the same duplex or apartment building. Rachel had short, tight, curly red hair, and everything about her just screamed *fun!* She was hilariously funny and reminded me of Phyllis Diller, an actress and comedian known for her wild hair and clothing and an uninhibit-ed laugh. And she indulged me in just about everything. Whenever we went over to her place, there was always an electronic item that needed to be fixed. She would hand it to me, declaring me "the ex-pert." Frankly, I think she broke these devices on purpose, just to entertain me. I also have fond memories of making scrumptious Jiffy muffins with Rachel, which we did every time we rendezvoused. She let me be the "head chef," and she was my assistant. I always enjoyed my time with Rachel and could never quite understand how she and Miriam had come from the same family. They were as different as night and day.

My other grandmother, Helen, was more like Rachel. She had an eccentric personality and brimmed with positivity and liveliness. Whenever I passed through the threshold of her door, her wide smile emanated deep love. She is the one who took me to the "stinky place" pet store on Saturdays and never complained of being tired of going. Nana, as I called her, had been a dancer on Broadway when she was young, even appearing in the famous *Ziegfeld Follies* spectacu-lars, and it wasn't uncommon for her to break out into a song-and-dance routine in the living room. We would take out old copies of her *Playbills*, and she would let me pick a show that we would be dancing in that evening. Then, of course, we needed to play beauty parlor to gussy up. I always walked away with brightly colored nails and fancy lipstick. She was the best playmate ever. She had no ex-pectations of social norms, and I felt free to disclose all of my mind's scary stories to her.

I spent many weekends with my dad's parents. My grandfather Ernie was a quiet, kind-hearted man who had retired from the dental laboratory where he'd worked his entire life. By the time I was old enough to notice the world, Ernie had grown quite elderly, as he was twenty-five years older than my nana. Yet, he still had a full head of thick white hair and dashing aquamarine eyes. He spent most of his days in a chair by the window that overlooked Schwartz Brother's Funeral Parlor off of Queen's Boulevard. He never had much to say other than commenting on who was getting buried that day.

My nana was a mind-blowing cook and made everything from scratch. She never cut any corners. She made the best matzo ball soup in the world, and while her cooking could have won awards, she always indulged me with lunchtime adventures to McDonald's, where I invariably gobbled up a hamburger Happy Meal with extra ketchup, extra pickles, and no onions.

According to family lore, my nana was somewhat "unstable" while my dad was growing up. Her symptoms are descriptive of possible bipolar disorder (though she was never formally diagnosed), prescription drug abuse (specifically Miltowns, which were tranquilizers), and alcohol abuse. My father tells stories of my grandmother being carted out of the house and taken to a sanitarium on several occasions.

When talking about this painful experience, my father's manner does not match the gravity of the story. Instead, he focuses on the great time he had in his mother's absence when he was sent to stay with his cousins on Bantam Lake in Connecticut. I know that he loved his parents deeply; perhaps seeing them in so much pain was just too much for his young soul to bear at the time.

By the time I came along, my nana was post-menopausal, which, for some, can ease symptoms of bipolar disorder. While both Ernie and Helen continued to drink every day, the quantity and effect had radically decreased. I suspect both tried to quit drinking on multiple occasions, as we would play card games and bet using her "poker chips," which I think were actually Alcoholics Anonymous tokens.

It's hard for me to imagine my nana as "mentally unstable," as this suggests a stark contrast to what I remember about her. Perhaps I only remember what I chose to remember. Still, she was a true friend and the one person who indulged my obsessions and quirks, such as letting me collect unlimited paint swatches from the local hardware store and ritualistically lay them out across the dining room table. Paint swatches were so fascinating to me because of the gradation in each row. Fixating on each color fragment, I could imagine a lighter shade being mixed in to create this new color. I also enjoyed lining the swatches up and zooming my head back and forth over them so that the colors would appear to mix together.

Nana embraced me "as-is." When I started to develop psychotic symptoms, I could be honest with her about them, disclosing all of my scary thoughts and experiences. I don't know whether she understood that these frightening symptoms were real to me or whether she simply chalked them up to an active imagination, but either way, she listened. I would often lie on the couch while she stroked my hair and firmly rubbed my back. I was always able to turn to her when I needed a sympathetic ear.

Helen passed away thirty-six years ago. Now, when I'm upset or experiencing some kind of mood instability, I will often call my mother. She will always hear me out, but she has trouble coping with my mood shifts and always tries to fix the problem, when I only want someone to listen. This was true even when I was a child. I think my changeable moods seem strange and uncomfortable for her, and she only wants me to "get better." However, bipolar disorder is a life-long disability; it's not going away. I wish I could "fix" it for her. My father, on the other hand, largely denies and ignores my symptoms. Emotionally, he just can't handle it. On the rare occasion when I discuss my experience with bipolar with him, I'm often met with comments like, "You don't have a problem," "You're just fine," or "Think about how this could ruin your business." None of these responses are helpful.

When I was growing up, my parents always treated me as if I didn't have a disability. They had the same expectations for me as any other child and refused to dance around my quirkiness. On some level, this meant that I grew up with a feeling that I could never live up to their expectations. On another level, though, I suspect that if they had catered to my disabilities more, I never would have experienced the successes I've had in my life. I wouldn't have fought so hard to get out of the institutions, and I would have believed the doctors and educators who constantly said, "You can't," "You won't," "Not with your diagnoses." For my parents—and, to an extent, for me—having a disability was just not an option. However, I *did* have a disability, and the symptoms were so frightening that I often just kept my mouth shut about them.

When I was growing up, we moved around a lot. In fact, there was a family joke that my mom didn't redecorate; we just moved! We started in Queens in New York City, then moved to Long Island, then Morgan's Island due to a fire, and then to Manhattan in New York City.

My years attending public school were marked by social isolation. Ironically, I remember being reasonably happy until fourth grade, although when researching my records for this book, I found a note in my first-grade report card that read: "It's hard to know just what kind of mood Alex will walk through the door in each day. Some days she is compliant and easy to work with whereas others she is loud, angry, and unpredictable. She has challenges with peers. This month we moved her desk away from the other students, and this seems to have helped a bit." That doesn't exactly sound like a happy child. Perhaps my memory is a little skewed, or perhaps, when compared to my subsequent years of schooling, early elementary school simply felt tolerable.

At school, I never knew the right thing to say or do. It felt like someone had written a list of social rules to which I was not privy. There was no manual, and yet, magically, everyone else intuitively just got it. I carefully studied my peers' play at recess; everyone seemed to know *how* to play, which was an activity that still baffled me. I didn't speak the language of interaction. It was a foreign tongue. I desperately wanted friends, but I didn't know how to make them or, even more importantly, how to keep them.

From kindergarten through third grade, I didn't have any real friends except the neighbor across the street who was blissfully oblivious to my deficits since he had nerdy interests and social challenges of his own and my parents' friends' kids, who played with me only out of obligation. There were other kids in the neighborhood who included me in some of their play, but they also tormented me.

Multiple report cards sounded warning bells about my developmental delay, but from my perspective, I was happy. At recess, I would sit in a sandpit by myself under the school's triangular climbing structure or look for frogs in the water grates. After school, I loved to go by the tape factory, where they manufactured various sizes of colored duct tape. It was housed in a huge, inviting brick building and was near my home. Whenever I had a free moment, I would ride my bike to the factory and collect all of their rejected tape from the dumpster. Then, at home, I would bubble with excitement as I spent hours organizing the tape first by size and then by color. The tape factory's rejects were my treasures. Tape made sense to me. There was no mystery about it, it was always consistent, and it was preservative in nature, which I valued.

My earliest odd behavior that I can recall started in kindergarten. My teacher, Mrs. James, had a bright and lively classroom with bold colors adorning the walls and a glorious circular ABC rug, which held our whole class. Mrs. James was a strict but loving teacher with straight, waist-length brown hair that she always wore pulled back. Her smile seemed to radiate outward to us all. One of our "jobs" that year was to memorize our phone number, which I mastered within a few days. Each morning for the entire year, we would sit in a circle on the ABC rug, and Mrs. James would ask each student to recite their phone number aloud. There were about twenty kids in my class, and it was pretty boring to listen to everyone else spit out their phone number; after all, it wasn't like I was memorizing it for a play date! To pass the time, I often gazed out the window and counted the windowpanes over and over. There were sixteen altogether—eight windows, each composed to two enormous panes of glass.

Above the window was a number line, a long piece of paper with the numbers 'one' through 'one hundred' written horizontally. One day, I visualized putting one number in each of the window-panes until I reached sixteen. It took quite a while for Mrs. James to get through the entire class's phone numbers, especially since Danny would always fumble, so I had more time to kill. I started adding the numbers of the corresponding windowpanes together: window one, plus window two, plus window three, plus window four... On and on I went until I had added up the value of all the windows, which equaled 136.

Shortly after I had figured this out, I started compulsively adding all the digits in numbers together until there was one single digit. For example, since the windowpanes totaled 136, I would then add one, plus three, plus six and get ten. Then, I would again add the one and the zero to achieve the single-digit number one. That done, I mentally assigned the windowpanes the number one. I was fascinated with this idea, and from then on, I assigned everything a number based upon simple equations. I sometimes still do this today for fun, especially with license plates. Unlike people, numbers just make sense.

About mid-year, Mrs. James announced that we would start to have weekly visitors. First, Mr. A, a gigantic blow-up cartoon char-acter who had an "A" printed on his stomach, was coming to help the students learn their letters. When Principal Edwards brought Mr. A into our classroom, I freaked and immediately bolted out the door, screaming. I don't know if it was the pure size of the character or his flashy, jagged silver teeth, but this character frightened the hell out of me. Mrs. James ran after me, grabbed me by the wrist, and marched me back into the room to confront the evil character. "Sit down, Alex," she said with a firm tone and a sharp tug.

As I nervously sat on the carpet, I could see my heart pounding through my shirt. I tried to look anywhere but in the direction of the evil character. Glancing at my favorite windowpane, I made a mental leap and decided to associate each letter with a number and started perseverating on this. This distraction calmed my nerves and from this day on, all letters would be assigned a number and then added. For example, the word "I'm" would equal four because "I" is the ninth letter in the alphabet and "M" is the thirteenth letter. From there, I would add nine and thirteen, which equals twenty-two. Two plus two equals four. Thus, the word "I'm" equals four.

Sometimes, I would simply count the number of letters in the word, so that "I'm" would be a two. Spelling and punctuation didn't count in kindergarten when I made this rule, and there was no rhyme or reason to why a word would be assigned a particular method of counting over another.

The rest of kindergarten went off without a hitch, except whenever the next "letter of the week" came to visit. They continued to frighten me, and to keep calm, I learned to just focus on the number line over the window.

In second grade, I had a fantastic teacher, Mrs. McCarthy, who sported a muted Irish brogue. She was jovial, had red cheeks, and was quite portly. Mrs. McCarthy often sat on a wheeled stool, and she slid around the classroom on it. I enjoyed Mrs. McCarthy because she was exceptionally kind to me and told hilarious stories, like the one about the day she moved her daughter's bed and found the wall covered with boogers. To a second grader, boogers are hilarious.

Third grade proved to be more challenging. Mrs. Carter, my snarly teacher, was always raising her voice and telling me how irritated she was, but I could never figure out why. One day, she took me by the hand and escorted me to the principal's office. I truly didn't have a clue as to why I was there. As I peered into Principal Edward's office, I overheard my teacher whispering to him about me. She quietly referred to me as "retarded," and the principal nodded in agreement.

I'm not sure what led her to this conclusion, but it really hurt my feelings. I don't think I fully understood what "retarded" meant, but I knew it wasn't a compliment. This overheard comment wedged itself into my mind like an aneurysm waiting to explode. Years later, when I learned the true definition of the word "retarded," it stuck to me like a piece of duct tape, poking at my self-esteem and making me forever doubt that my intellectual functioning matched that of my peers. Even today, I'm incredibly uncomfortable when people tell me that I'm smart. I always feel like they are lying.

Later that year, things were beginning to look up for me socially. I became a commodity, which I mistook for being popular. Each day, I would grab a handful of change from my father's dresser drawer and shove it into the pockets of my terrycloth shorts so that I could buy extra cookies at the cafeteria. One day, Stephanie Tumbler approached me and noticed my extra cash. She said that if I paid her, I could play with her and her friends after school. It would only cost fifty cents, which bought a candy bar and some gum from the convenience store. But even with that price of admission, entering social situations was like trying to navigate a jungle in the dark. I simply never knew what to say or do. At some point, the other girls left me on my own—though they were willing to have me pay them again for the privilege.

In hindsight, I realize that I had no desire to compromise, always wanted things my way, and would sternly critique others if I felt they were wrong. For me, there was only one right way to do anything. I honestly didn't know how my actions influenced others' responses. Kids baffled me. From a distance, I would watch them interact and wonder how they knew what to say. People just seemed inherently comfortable with each other and got along. Adults were easy to adapt to, as they were always willing to work around *my* interests and engage me. My peers, on the other hand, presented an exceptional challenge. They weren't willing or able to accommodate me, and we had little in common.

As an adult looking back, I am able to surmise that the overarching difficulty with playing was that while my interests were similar to those of other kids, such as putting together Lego sets, I only enjoyed the set-up and not the actual imaginative play schemes that emerged once the sets were together. During most of my paid play dates, I sat and watched the other kids play, which wasn't actually any fun. Similarly, I collected baseball cards but didn't care about the sport, nor was I interested in discussing, sharing, or trading the cards. I did, however, like the gum that came with them!

There was one popular game at my elementary school involving baseball cards that I *could* play, though, and I finally began to collect social credit through it. The object of the game was to throw a baseball card toward the wall. The person whose card landed closest to the wall won. You could tape together as many cards as you wanted or alter the cards in any way. Thus, my love of physics and trajectories was born. After a few hours of good thinking and reading through my prized leather-bound, gold-leafed *World Book Encyclopedia* collection that always retained their "new book" scent, I figured out that if I taped specific coins in specific locations between two cards sandwiched together, I could win every time. My card would hit the wall and fall perfectly against it. After this, I was dubbed the "recess ringer," and for many weeks, kids asked me for my secret. Finally, I was popular! Naïvely, I opened the cards and showed everyone my secret. Once they were able to duplicate my system, I returned to being a social outcast which was heartbreaking as I thought I finally had broken through.

As I grew up, social interaction became increasingly difficult. Each year, it was as if my peers were awarded with new social savviness that I had failed to gain. In retrospect, I realize that part of this was due to the fact that I was primarily interested in my own agenda. In fact, I didn't even realize that there were other agendas to attend to, which makes for rocky friendships. When I learned perspective-taking as an adult, a colleague shared this technique: count the people in the room and divide them into equal portions. If there are five people present, that means you should take up about twenty percent of the conversation and no more. It was a useful intervention that was easy to apply; I only wish I had learned *that* in elementary school!

After a particularly hard day at school, I would often rant and rave about whatever atrocity had occurred. One day, my mom, probably frustrated and wanting me to shut up, said that I ought not to rant for more than five minutes, as people would lose interest and become angry with me. Now, *this* was helpful! I didn't like it, but it was concrete and something that I could apply and generalize. Employing this rule helped me socially "pass" and be less annoying.

Having a toolbox of "rule-based logic" interventions can make or break a social interaction for people with autism. For me, these were all important elements of helping me learn how not to be annoying. One can learn social skills, such as how to make a friend, by teaching specific overtures, but teaching people with autism the fundamentals of pragmatics, such as how to *keep* a friend, is equally as important.

While social skills were hard, conceptually, math was the one area where I didn't need instruction; I just seemed to get it. Answers to equations tumbled out of my mouth, never requiring written output. With math, I could gain some dignity and praise from my teacher— though not in fourth grade with Mr. Meaner (yes, that was his name). Before he could even finish explaining to the class how to solve the math problem, I would (annoyingly) call out the answer. Not only did this irritate him, as he bluntly let me know, but it must have exasperated my classmates, too, as I spent fourth grade picking spitballs out of my hair. Mr. Meaner eventually grew so frustrated with me that he took matters into his own hands by putting me in the wooden coat closet with squeaky bifold doors. I would peer out of the cracks to see the chalkboard and continue to call out the (muffled) answer. One day when I was in the closet, Mr. Meaner opened the door and put his hand over my mouth. It smelled funny, like tobacco, and I licked his hand. It tasted gross.

And my situation was about to go from bad to worse.

One day, my classmate Sam told me to meet him on the upper field after school if I wanted some candy. I might have been labeled "retarded," but I wasn't stupid. Hearing this offer of candy, I ran with gusto! Approaching the field, I noticed that there were eight other kids with their bikes. Sam held a satchel, and the other kids were eating Kit-Kat bars. Sam pleasantly extended the satchel toward me and said with enthusiasm, "Everyone already picked theirs. Your turn." I forcefully plunged my hand into the satchel, but there was no candy waiting for me. Instead, my fingers grasped a mound of mushy dog diarrhea. The other kids started laughing and bellowing insults: "Moron," "Crazy," "Imbecile," "Freak!" Then, Sam punched me in the stomach, and he and his cohorts mounted their bikes and rode away. I had heard names like this before, but on this day, I understood that they were derogatory and, more importantly, that they were aimed at me. I walked home with my hand covered in dog poop, a sunken heart, and the realization of just how different I was.

After the dog poop incident, I didn't want to play with anyone—not even for free.

In June of 1982, as elementary school came to a close, my grandfather Ernie died. I felt profoundly sad and angry about his death. This was the first loss I had ever encountered. When the call came from my nana, we piled into the car and dashed to Deepdale General Hospital. As we walked in, I spotted my nana sitting on a bench in the hall with her head buried in her hands. Her wailing reverberated down the corridor's walls. I didn't know what to do, so I ran toward her and hugged her tightly. As we all huddled together and shared our tears, I noticed that we were all feeling the same thing: profound sadness.

Suddenly, a man stepped up to our group and asked calmly, "Helen?" I glanced up and saw that he was short and wore a white doctor's coat. Our huddle broke up.

My nana took a deep, shuddering breath and replied, "Yes, I'm Helen."

"Please come over here. We have some papers for you to sign."

Nana was drowning in grief and could barely communicate, so my mother took over for her. She helped with the endless paperwork: Medicare, the funeral home, arranging services, waiving rights… It all seemed like gobbledygook to me.

I wanted to see Ernie one last time. I peeked into the hospital room next to the bench where Nana had been sitting when we arrived. There was a man lying in the bed. I looked closer and realized that it was Ernie. He was still. Very still. It was in that instant his death became a reality. I had never seen a dead body before, and I was as curious about death as I was sad. I started inching toward him. It was definitely my grandfather, but he was very pale, lifeless, and slightly cold when I poked him. It was a little eerie. I kneeled beside his bed and said a little prayer that my nana made me say every night. In some way, I felt a sense of closure.

After all the paperwork was signed, we drove back to Nana's apartment to pick up a few things so that she would be comfortable staying with us for a short while. As I stood on the threshold of their bedroom, waiting for Nana, I froze, my eyes focused on Ernie's recliner and the window that overlooked Schwartz Brother's Funeral Parlor. *That's where his funeral will be*, I thought. *Weird.*

While my mother, father, and I were upset, Ernie's death took its greatest toll on my nana. They had been the perfect couple and very much in love. I don't think she knew how to carry on without him. None of us did. But, despite the pain, we all marched along.

After my mishaps in elementary school and the death of my grandfather, I looked forward to a new start in junior high. Perhaps a physical change in location would be good for me.

CHAPTER 3

THE SMELL OF JUNIOR HIGH

ON SEPTEMBER 7, 1982, my mother dropped me off at Jefferson Junior High School, which was a nondescript two-story brick building that had been built in the 1960s and housed seventh and eighth graders. As I opened the car door, a wave of oppressive heat bowled me over as I kissed my mother goodbye. Walking toward the school, a kind of mugginess filled the air, making my shorts stick annoyingly to my thighs. I was hot and slightly miserable. This was not a good way to initiate my fresh start. Many people with autism exhibit little tolerance for being uncomfortable, even if the sensation is considered "acceptable" by societal norms.

Regardless, I was starting junior high. Opening the school's heavy grey metal door, I immediately noticed a gaggle of loudly giggling girls conversing around one locker. About what, I didn't know and didn't care. I successfully avoided the catty girls. As I darted past them, I gave myself a pep talk, *You can do junior high! I know you can!*

But now there was something else. My nose began to twitch, and the sensation worsened the farther I went into the building. It was overwhelming. *What the hell is this smell?* I couldn't put my finger on it, but I was determined to super-sleuth it out. As the bell rang, several boys ran past me, and the odor wafted close by. With a jolt, I realized that it was body odor. *Don't they know about deodorant?* I mentally grumbled. Immediately, my doomsday-focused mind went right to gym class. *What will happen there? Won't the smell grow exponentially? I know it will.* I already hated gym. Luckily, I had learned in elementary school that a doctor's note would excuse me from gym. I'd have to find a way to get one.

In addition to the unsettling smells, I soon noticed that several boys had pimples and a tiny few of them sported wiry black threads sticking out of their faces. I stumbled into my first-period science class a few minutes late, since I was still getting my bearings, and the only open seat left was next to Danny Beischel, a peer from elementary school. As I sat beside him, I couldn't help but stare at the five short, wiry hairs emanating from a mole on his cheek. I reached over and grabbed one to pull it out; after all, they didn't belong there. I was just helping him out. However, this behavior did not endear me to him, and Danny, who was proud of his "beard," told everyone what I had done.

My own body had begun to change that summer as well. I was not fond of hair, period, and I was even less fond of hair growing in places where it had not previously been. Over the summer, my hair became thicker, like that of many adolescents. I hated the way it felt when it rubbed against my clothing. Even worse was the sensation of the wind blowing against my skin. It felt like I was being constantly poked. It was a hellish sensory experience, akin to having hundreds of ants crawling all over my body. Every day, I had to muzzle my screams of agony.

One afternoon before the school year began, I had a keen idea and grabbed my mother's Chic Lady razor from my parents' shower. Proud of my plan, I started removing this bushy new hair growth from my arms, armpits, and legs. When I was done, it looked like I had used a chainsaw, given all the accidental cuts and nicks I had inflicted on myself. However, as I inspected my almost-hairless body, a light bulb went off. What if I eliminated *all* of my body hair? With a twinkle in my eye, I gazed into the mirror and began removing my right eyebrow. Halfway through, I thought, *Oh no! This looks awfully stupid.* I was sheepishly humiliated. Putting the weapon down for the day, I left the bathroom, hoping no one would notice my fatal error.

Fortunately, my eyebrow had just about grown back by the time school started, so I only had to face the humiliation of this self-inflicted experience from my own family. My mother was pleasantly understanding and taught me how to properly shave my legs and underarms—but *only* my legs and underarms! I couldn't quite articulate why I hated the sensation of my hair, so she couldn't understand why I wanted it all gone. My parents were fairly oblivious to my differences, and they would only accept normalcy. All of my quirks were dismissed and swept under the rug. To be fair, I also didn't have the vocabulary to explain why or how my sensory processing system was different, as I fundamentally didn't understand that difference. I thought everyone experienced the same things I did.

The natural pleasures of getting older, such as growing taller, were entirely off-putting to me; I have a disdain for change. Disorientation abounds with change. Change evokes unpredictability, and when things are unpredictable, I don't know how to respond. Predictability is consistent and requires no challenge mentally or to my sensory system. Change elicits vulnerability, which often taxes my skills or requires a skill set that I lack.

When my body began to change, it completely changed the way my sensory system functioned, which is vital for perceiving and interpreting information correctly. When I was younger, I had invented various coping strategies to compensate for my faulty sensory system, but each time I grew, these strategies lost their effectiveness or required recalibration, which was arduous and, at times, seemed impossible.

When I first entered the junior high building and smelled the boys, the scent was like a tidal wave constantly poking at me. A "normal" person's sensory system is akin to the ocean's waves. At first, the sensation heightens, and then it crashes down, always leaving the person in a balanced, recalibrated state. For those who are more sensitive—and this includes many people with autism—the wave is much larger and scarier. Plus, the recalibration at the end is not automatic or may not occur at all. As an adult, I learned some rule-based logic, deep breathing exercises, and meditation practices to help me ride the wave, but in junior high, I was defenseless.

There are three core aspects of sensory processing, all of which I struggle with: (1) **Intake**, or how information is perceived or taken in through the senses (for example, seeing a small, round, bouncing object); (2) **Interpretation**, or labeling and analyzing what we experience (we recognize that a small, round, bouncing object equals a ball); and (3) **Output**, or how we react to what we perceive (we play with the ball).

Junior high was a new sensory hell. I couldn't even find my A-game, let alone be on it. A few months in, I was sitting in the cafeteria one day with another outcast student, Thomas. He tapped me on the shoulder (the tap is a sensory **intake**), but I **interpreted** the light touch as a smack. In response, I hit Thomas very hard because I felt attacked (**output**). While it's never okay to hit another person, this type of false interpretation from my sensory system can lead to a host of cognitive distortions.

Mrs. Gorman, the plump, nightmare-ish lunch lady, witnessed the incident and sent me to the principal's office.

When I arrived, the principal sighed and asked me, "What did you do *now*?"

I tried to plead my case. "Thomas hit me first! I was just defending myself…"

The principal, who never even glanced up from his messy desk while I babbled, looked like he wanted to be anywhere but there. He finally interrupted me and said, "Don't do it again, and get out of my office! Now!"

I thought to myself, *Whoa, I just avoided a major punishment.* I went back to the lunchroom, stuck my tongue out at Thomas, and finished my roast beef sandwich.

To exhibit appropriate output, one must "select, enhance, inhibit, compare, and associate the sensory information in a flexible, consistently changing pattern; in other words, it must integrate it" (Ayres, 1972). Integrating one's senses to produce appropriate output is no easy feat. Even internal sensations can be askew. For example, I can never tell the difference between being sick and being tired within my own body. They register as the same thing to me. To cope, I keep a thermometer and Tylenol on my nightstand. That way, I can easily check whether I have a fever and am sick. If not, it's probably time to go to bed.

Our sensory systems play the starring role in helping us make decisions and guide our behaviors. When you're about to sit in a chair, how do you know when to shift your weight from your legs to your buttocks? When driving through a small tunnel, how do you know that your car will fit? How do you know whether you are hungry or need to pee? Your sensory system is continuously providing you with feedback to guide your decisions. Sensory processing and regulation deficits are prevalent in people with autism, but you don't need to have autism or a mental illness to struggle with it.

In my case, I cannot correctly perceive the input from most of my senses. Unquestionably, smell is an issue for me, but so are taste and sound. It is difficult to attend to the world around me when my senses are under assault. When I was a child, my parents and I often frequented restaurants. Loathing variation, I always ordered an extra glass of water with my meal. I would dip my meat in the water, which diminished the flavor, resulting in consistency. If water was not an option, Heinz ketchup was an excellent alternative; I'll eat almost anything with a good dose of Heinz! Many parents describe their child as a "picky eater." I wasn't picky because I didn't like certain foods; I was picky because my pallet felt like it was under attack.

Despite my frequent trips to the principal's office and *Dennis the Menace*-like tendencies, I was generally a good kid. When I had tantrums, I believed they were warranted. One day, my mother, Meri, and I went shopping in New Jersey and stopped for lunch at

McDonald's. Now, I love McDonald's and often went to the one on Queens Boulevard in New York with my nana. So now, I ravenously threw open my Happy Meal and thrust my burger into my mouth. As soon as I tasted it, I jumped up, threw my burger on the floor, and started screaming incoherently. Initially unable to articulate the problem, I finally screamed in terror, "Get it off! Get it off! There's mustard on my burger!!!" Apparently, in the 1970s, New Jersey, unlike New York, put mustard on their burgers or it was simply a mistake. I don't know which one it was.

My mother and Meri were embarrassed as the other customers stared.

"What are you doing?" my mother demanded. "Sit down right now!" She was clearly upset by my display.

Taking a deep, thoughtful breath, Meri whispered to me, "I'll get you another burger without mustard. This isn't a big deal!"

While this was a solution-oriented overture, I still had the slimy and sharp taste of mustard on my tongue. Dipping my napkin in my Coke, I started to remove this disgusting substance.

Not only were my olfactory system and taste buds defective, but my hearing was flawed as well. Anytime my mother ignited her hairdryer or the vacuum, I hid under the covers with a pillow over my head. Quite frankly, these noises were painful and made me miserable. Higher frequency sounds felt like a long-beaked bird repeatedly pecking at my eardrum. I *hated* having my hair blow-dried, even in the dead of winter. My mother playfully called me "Nancy Knot" because my hair was always snaggled, and she and I constantly tussled over the blow-dryer. I always won out; walking to school in the winter with wet hair that would freeze seemed like a better option than being subjected to the sound of the deadly blow-dryer. Fortunately, in my early twenties, I boarded a Delta flight with a double ear infection. During the fight, my eardrums burst, and while it was painful at the time, ultimately, I was left with decreased hearing—like that of a "normal" person. While I still don't like hairdryers and vacuums, I can now somewhat tolerate their sounds.

Another trial I had to endure in junior high was the bells. Every forty-three minutes, five loud bells clanged, holding my ears hostage and signaling a shift to a different classroom with different sensations. Elementary school had been considerably more comfortable, with just one primary classroom, a few special rooms, the lunchroom, and the recess yard. When it was time to transition, everyone lined up alphabetically and tiptoed quietly through the hallways, motivated by winning "the quietest prize." I missed that. Lost in a reverie, I moved through the junior high corridors whispering to my peers, "Please don't touch me."

I hated walking through the overwhelming halls, where hordes of smelly students barreled over each other. Eventually, I learned to ask the teacher a nonsensical question right at the end of class so that we could engage for a few minutes while everyone else rushed out into the halls. Or, I would dart into the bathroom and make my way to my next class once the hallways were clear. I was generally a few minutes late to class, but no one seemed to care.

One day in seventh grade, Scott Spenser approached me as I was darting from math class. He karate-chopped the books out of my hand and berated me, "You have BO, dumbass. I saw you smelling your desk in math. What are you, a freak?"

"Ha ha. I was smelling you! When was the last time you took a shower, stinkball?" I shot back. I felt satisfied with my good comeback.

Overall, junior high was exhausting. Every day after school, I barely had enough energy to play with my Atari.

Shortly after the Scott Spenser incident, my father came into my room to kiss me goodnight before I went to bed. He could see that I was upset. "What's up, chum? You look down," he observed.

"I hate junior high, Dad. All the kids are mean to me," I said, wiping my nose on my pajama sleeve as tears welled up.

"How could that be? Don't they see what a terrific person you are? They're just not looking hard enough. There's no reason to be mean to you," he said. "Maybe you're just taking this too hard. Perhaps they're just playing around."

The more he tried to explain away my experiences, the more upset I became. My tears flowed fast and hard as I contemplated whether this might all actually be my fault. I tried to reply, but my sobbing prevented me from forming a coherent sentence.

"Hold on," he said. "I'll be right back." I assumed he was going to get my mother, but instead, he returned with a little round peach pill. "Take this. You'll feel better." He was my dad, so I listened. About thirty minutes later, I did feel better, though a little woozy.

"What was that, Dad?" I was honestly curious.

"Valium. They're great for calming down."

While Valium did not solve my problem, it did dampen my sensory system, effectively calming my anxiety. I've been taking Valium on and off since seventh grade, and I have to admit that Dad was right about its effects. Valium is my drug of choice even today, though now I only use it occasionally as a one-off, short-term solution to a problem.

Following that night, my dad would sporadically and infrequently act as a Valium dispenser. Eventually though, I found another, more potent remedy.

One Saturday when I was in seventh grade, my mom took me roller skating, and I mildly sprained my ankle. As we tightly wrapped it with an ace bandage, I noticed a funny squeezing sensation. The normal hypersensitivity on my skin and inside my body seemed to diminish. It wasn't that I didn't feel the blood rushing through my foot and ankle, but it was tolerable, and that part of my body no longer hijacked my attention. When the wrap was fully pinned in place, relief instantly flooded my nervous system.

Hmm… I thought. *What if I ace-bandaged my whole body?* Applying my father's old adage, "If one is good, ten are better," I asked my mom to purchase many more ace bandages. It was now fall, and I was wearing long-sleeved shirts and pants, which unintentionally and coincidently would hide the evidence of my plan. Before school on Monday morning, I stood in front of my bathroom mirror and tightly wrapped myself from chest to ankles. I immediately felt better. For the first time, I was on a level playing field with my internal sensations. When I went to school that day, I also discovered that dulling my internal sensations also increased my tolerance for others.

I wrapped myself every day for weeks and showed my smile for the first time in junior high. Gym class wasn't a problem because I had an ongoing knee injury and a doctor's note excusing me from having to participate.

Then, one day, an announcement came over the school PA system: "All 'Team A' seventh-grade girls please report to the nurse's office." We were being screened for scoliosis. I didn't even know what scoliosis was, let alone why I needed to be screened for it.

As I waited in line at the nurse's office, Lena Norwak, the most popular girl in school, stood right behind me. Curious as to what scoliosis was, I peered around the girl in front of me and saw Mrs. Sheehan, the nurse, instruct each girl to take off her shirt and bend forward at the waist. Then, she ran her hands over the girl's back. With deep apprehension, I thought, "This is going to end badly." I was so focused on the idea of Mrs. Sheehan touching me that it didn't even occur to me that she might react badly to my ace bandages.

"Next! Remove your shirt," Mrs. Sheehan bellowed when it was my turn.

As I stripped in front of the other girls, Mrs. Sheehan jumped off her stool. "What is this?" she asked gravely. She seemed concerned as she eyed the ace bandages encasing my whole body.

Proudly, I said, "Oh, I figured out a way to stop my body from hurting. You know, to stop the creepy-crawly feeling."

She looked dumbfounded and clueless as to how to respond. All the girls behind me were laughing. I genuinely didn't understand Mrs. Sheehan's disapproval or my peers' reaction. Without a word, she unraveled my bandages and tossed them in the trash. After she checked me for scoliosis, I sorrowfully walked out to the recess yard. And, no, I don't have scoliosis.

As soon as Lena burst through the recess yard doors, she made a B-line for me, making offensive comments about how weird and crazy I was.

In that moment, I'd had enough. I had lost my cherished ace bandages that had provided so much relief, I had endured being touched by Mrs. Sheehan, and now, Lena was calling me names. She was a girly-girly who clearly didn't know how to fight, whereas my dad and I play fought all the time. I knew how to twist her arm throw a punch. And so I did. I broke her arm and momentarily felt vindicated. However, my mother was none too amused and made me pay for Lena's doctor's bill. Still, it was worth every penny!

Recess had always been a social struggle for me. Built-in activities such as sand play and searching for frogs had been abundant in elementary school. However, junior high was different. After lunch, the students were let outside for a short time, but the metal playground equipment was gone, and we were left with just brick walls and a broken basketball hoop, which the boys monopolized. The girls generally huddled together talking or putting on makeup. Neither of these activities interested me. Even worse, there were now more social norms that I didn't comprehend or care about.

One day in seventh grade, I spotted my neighbor Eric Anderson on the recess yard. He was a year older than me and the one person who was always either blissfully unaware of my differences or didn't care about them. We had often played together at home, and now, we attended the same junior high. He was an outsider, sweet, weird, and nerdy, just like me. With the hope of having found a life raft, I moseyed over.

Spread out in front of him and a few of his friends was a Dungeons and Dragons map. As I approached, he looked up and said, "Hey, Alex! Guess what? My recess time changed, and now we're together. We're recess mates!"

I could feel my entire chest melt with relief. "That's amazing!" I replied with a grin. With Eric as my protector, I had a posse! I didn't need to be popular, just to belong somewhere.

With Eric lending me his circle of nerd-friends, I was socially set. Now, I just needed to contend with my faulty sensory system.

Then, one magical outing with my mother to Astoria Federal Bank led to a solution. I always *loved* visiting the bank because everyone spoke softly and the thickness of the walls served as sound insulation. And, as a bonus, the vault's thick walls and colossal shiny silver lock always fascinated me. I was having a particularly uncomfortable sensory day, and as I looked around, I suddenly drew a parallel between my sensory system and the bank.

I came up with a sensory budget that worked like a bank account. I listed all possible daily activities that I engaged in (getting out of bed, peer interactions, playing with Legos by myself, eating white bread, and so on) and assigned a numerical value to each one based upon how irritating they were to my sensory system. Some activities, such as eating bland white bread, only ate up a small portion of the budget (say, $0.50). In contrast, activities such as social interactions with non-preferred people and topics and unpredictable situations ate up an exorbitant amount of my budget (as high as $25). Each day, I started my budget with $100, and I knew that I needed to live within that to remain stable. Any activity that came with anxiety, unpredictability, or a need for me to be flexible was entirely consuming, no matter what it was. Once I had "spent" close to $100, I needed to end my day or replenish my budget by engaging in pro-sensory activities, such as running, riding my bike, or sleeping. This intervention provided me with rule-based logic to guide my behavior, and to this day, it is one of the most useful tools I have.

At school, when I ran out of sensory points, I intentionally got in trouble so that I could sit on the principal's "quiet bench." This strategy was effective in a pinch. When he called me into his office, the principal always asked probing questions about why I was in trouble (again) and how I would change my behavior in the future. I could never muster up a good answer, although I tried.

In eighth grade, he introduced me to Mrs. Vigstein, who always spoke slowly and softly. She had long brown hair and stunning jade-green eyes with unusual yellow speckles that I found distracting. Mrs. Vigstein was from the guidance department and took me to her office to talk and "play games," which, in retrospect, from what I could gather, was a euphuism for an assessment.

When I reviewed my records for this book, I found her notes from our meetings: "Alex is complicated to figure out. At times she's an exemplary student, yet often misbehaves…Her testing indicates that she is cognitively intact, but lacks emotional insight into her challenges…She doesn't seem to have a peer group which staff on Team A is concerned about…"

This school seemed to be full of smart educators, so why couldn't they figure out that I was purposely getting in trouble? Furthermore, it's frustrating how they all turned a blind eye to the fact that I was frequently bullied.

By December of eighth grade, junior high in general and rushing around every forty-three minutes had started to feel familiar. Taking the plunge, I also extended myself and spoke to a few of the popular girls in my math class. I thought that if they liked me, I would be popular, too. They asked to cheat off my tests, and I thought friendship was a good trade-off. Eva, Diane, Krisa, and Doreen all sat around me, imitating the pop star Cyndi Lauper with her wild makeup and big hair. While I had no interest in wearing makeup or changing my appearance, I felt respected that they would even talk to me. I also secretly enjoyed watching their punk-rock black makeup start to smudge around their eyes at the end of the day. The effect looked interesting, like a Salvador Dali painting.

The more I let them cheat, the more the girls took me under their wing and taught me what was "cool" and how I should talk and act. At the time, speaking like a "Valley girl" was all the rage. To do so, one would commonly start a sentence with the word "like." Then, throw in several "totally"s and mix it with a few "radicals" or "rads." With these rules, I was set and could now say things such as, "Like, what totally should we do now? Like, something totally rad, I hope." I could handle this.

In many ways, these lessons helped me socially far more than Ms. Vigstein's "talk therapy." Eventually, I thought I was popular because

I was friendly with the cool girls, and I refused to meet with Ms. Vigstein anymore.

In return for their cultural education and protection from the other students, not only did I pay them in good grades in math, but also something they really wanted: scotch and tequila. On Saturday nights, they would arrive at my house around eight p.m. when my parents left to go clubbing. My parents hosted countless parties at home, so there was always an abundance of alcohol around. Back then, people didn't lock their liquor cabinets, I think, and I frankly doubt that my parents ever noticed the alcohol was missing. If nothing else, they never said anything about it. This is when my love of tequila began. Initially, I didn't like the taste of liquor, but eventually, it became something I craved.

These antics went on for several months until the spring trip to Washington, DC.

For this eighth-grade rite of passage, students submitted their roommate preferences. Crowds congregated as results were posted, and my nose was close to the list. As I scanned the list and saw the names of my friends, but not my own, I muttered aloud, "What? What? Something's wrong…" When I finally found my name, I was shocked to discover that no one wanted to room with me; I was assigned to share a room with Mrs. Lewis, our English teacher. Holding back the tears, I thought, *What happened to my math and Saturday night friends? I really thought they liked me. But if that's true, then why didn't they request to be my roommate?*

I confronted them. "Hey guys, can I room with you?" I asked.

Eva said snarkily, "Like, can you sneak in some scotch and tequila on the bus?"

"A-ah, I don't think I can," I said. "That's against school rules."

Diane chimed in, "Sorry, then. Totally no room in the inn!"

Doreen rolled her eyes. "Like, we're going to Washington to have a totally good time, and you'll just ruin it. It won't be rad with you there."

In a pack, they walked away flipping their hair and giggling.

I had thought these girls were my friends, but apparently, I was wrong. On some level, I had always known they were using me, but I had thought it was worth it. Only in retrospect did I realize that this situation was similar to Stephanie Tumbler's "pay-to-play" offer in elementary school.

I tried several times to talk to my mom about the Washington, DC, room assignment issue, but was too apprehensive to bring it up. I was embarrassed that these girls had been using me, and I also didn't want to confess how much liquor we drank.

Coincidently, the wretched stomach pains that I'd had for years were getting worse around this time and I was prescribed Belladonna, a tranquilizing anti-spasmodic. This medication did help my physical discomfort, but it couldn't touch my emotions. When the Washington, DC, trip came around, my pain was so intense that I had to stay home. While this wasn't a conscious choice on my part, I do think it was my way of avoiding social loneliness and rooming with Mrs. Lewis. My parents were reasonably attentive to my physical ailments, yet they avoided anything emotional like the plague, so they let me stay home and didn't ask any awkward questions. I was relieved.

That weekend, my dad was away on a business trip, which afforded my mom and me some quality time. She took this opportunity to give me a "heart-to-heart" about my toys. These were my treasures, and I struggled to see what might be objectionable about them. My mom pointed out several toys that were geared for much younger kids, such as the Play-Doh Fuzzy Pumper Barbershop and my beloved Matchbox car collection. In a kind manner, she explained that other kids might think I was weird if I played with toys meant for a seven-year-old. "You're twice that age now," she gently reminded me. I took her words under advisement.

However, when I returned home from school on Monday, I discovered that she had thrown away all of my toys and replaced them with makeup and hair clips. I was furious. I had agreed to consider her advice, but I wasn't ready to let go of my prized possessions! Still, I must admit that her actions nudged me closer to fitting in.

I was miserable. My "friends" would no longer talk to me, Eric Anderson and his cohort were now in high school, and the noisy lunchroom frustrated me beyond measure. I was back where I had started: alone.

While I was sinking socially, academically, I was thriving. Despite my third-grade teacher's assessment that I was "retarded," academics came easy to me.

That year, in Mr. O'Sullivan's social studies class, we engaged in a persuasive essay contest. The finalist would give an oral presentation on their topic of choice. Perhaps because I had been depressed for most of my childhood, I became obsessed with Jack Kevorkian, an advocate for the right to die and physician-assisted suicide. If someone was suffering so much that life didn't seem worth living, I believed that they should have the choice to exercise that option. Not only was I a finalist in the essay contest, but I also won the oral presentation. The material was personal and eerie; I gave details from my own life about wanting to die. If this were today, the guidance department would have immediately sprung in, but my conversations with Ms. Vigstein ended months back. This paper was a cry for help, and thankfully, Mr. O'Sullivan stepped up.

Mr. O'Sullivan was a short man with reddish hair and a great sense of humor; he kind of looked like a leprechaun. I don't think he knew what specifically was wrong with me, but after my presentation, he let me eat lunch with him every day. At least now, I knew that I would have a calming forty-three-minute reprieve. Mr. O'Sullivan and I talked about all sorts of things. Fortunately, most of them weren't related to his social studies class, which I found boring. He told me about the poor relationship he had with his father and how his dad was never there for him. He also vowed to not make the same mistakes with his boys. He introduced me to Harry Chapin's song "Cat's in the Cradle," and the lyrics adhered to my cerebrum. Mr. O'Sullivan had a tape deck in the back of his room, and every time he hit *Play*, I teared up.

Because I had become an authority on suffering, I felt that I could relate to him. I disclosed my destitute social life and other things that were bothering me at home. He was sympathetic but never flinched. Mr. O'Sullivan became my rock, and I finally looked forward to attending school because of him. They say it only takes one teacher to make a difference in a kid's life, and mine was Mr. O'Sullivan.

Aside from my time with Mr. O'Sullivan, school in general was still stressful. Luckily, my home life remained fairly stable. I confessed to my mother that I had thrown away the makeup and hair accessories she bought and asked if we could redecorate my room. She gladly obliged. My mom and I took a trip to Nick's Design Studio and picked out a beautiful pattern of navy-blue wallpaper with small white flowers the size of a thumbnail all over. I loved it. The colors were soothing and didn't eat into my sensory budget *at all*. We decorated my room with things I considered important, such as slings to hold my stuffed animals, pictures of turtles, and a huge fish tank. However, my favorite object was my new stereo system with two tape slots, which I could use to make mixtapes. Music was, and still is, one of the best remedies for my sensory system and moods. I created a tape for every possible emotional state, which was extremely helpful. I relished my new bedroom, which became my oasis.

CHAPTER 4

HOUSE OF CARDS

IT WAS EARLY June 1984, and I recall thanking God that junior high would be over soon. I looked forward to sleeping in, riding my new ten-speed blue bike, and hanging out with Eric and his sister, Sarah, who was two years my junior. Their house was directly across the street from mine and cascaded with amazingly colorful toys. I clocked many hours there. We both had swimming pools in our backyards and ran, screaming like banshees, in our bathing suits from one pool to the other, seeing who could get there first and make the biggest splash.

One Saturday, my parents were hosting a high school reunion for my father in our back yard and expected about fifty people. The caterers were outdoors putting the final touches on the tables and chairs and lining up the liquor on the outdoor bar. I left Eric and Sarah's house, where I had spent the morning, and trotted across the street to help with the final touches. The back yard looked beautiful. As I was absorbing the atmosphere, I realized that I was thirsty. My dad had told me to leave the drinks at the bar for the company, so I went inside to our kitchen. I picked up a can of Coke and sauntered down our long, off-white hallway, running my fingers across the scratchy textured wallpaper. I stopped at our house's entranceway.

All of a sudden, I started to cough forcefully, and my brow began to sweat. Charcoal smoke filled the air. Looking up, I was overcome with terror as I saw scorching flames shoot from the ceiling and the tops of the walls. Our house was on fire. All of the fire-safety rules that we practiced each year in school (stop, drop, and roll) went right out of my head. I panicked and ran to the backyard, screaming, "The house is on fire!" I'm not sure what my parents did because I immediately turned and ran to my bedroom. I grabbed my stuffed bunny and then hid in my closet. Scared and unable to formulate a cohesive thought, I was helpless as image after image of fire ran through my mind. My soul was burning down with the house.

Fortunately, I had one of those bright-red "tot finder" stickers placed prominently on my window. I assume the firemen immediately recognized it. Soon, a fireman was carrying me—and my stuffed bunny—out of my closet to safety, just like in the image on the sticker.

While I was grateful that my parents and cat were saved, everything else important to me was gone. We lost it all. Now, no place felt safe. I experienced a swirl of sadness, anger, and fear. As we sat on Eric and Sarah's front stone wall, my mom, dad, and I watched the firemen drag their thick, coffee-colored hoses into our home, which was already crumbling. I disclosed to my mom that I was quite upset about this loss. We had just redecorated my bedroom, and now, all of my important possessions, with the single exception of my stuffed bunny, had disappeared without warning.

I started to cry.

My parents are very practical and always look at the logical side of things. While I was having a visceral reaction to this loss, my parents tried to remind me that we had only lost material possessions, all of which could be replaced; everyone was unharmed. This, of course, is a healthy analysis of the situation, but my grief process wasn't there just yet.

That night, we stayed with my parents' friends, Alice and Adam. In the morning, the fire department called with news that the fire had rekindled overnight and that the house had sustained catastrophic damage. It was now a total loss. The cause was faulty electrical wiring. Hearing this news, I slowly walked into Alice's bathroom and stared at myself in the mirror. I started slapping myself in the face, expecting to feel something, even a tingling, but I was numb.

After that, we moved to a waterfront home on Morgan's Island, a tiny patch of land in the Long Island Sound, for about a year. There weren't many homes on the island, and the isolation gave me a sense of comfort.

While living on Morgan's Island, I continued to attend Jefferson Junior High and later the town's high school. Between the stress of junior high school and now losing everything, my psychiatric stability began to slip. Around this time, I started having erratic mood shifts and paranoid delusions that felt out of control. Before the fire, I'd had hallucinations once or twice around age ten, but nothing like what blossomed in my brain now.

I was walking past the picture window in my family's guestroom one day when, out of nowhere, I saw a plane hovering overhead. Paratroopers were climbing down to the ground on tan ropes and pointing machine guns at me. They began to shoot, and I was hit! At least, I thought I was, despite the lack of blood or bullet holes. I ran screaming to my mother, who brushed it off as my "active imagination." Not having the vocabulary to truly describe this experience, I started calling such incidents "daymares," since they were similar to nightmares. I tried to tell my nana what was happening to me, and she was at least sympathetic. With her delicious matzo ball soup and head rubs, she knew just how to make everything better. And for a while, it helped.

However, eventually, even nana's matzo balls couldn't do the trick. *What is going on with me?* I repeatedly thought. *I can't trust my mind. It keeps tricking me. I'm scared. So scared.* Like a noose, my disturbing intrusive thoughts choked me and grabbed hold of my mind. The frequency of these daymares gradually increased from "occasionally" to "sometimes" to "most of the time." There were so many distortions; my mind became jumbled. I thought I had caused Ronald Reagan's cancer. I was convinced I had set fire to our old home. Once, I thought I was the owner of our local Pathmark supermarket.

Other times, I thought that I was a criminal and that the police were stationed around my house, ready to pounce. I often heard people whispering derogatory comments about me. These thoughts and sensations all felt *real*. They weren't like some passing fancy.

In time, I could no longer distinguish reality from fantasy. In my more lucid moments, it was glaringly obvious to me that something was wrong. Still, I decided not to tell my parents. They are very logical people and don't react well to emotional issues. Luckily, now that we were living on Morgan's Island, I was socially isolated, which kept my secret secure. I felt it was best to keep this development between myself and my nana, the only person I could trust fully.

While I was psychologically struggling, paradoxically, Morgan's Island offered me safety in a way that I'd never experienced before. The sound of ocean waves breaking on the shore was tranquil and soothing. There was a door from my bedroom that led right out onto the beach, and I was able to boat, fish, and walk along the jetties whenever I wanted. My parents' bedroom was upstairs on the other side of the house, which might have been another continent, as far as I was concerned. I had many midnight walks along the beach and found much-needed solace there.

That summer, my nana rubbed my head. A lot. At one point, she pleaded with me to talk with my parents about my symptoms. I suspect that with her own former mental health issues, it frightened her to see me stray down the same path. I begged her not to tell them, and I believe she acquiesced.

One September day, I caught my parents unexpectedly scurrying out the door. I didn't understand their atypical behavior. When they returned a few hours later, my father was crying. I had never seen him cry before. Mom and Dad were quietly mumbling to each other, but I couldn't quite hear them. Finally, I demanded, "What's going on?"

My mother said, "Nana has lung cancer, which has metastasized into her bone marrow."

"The doctors don't know how much time she has left," my father added solemnly.

My thoughts began racing a mile a minute. *How can this be true? Why does God keep punishing me? I must be a bad kid. What will I do without Nana?* I loved her. She was the rock of my stability and acceptance.

After that, I spent every moment with her that I could. At night, I skipped many rocks into the ocean as I struggled to accept this development. Nana knew that she was going to die, and we frequently conversed about the inevitable. She imparted many pearls of wisdom to me, such as, "Always treat others with respect," "Listen to your parents," and "Don't die defending the right of way," referring to my tendency to dig my feet in whenever I thought I was right, despite the consequences or another person's feelings.

As one of her final acts, Nana gave away many of her possessions. I was the recipient of her Broadway dance shoes, some *Playbills* from the shows she was in, her childhood cross, and her cameras. As the months passed, she grew weaker and got out of bed less and less often. On Thanksgiving, I kept her company while the rest of the family was in the living room.

She died the day after Christmas.

I still miss so many things about her. She played with me. She would simply listen to me and not judge. She didn't care how disordered my thinking was. She never gave up on me. She was proud to call me her granddaughter and showed me off to her friends. She always hung my artwork on her fridge. She never tried to change me. And, above all, I felt "normal" around her. Everyone needs at least one person who believes in them and loves them unconditionally.

My nana's death pushed me over the edge. My mind was now fractured. With her gone, I knew that the bottom had fallen out of my life in a way that walking along the jetties and skipping stones couldn't repair. My world simply crumbled.

As my parents made funeral arrangements, they began their own unique grieving processes. My mother grew more organized and preoccupied with rebuilding the house that had burned down. My dad worked even harder and came home later. They were emotionally distant and didn't notice my slow eight-month descent, which culminated in an extreme explosion of mania with psychosis, followed by a despondent depression. At least, I like to think they were too preoccupied to notice. In retrospect, my illness was fairly obvious. It is distressing to think that they might have been ignoring the signs.

During this time, both at home and at school, I experienced periods when I was not lucid at all and had little insight into what was reality. I suspect I flew under the radar at school because these psychiatric symptoms, while present for months at a time, the intensity waxed and waned throughout the day. When I experienced hallucinations, I simply left class, often with very little follow-up by the teachers. Additionally, due to my autism, I had no real friends. There was no one for me to confide in, bounce ideas off of, or be my eyes and ears when my thoughts seemed to go crazy.

I had no idea what I was experiencing; I only knew that it wasn't normal. I was trapped in a 1980's horror movie like *Motel Hell* or *The Shining*. My moods shifted from grand elation with extreme giddiness and intense euphoria to frank psychosis. I think my parents mistook my mania for happiness, and they were just glad that I appeared to have overcome my nana's death. I didn't dare tell them about my hallucinations and delusions. I was afraid of how they would react. Plus, then, I would have to actually deal with my instability. On the other hand, I was also equally afraid that they would ignore what I had to say. Both options seemed terrible, so I kept my mouth sealed.

This eight-month period during my first year at our town's high school was challenging, to say the least. Surprisingly, in high school, I found that I could disappear into the walls and simply be ignored by my peers instead of being constantly picked on. I don't understand the reason for this change in social behavior, but it was preferable to all of my other educational experiences. My stomach spasms were also getting worse, and they frequently kept me home and certainly excused me from gym class.

As my symptoms got worse, my mania seemed to be toughening up and becoming brawnier. Episodes of verbal diarrhea were common, which resulted in constant inappropriate "blurts" and comments during class. While I could hide my autism symptoms to a degree when mania hitched a ride, my coping skills and sensory budget vanished. Mania takes over the brain's reasoning center, and whatever impulse I thought or felt became my actionable top priority. Because my perspective-taking skills back then were skimpy, I don't know what my teachers or peers thought, but I can imagine that it was not kindness or understanding.

A few times throughout this year, the guidance department called me in for "a talk." I always promised to stop blurting things out in class, but the babbling continued. I couldn't control my bipolar disorder. No one can.

While my parents were very supportive in terms of making me self-sufficient and always looking on the bright side, they also ignored signs that something was seriously wrong. Because of this, I lacked opportunities to gain missing skills and overcome my disordered thinking. My parents and I were like the yin and yang symbol, each living in our own very different worlds. I often wished that they could see my perspective and embrace me and *my* interests, such as running, bicycling, photography, and, of course, the tape factory!

One evening toward the end of ninth grade, a tall gentleman came to our house bearing colorful brochures advertising a European tour for teens that summer. With good intentions, my parents thought this trip might be just the distraction from school that I needed. Plus, they were always pushing me to engage with "normal" kids, as if I could absorb their stability through osmosis. Within a week, they had signed me up for a whirlwind tour of northern and western Europe. I didn't want to go, but my fear of disappointing my extremely excited dad won out.

The European countries we visited were beautiful, and I enjoyed the landscapes and cities. I took my nana's camera with me and bought ten rolls of film with a combination of ISO 200 and 800, which helps determine the exposure. During the day, I could ignore my peers and focus on photography. The evenings, however, were horrific. I was the youngest person on the tour, and the other kids were mean. While I could hold my liquor, they all smoked heaps of pot, something I hadn't experimented with, and teased me mercilessly about my refusal to smoke. It wasn't that I didn't want to try pot, but I was petrified that my frightening thoughts and visions would creep out of my head into the real world. I quickly came to hate the trip and counted down the days until it was over. Plus, my stomach was acting up again and felt as if it were hemorrhaging. I was under too much stress.

When we were in Paris, the counselors took us out to a disco one night. It served alcohol to everyone and didn't seem to mind that people were smoking pot. I sat down at a table by myself. The blaring music which pecked at my ears reminded me of my parents' parties in the seventies. I was overstimulated and needed peace and quiet. I had to get out of here.

Through the smoke, I spotted Toni, one of the counselors, and made my way over to her. "Would it be *possible* to go back to the hotel?" I asked.

Matter-of-factly, she stated, "No, I'm sorry. We all need to stay together." She patted my arm and said with a slightly drunken smile, "Have fun! Go out on the dance floor!"

Frustrated by her answer, I decided that my best option was to join in the revelry. I began downing tequila shots, my old standby. The more drunk I became, the less organized my thinking was. I could no longer stand this nightclub and the tour itself. My stomach was killing me. Tears began cascading down my face. I hated my life and was done with everything and everyone. I wanted to be with my nana again. I missed her so much. There was something very wrong with me, and I needed it to be over. I wanted the pain to end. *I wanted to die.*

Slithering into a corner table, I sat by myself, took a full bottle of Belladonna out of my bag, and seductively caressed it. With tequila onboard, increasing my impulsivity, I unscrewed the top and ingested the whole bottle within minutes.

I only remember snippets of what happened next, so I was probably floating in and out of consciousness. I do remember Toni at my side in the nightclub, holding my hand gratefully thinking my life will be over soon. Despite the chaos around me, I *finally* felt peaceful. I heard blaring European medic sirens, which sounded familiar with their *non-e, non-e, non-e* drone. Someone in a white and red outfit picked me up. I have a vague memory of vomiting all over him and myself at the hospital. After that, my mind is completely blank until the next day.

There was a flurry of action around my bed when I opened my eyes. It all felt like a dream. But it wasn't. I really had tried to kill myself, but clearly didn't succeed. Damn. The doctors and nurses were all speaking French, and I didn't understand a word. All I knew was that my throat was sore, my stomach hurt, and I didn't know how to ask for red Jell-O in French.

At that moment, Toni came into my room. I had never been so glad to see her face. "Are you okay?" she asked.

"I don't know," I replied in a monotone voice. "I'm really sad, and I don't want to be alive anymore."

"Can I just sit here with you?"

"I guess." I gazed out the window to avoid further conversation. I couldn't explain myself, let alone coherently verbalize it to another.

Someone from the teen tour called my parents and I assume let them know what had transpired. It was agreed that I needed to fly home. Immediately. My parents arranged for me to fly back to the States on the Concorde, a supersonic jet that flew from Paris to New York in three hours. I've heard amazing things about the Concorde, but to this day, I have little memory of the experience. My mind was still murky.

I should have seen a psychiatrist as soon as I got home, but instead, my parents brought me to the pediatrician's office. He concluded that I was fine. I'm not sure what criteria he used, but I was anything but fine.

That September of tenth grade, my mind was completely jumbled, and I started to believe that I could control electricity. Within one week of school beginning, I had collapsed in the hallway with crippling stomach pain and was rushed to North Shore University Hospital, where I was admitted for over two weeks. The hospital staff ran what felt like a million tests, all of which came back normal. However, I continued to have brutal stomach pain. I was placed on the opioid Demerol, which I took every two hours for about two weeks. During that admission, my parents often brought their friends Jason and Elizabeth to visit me, and they augmented my medication with sips of wine. Lying in the hospital bed I felt monumentally scared as I was aware that I couldn't control my mind and still had a strong desire to die.

At this point, going over the edge was inevitable, but with the supplemental enhancement of wine and my body not reacting well to the Demerol, my mind rapidly ruptured. I thought that the static on the television was sending me messages and that there was a colony of people living in the grains of wood on the oak door of my hospital room. I called them the "floor people" who lived in another dimension. Convinced that I had a specific medallion at home that was evil, I called my mother in the middle of the night and told her to throw it in one particular sewer on the road where we lived, so that I could save the world. Worst of all, I thought Dr. Cole, who was in charge of my case, was secretly trying to poison me. I'm not proud of this, but at one point when I was particularly psychotic, I lunged at her when she entered the room. Luckily, I was restrained immediately. When you are psychotic, there is only one reality. There's no way to pause and think.

At this point, the medical doctors had drawn their conclusion that I was psychologically ill. And despite their deep denial, even my parents could no longer hide from the fact that there was something severely wrong with me, both developmentally and psychologically.

I was fifteen years old, and this started my first journey in a mental institution.

I was scared shitless when they transferred me by ambulance from

North Shore University Hospital to Stonyfield Psychiatric Hospital, an institution in upstate New York, but everyone assured me that my stay would only be for two weeks.

It lasted almost a year.

As I peered out of the ambulance's window, we turned onto the long driveway leading up the institution. The entrance was flanked by sprawling bright-green lawns. I spotted tennis courts, a golf facility, and an enormous building of brick and stone, which looked like a European mansion. I thought this place looked like a country club and not something from the horror movies I watched on television, such as *One Flew Over the Cuckoo's Nest*.

As it turned out, my soul would be repeatedly raped at this institution over the next year. During the entire year, I never once played tennis or golf or strolled along that picturesque landscape.

The intake process took place in a fancy room with a gleaming hardwood floor, wainscoting, and big olive-green leather chairs, one for each of us. My parents and I met with Dr. Broodner, an older gentleman who put on airs with his stiff posture and condescending tone. Quite plump, he wore thick brown glasses and had white beard; I thought he looked like Colonel Sanders or Sigmund Freud. I felt like he was analyzing my every word.

Dr. Broodner asked me a ton of questions, some of which made me angry because I had just gone through a similar psychological evaluation at North Shore University Hospital. Many questions were uncomfortable, such as, "Do you ever see things that aren't there?" and "Do you hear sounds that don't exist?" I answered these honestly, but from my perspective, the things I saw and heard *were* real. In my chart, he wrote, "Patient and patient's parents refuse to acknowledge psychotic symptoms."

After this litany of questions, I was exhausted, and my parents and I were shown to Elbert-North, the unit I was being admitted to.

Elbert-North was an adolescent unit and looked nothing like Dr. Broodner's office. The walls were painted institutional white and were covered with scuff marks. There were two long L-shaped hallways with sparse bedrooms on either side. Where the hallways intersected, there was a community room, which sported three gross, coarse, stained couches and ashtrays overflowing with cigarette butts. Apparently, teens were permitted to smoke, so long as they had their parents' permission. There was also a small television with a scratch across the screen. The windows opened, but there was thick mesh wire obscuring the view. A few patients shuffled about. Overlooking this hellhole was a nurses' station behind plexiglass windows. Beside it sat an itchy-looking maroon chair that would soon become my closest friend.

My parents stayed with me on the unit for about ten minutes and were then ushered out the door. I felt quite vulnerable and sad once they were gone.

As soon as my parents left, I was patted down like a criminal, endured a cavity inspection, had my shoelaces removed, and was forced to trade in my street clothes for a hospital gown. I thought, *How am I going to play tennis in a hospital gown?* My possessions were stored away from me, and my room door was locked, forcing me to socialize, which only made my mental and emotional state worse. Being alone in a dark room in my bed had always been soothing, but this was not allowed here.

Complicating manners, I was completely manic. My mind raced endlessly. As soon as I was released into the community room, I panicked and bolted toward the door to go after my parents and beg them to rescue me. What kind of hell had they put me in? But the door was locked, and they were long gone. This bolting action alarmed the hospital staff, and within seconds, a loud buzzer went off and I experienced my initiation into hospital-aversive therapy.

Hordes of burly men dashed onto Elbert-North as one of the nurses bellowed, "Get her! She's running toward the door."

As they converged on me, furious words flew from my mouth: "Screw you! Leave me alone! Get me the fuck out of here! I don't belong here! I'm not crazy! Stay away from me! I bite!" My voice was like that of a tortured animal. *They aren't taking me without a fight*, I thought.

I was hysterical at this point, and when the men cornered me, I panicked and started swinging frantically. It was five gargantuan men against one lanky adolescent. I lost. In an instant, they had grabbed my arms and legs and pinned me stomach-down on the floor. Next, one of them lifted my hospital gown and ripped my underwear down, exposing my ass. I felt the sting of a needle filled with a hefty dose of some mind-numbing sedative enter my body. Then, the burly men carried me hog-style to the "quiet room," which reeked of stale sweat, like an old gym locker, and proceeded to tie me down with thick leather restraints around my wrists and ankles.

I was terrified and wondered if I would be here indefinitely. Was this the way my life would end? I tried to wiggle out of the restraints, without success. The more I wiggled, the more the straps cut into my skin. My body kept writhing, though; I was manic and absolutely couldn't calm down. Being restrained was the worst possible intervention. Having no control, I exercised what was not muzzled: my voice. I screamed. Loudly. And often.

Several hours later, I finally stopped wiggling and screaming, which prompted the staff to unleashed me from the restraints just before dinner. I now sported the first of what would be many sets of black and blue marks all over my body.

Soon after, I was ushered to the dining hall and directed to sit down at a white plastic table with other adolescents. Older heavy-set ladies with hairnets scurried around, balancing individual trays of food. The institutional gray tray was sectioned off for various foods.

When my tray was placed in front of me, my anxiety instantly escalated. I could feel my pulse rapidly throbbing in my neck. The gravy from the mystery meat had jumped over the guardrail and leaked onto my potatoes. In my autistic world, food could not co-mingle. Potatoes could no longer be classified as potatoes if they had gravy on them. I simply couldn't reconcile this. I immediately started screaming and jumped up, accidentally knocking my tray onto the floor.

In a snap, a twig-like staff member with deep cratered acne scars and stringy, greasy hair yelled in her thick New York accident, "She's going off! Hit the buzzer!"

A loud alarm sounded, and in an instant, hordes of enormous men raced into the dining hall and pinned me face down on the floor. As before, each beast grabbed a limb, and someone pulled my underwear down and jabbed a needle into my ass. Within minutes, I felt extremely woozy and stopped screaming and fighting. I was then carried back to the "quiet room."

When I was released again hours later, I requested my sketchbook and began to draw. I'm honestly not sure why I drew myself naked and looking out the window with my hands and legs tied to the wall, when I was actually restrained on the bed, but here's the picture.

For the next four months, I spent considerable amounts of time in that room. The "quiet room," as it was called, consisted of four thick white walls made of concrete cinderblocks, a window covered in dense mesh that overlooked maple trees, and the locked door, which contained a minuscule window at the top. The staff used it to leer in at me. Every time I was locked in here, I was convinced that I could escape, and every time, I was wrong. For me, an average stay in the quiet room was anywhere from three to twelve hours. Twice, it was overnight.

Because I was in the quiet room for so long, I often ended up needing to pee. I would screech this need, but was always met with silence. "Please, please!" I'd beg. "I can't hold it anymore. I promise I'll be good."

Crickets.

After having a heart-to-heart with my bladder, I eventually just peed in the bed. The staff was always angry with me for this, but honestly, what was I supposed to do? It wasn't pleasant for me, either. Fortunately, the peeing didn't happen that often.

While the adults were unhelpful, one of the rules that actually made sense was that whenever a patient was in the quiet room, a staff member (jailer) had to be watching at all times.

One day, two months into my stay, I was having yet another jaunt into the quiet room. At this point, I was rarely restrained anymore, just drugged and thrown in with the door locked. After the Thorazine sedative started to wear off, I looked at who was minding the store. It was Emmanuel, a heavyset Haitian mental health worker. When he noticed me looking at him, he rattled his keys and snickered, "You better get used to this place, 'cause you ain't never gonna get out of here."

Those words reverberated within me. I turned my back on him and looked at the remaining November leaves on the maple trees outside. That day, I realized that if I wanted to get out of the mental institution, I would have to help myself—and stop screaming! The only thing I learned from the adults there was to never trust them.

While I continued to receive psychological "treatment," my illness continued to fester. Although I didn't understand what was wrong with my mind, like a trained dog I also eventually learned that the correct response to the question, "Are you hallucinating?" is an emphatic "No!" With all of the "treatment," no one there ever explained to me what a hallucination or psychosis was. I simply just learned to shut up. It wasn't until I was in college that I learned that hallucinations and delusions weren't real and couldn't be trusted.

After a four-month learning curve, the restraints completely stopped, and I frequented the quiet room less. Instead, I was assigned to the chair outside the nurses' station, where Nancy, the nursing Nazi who wore a constipated smile, habitually peered at me. I was not permitted to leave that chair unless absolutely necessary, such as going to the bathroom, and when I did, I was escorted by a staff member whose job was to keep their eyes on me at all times. The bathroom stall door had to remain wide open, and my jailors watched me pee and poop. This protocol even extended to showering, where the doors remained wide open constantly. It felt voyeuristic and was quiet humiliating for a self-conscious teenager. Razors were also out of the question, and the hair growing on my body made me want to scream. But I now knew better; no more screaming.

I named my chair "Josephine." I don't know why, and I don't think there was any significance in my choice. Eventually, I grew fond of Josephine. She was a heavy wooden chair upholstered with scratchy maroon fabric, but she kept me away from the quiet room. Josephine also permitted me to experience limited social interactions, which was a huge relief, as I still hadn't found that social manual I sought. While I still felt far from normal, even by mental patient standards, I had access to my peers and the comradery of the Elbert-North crew. In some ways, I now fit in. Here, everyone struggled with a mental health challenge of some kind.

I wasn't permitted to attend the hospital's school because the staff felt it wasn't safe to let me leave the unit. They likely thought I might run away. As a result, I was pretty bored most of the time. Josephine and I thought and read a lot, mostly about Buddhism and physics. I only read nonfiction because I detested books that required perspective-taking. The staff also allowed me to use my Discman, which was helpful.

While I sincerely hated the hospital, it was the first time since my nana had died that I could just "be." I didn't have to try to be "normal," non-psychiatrically ill, and not autistic. I could finally breathe. Even though I was often intimidated and humiliated, the hospital staff could only touch my exterior. I would *never* let them get the best of me.

I listened to Whitney Houston's song "Greatest Love of All" over and over again on my Discman. While the song is quite clichéd, I played it incessantly for Josephine until we learned that we both had worth, even if the staff couldn't see it.

In time, I gained the self-confidence to accept my peers' overtures of friendship. My social skills were still wobbly, but I had enough under my belt to acknowledge—and tolerate being acknowledged by—the other inmates. Strangely, once it was clear that I was receptive, their overtures kept increasing. Whenever they walked by Josephine, they would throw crumpled white pieces of paper at me. These contained funny or encouraging notes, *and* they pissed off the staff who still kept their eyes on me at all times. They all carried a similar sentiment:

"You're great! Get off that stupid chair. We hate the staff!"

"Chris and Erin are dating!"

"We're on your side! Go, Alex! You can do it!"

"Guess what happened to Matt at lunch…"

One day, my new friend Melissa walked by Josephine and whispered in my ear, "The over-night staff, Raffi and Sue, will let you get up, go to the bathroom by yourself, and will let us hang out with you."

That night, I tried asking for those "privileges" and was thrilled to discover that Melissa had been right. I stayed up until three in the morning talking, laughing, and having fun with Melissa, Rachel… and the over-night staff! It was the first time I had belly laughed in months.

While things were quite different during the day, I also experienced some joy. On one end of Elbert-North, there was a piano, and one of my fellow patients, Becky, a slightly overweight, jovial girl with thick blonde hair and a huge personality, was quite the pianist. She could play anything, even without sheet music. While I wasn't permitted to visit Becky's piano—that would mean leaving Josephine, after all—the other patients were, and they often gathered around the piano and sang along loudly. The piano's sound reverberated down the hall as Becky played the unit's favorites: "The Rose" by Bette

Midler and "Piano Man" by Billy Joel.

The other patients also created a song with disparaging remarks about the staff that made me chuckle. They would line up in front of Josephine and sing at the top of their lungs. Whenever this happened, the staff would lunge out of the nurses' station to shoo away my friends, but I reveled in the short amount of time when the patients were in control.

During what felt like a prison sentence at Stonyfield Psychiatric Hospital, my mother came to visit a few times a week, and my father came at least once a week. When I was in the quiet room or floridly psychotic, they were not permitted to see me, despite having driven more than two hours from the city.

I was also constantly frustrated and angry with everyone. I fumed at the institution staff for their maltreatment. I was furious with North Shore University Hospital for discharging me here. I was livid with my parents for not having taken action earlier when I was in trouble. And I was furious with my nana for dying. All around, I was a pretty angry kid. When my parents were able to visit, I often turned them away at the door, demanding they leave. I wasn't able to consider their perspective and cope with my rage.

About five months into my stay, I was freed from Josephine and allowed to roam around the unit and partake in Stonyfield Psychiatric Hospital's comprehensive treatment regimen, which involved family therapy.

My parents are fun-loving people, and they don't take life too seriously. When I was growing up, they worked exceptionally hard, but they also partied hard. I did not have the same relationship with them that I did with my nana. Sharing my thoughts and emotions with them in therapy was torturous. I just wanted my parents to love me, and based upon learned experiences I didn't know how my honesty would sit with them. I continued to keep my thoughts and symptoms to myself.

The social worker who conducted our family therapy, Erin Gaynor, was a tall, thin redhead with a soft-spoken voice. Erin was brand new to the field, and Stonyfield Psychiatric Hospital was her first gig, God help her. My parents are gregarious and charismatic, which overshadowed most of our sessions. They had many conflicts with the hospital staff, ranging from the hospital's lack of permissiveness to my treatment to my doctors' critical view of me. At one point, my parents even tried to persuade Erin and Dr. Alona Weismann, my psychiatrist, to give me a two-day pass so that I could attend my mother's fortieth birthday booze fest in Canada. Obviously, this proposal was shot down!

During our sessions, my parents would often make fun or light of my illness. I understand their belief that it's important to not take life too seriously, but Erin, Dr. Weismann, and I needed them to grasp the gravity of my situation. Since childhood, I had known that there was something wrong with me, and now, someone was finally identifying what that "something" was. I needed my parents to hear, understand, and accept this.

In truth, I never looked forward to these sessions, which were only made tolerable by the off-grounds pass that accompanied the session. Afterward, my parents would take me out to eat dinner in the community. At the restaurant, I could always count on my father to imitate Dr. Weismann's nimble, trembling, high-pitched voice and her pathetically limp handshake while saying, "Hi, I'm Alona Weismann, and I'm sitting on a vibrator while I talk…" Dr. Weismann had a flat affect and no personality, and while Dad's comments were inappropriate, they always made me laugh.

In reviewing my records from Stonyfield Psychiatric Hospital, I saw that synonyms for "grave" abounded. There were also several references to how "the patient's parents cannot accept the gravity of her diagnosis and prognosis." I'm honestly not sure whether they couldn't *accept* how sick I was or simply didn't want to *give up* hope that I would get better.

One afternoon, I was out with my mother, on a pass from the hospital. As we were driving back to Elbert-North, the song "Don't Give Up on Us, Baby" by David Soul came on the radio, and my mother started crying hysterically. I didn't know what was wrong, but intuitively, I started to listen to the lyrics: "Don't give up on us, baby. Don't make the wrong seem right…We're still worth one more try…Don't give up on us. I know we can still come through…" I was soon a little teary-eyed myself. I didn't want to give up on them; I just wanted to be free from pain. But I got it; Mom did know that there was a problem. While my parents had many issues and struggled to accept my disabilities, they never stopped believing in me. And for that, I will always be grateful.

Ten months after my initial admission, nothing had been accomplished in my treatment, but I was submissive and quiet enough to be released from the institution—or maybe my insurance ran out. I'll never know which it was, since this wasn't in my records. And trust me, I looked! Either way, Erin and Dr. Weismann assembled a discharge plan without my input or consent. I assume they involved my family, but honestly, I'm not even sure of that.

I would attend a private special education school in New York City, where we lived at the time. The school specialized in students with emotional problems. At Stonyfield Psychiatric Hospital, my autism had not seemed severe enough to warrant a diagnosis, despite the multiple references to "autistic-like" behavior and "childhood schizophrenia with autistic aloneness" dating back to my elementary school records. Asperger's syndrome, which best fits my profile, was not even a diagnosis yet. To this day, I wonder if my treatment and ultimate outcome would have been different if such a label had been available back then.

In addition to my "emotional problems," I now carried the trauma of having been confined, drugged, restrained, and tortured. It took me over thirty years to eradicate my nightmares and wear anything tight around my ankles or wrists, such as high-top sneakers, boots, bracelets, or watches. The trauma of having been tied down with tight leather restraints was too deep.

Regardless, on June 23, 1986, I walked out of Elbert-North's door with my mother. We drove past the sprawling lawns that I had never explored and headed home. Neither of us said much on that drive; mostly, we just listened to music. In hindsight, I think she was as nervous as I. Matt, my best friend on Elbert-North, had been discharged two weeks earlier. Soon after, he had called his mother at her office toward the end of the day. Her secretary picked up, since his mother was on her way out the door. She called from the hallway, "Tell him I'll be home in twenty minutes, and we can talk then." When they hung up, he shot himself in the head. And died.

There had been a very brief Elbert-North community meeting announcing Matt's death by suicide. The blood rushed from my face when I heard the news, and I was overwhelmed with emotions of sadness, loss, and grief. I also felt a bit angry and betrayed. Matt had been one of the good guys; he had always made me laugh. We had plans to meet up on the outside and were going to prove everyone wrong and succeed. A few days later, Rebecca, another patient, told me the details of his suicide, and we talked about it at a discharge planning meeting.

Knowing that could easily have been me, I was as nervous about leaving as I was excited.

As we drove home, I took a pulse on my emotions. I could tell that my mood was relatively elevated and ever-so-slightly delusional. It was nice to be going home, though.

The first thing I did was flop down on my bed and snuggle with my poufy green flowered comforter. I reveled in eating with real silverware and glassware. Best of all, I loved having free access to my razor again! I also appreciated my privacy and not being checked on by someone every fifteen minutes. However, my parents did take on that role, and multiple times a day, my mother asked me how I was. It was her way of showing that she cared, and I appreciated her attempts to connect.

The next day, I was compelled—as if by a driving force—to visit the stationery store around the corner from our apartment. I was on a mission to order business cards that read, "Alexandra West, MD." Sparing no expenses, I selected white linen parchment paper with black type. While my yearlong "internship" at the hospital didn't exactly give me a license to practice medicine, having these cards seemed like a step in the right direction.

This delusion that I was a doctor actually began as I was driving away from Stonyfield Psychiatric Hospital, and blew up over many years. I began to subscribe to the *New England Journal of Medicine*, watched the Surgery Channel exclusively, and picked up numerous medical paraphernalia, such as a stethoscope, otoscope, and glucometer, at a Duane Reade drug store. I had a healthy savings account, so the cost was not a factor. I likely thought that if I were a doctor, I would somehow be protected from my symptoms.

My parents interpreted this delusion as a healthy interest in going to medical school and becoming a doctor. To give me some work experience in a medical-related field and to keep me out of trouble, they insisted that I work at my father's dental laboratory for the summer, answering phones and delivering packages of teeth up and down the streets of New York City. The job started at six in the morning, and we arrived home around seven at night. It made for a long day, but the structure was essential for me; I had less time to live in my head, and it forced me to rein in my emotions. My only reprieve from the constant work was seeing my new psychiatrist and psychologist each week, the latter of which seemed good enough.

Wanting to please my father, I threw my heart into my responsibilities. Being slightly manic helped, as I could multitask at the front desk and made deliveries quickly. There was little social interaction required at the lab, which was perfect for me. It boiled down to saying, "Good morning, Perfect Smile," before transferring the caller. Package deliveries involved another line: "Here you go!" I could master that. I spent the rest of my time listening to music on the subway and in the office. While I had a list of tasks to accomplish each day, I had complete sovereignty over when and how my list would be completed.

To this day, my father takes credit for my functioning so well.

He boasts, "The hospital didn't teach you anything, but I did. You learned the value of hard work, and you didn't have any more problems." Even today, he has a hard time accepting my struggles. When I bring them up, he says, "That was in the past. You're fine now." I'm saddened that he cannot accept my illnesses, but despite this fundamental flaw, he's a great guy. I enjoyed working for him.

When I returned home each night, my family and I ate dinner together while I soaked up the urban landscape. Then, we went off in our own directions. I often took a walk around the city or retreated to my bedroom to read and listen to music.

We lived on the thirty-third floor of a lovely building on the East Side of Manhattan. Our apartment afforded panoramic views of the city, with windows that opened wide. My bedroom window was always open, as I loved the smoggy air and faint sounds below.

There was a small ledge outside my window, and sometimes, when I lay in bed, I heard a man's voice encouraging me to walk out onto the ledge. It's sometimes hard to tell a hallucination from reality and even harder to distinguish good choices from bad ones. Still, at first, I was scared and resisted. Then, I started taking a few tiny steps out on occasion.

During a "full disclosure" session with my psychiatrist, I told her about the voice. She verbalized how alarmed she was about this and prescribed another anti-psychotic, Moban, on top of the Thorazine I was already taking. After that, the hallucinations subsided, but I had yet to be diagnosed with bipolar disorder, so I continued to struggle with my mood. In the psychiatric community, back in the 1980's, pediatric bipolar disorder was not commonly accepted as a diagnosis.

I was living a dichotomous life. On the one hand, I held my "mental patient" identity close, yet I was also now marginally functioning. When my mood wasn't elevated, I felt sad and hopeless most of the time. Matt's death had hit me hard, and my near-fatal overdose in France had shown me how fragile life is. Yet, I appreciated being alive... most of the time, anyway. And working was a great distraction.

This distraction from my problems was not the only benefit of that job with my dad's company. I also experienced my first crush there, which was just what the doctor ordered!

CHAPTER 5

'CAUSE YOU GOT TO HAVE FRIENDS...

ONE OF MY father's business partners at Perfect Smile was named Vincent Mancini. His daughter, Francesca, was the same age as me, and she often came by the office during that summer to visit her dad. She had dark, tanned, flawless olive skin, beautiful chestnut eyes, and thick, wild, brown hair. Her lipstick-adorned mouth always emanated calming words. My desk was across from the elevator, and whenever it opened revealing her, my heart skipped a beat.

Initially, I wasn't sure what this meant. Though my parents had numerous gay friends, I hadn't entertained the idea that this might be a crush.

Betty, my therapist, was quite elderly but also pretty hip, and she endured my rants on this topic incessantly. Methuselah, as I lovingly called her, strongly encouraged me to disclose my feelings for Francesca, but I was never comfortable with this suggestion. I would be heartbroken if she didn't feel the same way. I wasn't proficient at reading non-verbal cues, so I was oblivious to her inner mind. If I didn't tell her, I could at least keep my fantasy that she might someday be my girlfriend.

That summer, Francesca and I hung out every chance we had. On the outside, we didn't seem to have much in common. She was outgoing; I was not. But in reality, she had few close friends and struggled with some mild mental health concerns of her own. In this regard, Francesca proved to be an excellent sounding board. We truly enjoyed each other's company, and she seemed to take my social quirkiness and mental illness in stride. We shared a love of tasty cuisine and made many expeditions all over the city to find the perfect diner cheesecake. The Glass Box, a tiny hole-in-the-wall diner on First Avenue and Forty-Ninth Street, won out every time!

My parents had a summer house on Fire Island, which is a large barrier island on the South Shore of Long Island. Parts of Fire Island are known for its gay population, and my parents' friends, both gay and straight, frequented their home. Francesca and I flocked there every weekend. We laughed incessantly. We bathed topless on the beach, which was legal, I think... We even slept in the same bed every night, spooning each other. My feelings for Francesca amplified as the summer went on, but nothing ever happened between us. To this day, I don't know if she felt the same things I did; I never had the courage to ask.

In addition to being my "girlfriend," Francesca was my social mentor and let me know when I missed a social cue. At this point, I was proficient at detecting when someone was experiencing a specific emotion, but I rarely understood why. I was much better in one-on-one situations than in groups, probably because there was less interpersonal dynamics and therefore less information to analyze. Plus, it was easier to find the right balance of listening and speaking in two-person conversations, and I could pause the conversation to ask a question or clarify information without seeming out of place.

As the summer came to a close with work and Francesca, I had to face going back to school. Francesca and I continued our friendship, as we both lived in the city, but we would be attending different schools.

Right after Labor Day, I started eleventh grade at Milton Academy, the private special education high school. At first glance, it was a weird school. It was located in a brownstone on the Upper East Side and housed forty students in grades nine through twelve. The classes were extremely small—no more than four-to-six kids—the teachers were all hippies, and the headmaster had a witch's nose, a real wart, and plenty of attitude.

I was sitting on the front stoop when the first morning bell rang, sending my sensory system into overload. Then, I was pummeled by students climbing up the brownstone's stairs. This was not a great start.

Due to the petite class sizes, I became acquainted with my peers rather quickly. Plus, I wasn't completely unfamiliar with Milton Academy. I already had ties. Some of my grandmother Miriam's relatives also went to school there, such as my twice-removed cousins David and Gabe. In addition, the brother of my friend Becky from Stonyfield Psychiatric Hospital was also a student. I already knew that most of the students abused drugs, which was not my scene. As on my European tour, I was petrified that if I smoked marijuana, my daymares would slip out.

Milton Academy was a fertile learning ground for social interaction. There were no jocks, no popular crowd, and no cattiness. Everyone was just a little quirky. I wasn't teased, though I was initially ignored. This was quite refreshing, compared to my past educational experiences. Milton Academy was like Stonyfield Psychiatric Hospital in a way; everyone bonded due to their circumstances. It simply didn't matter who you were. I had been given a fresh start and didn't want to blow it. I still wasn't proficient at reading social cues, but I had picked up enough tricks to get by at Milton Academy.

The academic content at Milton Academy was kind of a joke. Even having missed an entire year of school didn't seem to impact me. I quickly ascertained that if I wanted to gain any scholarly information, it would have to be on my own time. Luckily, I was studying my MCAT prep books, as I still had the delusion that I was a doctor, or at least, would be one soon.

While it had now been many years, the phrase "she's retarded" continued to ricochet around my brain, making me doubt my abilities.

I was uninspired at school and frequently skipped class. Then, about six months in, my advisor, Shauntelle, whom I adored, and "The Wart" presented me with a proposal.

"You got a ninety-eight percent in math," The Wart said in her witch's voice. "Out of the entire test, you only missed one question."

"What are you talking about?" I asked. I was puzzled and a little creeped out.

Shauntelle placed a typed piece of paper in front of me. "Your Regent's score. Here, look. Remember the standardized test you took recently?" she asked.

"Uh, yes," I said with some skepticism and trepidation. "It must be wrong, though, because I never really attended tenth grade. Remember, I was in the hospital."

"Well, your scores tell a different story," Shauntelle said. "We have a proposal. How would you like to teach Algebra II and Trigonometry to Grayson, Marcus, and Jamal? We know you help them all through class anyway. They would benefit from an even smaller class with more attention."

I wasn't sure how I felt about this. It was one thing to coach them, but something else entirely to be responsible for teaching them the content. *I'm not a licensed teacher! I can't even vote yet. How is this legal?* I wondered.

Still, after having a good think, I decided to take on the challenge. I needed something to stimulate my brain, and while these kids were not my favorite, I thought I could make a difference in their world.

Incidentally, this proved to be my favorite part of Milton Academy. There was something about imparting knowledge that gave me a sense of pride and accomplishment. I've always loved math, and when the topic of conversation is interesting, my banter is more natural, which conceals my autism. Plus, when I taught, the prescribed agenda and topics of conversation were created and guided by me. Still, by accepting this teaching assignment, I was put in limbo. I wasn't a teacher, yet nor was I entirely a student. Although happier than ever before, I still felt like I didn't exactly fit in anywhere.

Milton Academy was considered an "alternative school," and many of the rules were unconventional, such as lacking mandatory attendance. Before I started teaching math, I often skipped class and spent many days at the Guggenheim, the Museum of Natural History, and the Lenox Hill Hospital laundry vent—I just loved the way it smelled! I also spent about an hour each day with Sammie, a sweet homeless gentleman who lived under the Fifty-Ninth Street Bridge who held a cardboard sign indicating he had AIDS. I always brought him coffee and a sandwich, and we conversed about our lives.

However, teaching provided me with a higher purpose and a reason to come to school each day. Now, it wasn't all about me; there were others who relied on me. These students I taught had profound psychiatric illnesses, learning disabilities, and/or behavioral challenges. For the most part, we had a good rapport, and I was able to reach them. But I'll never forget my scariest experience teaching, which almost made me quit.

Shortly after I took on this project, Grayson kept his head down for most of the period one day. When I asked him to turn in his assignment, he reached in his concealed pocket, pulled out a gun, and pointed it at my face. I froze. Then, a voice emanating from somewhere in my gut said with absolute calmness, "Please put the gun away." If there was one thing Stonyfield Psychiatric Hospital had taught me, it was to *never* show your emotions. With that, Grayson put the gun back in his pocket. Crisis averted! I never told Shauntelle or The Wart what he had done. Fortunately, this was an isolated incident.

While math provided a distraction when I was at Milton Academy, all I could think about at home was Francesca. She attended a fancy college-preparatory private school downtown. We remained close and saw each other frequently at her grandmother's house in Brooklyn on religious holidays or when our parents feasted on dinner after work.

There was no real need to bond with peers at Milton Academy, as Francesca now came with a small gaggle of school friends in tow, which I borrowed. Yet, secretly, I missed our one-on-one time on Fire

Island. Still, she constantly provided tips on fitting in and graciously invited me along on whatever adventures she had planned.

Fridays were dedicated to *The Rocky Horror Picture Show* at midnight in Greenwich Village. Growing up in New York City, *Rocky* is a rite of passage. We would go to someone's apartment beforehand, down some alcohol while dressing up as the characters, and then grab our rice and spray bottles so that we could participate in the show. We all knew the alternative lyrics, and we sang. Loudly.

Afterward, with their fake ID's the crew would drop by the Platinum dance club, where I invariably departed their company. Dance clubs were too overstimulating for me, and I hated the smell. Plus, my suicide attempt at the French nightclub still haunted me.

Although rowdy, the consistency of each week's adventure soon became comforting for me. I finally had a group of friends, which is something I had always wanted. I belonged!

Francesca lived downtown in a building across from the Hudson River, which surrounds the Statue of Liberty and Ellis Island. One evening, our parents went to visit their friend Shelley at his apartment, and we were left alone at her house. We lay on her bed, listening to Queen's "Crazy Little Thing Called Love." Then, suddenly, Francesca pulled a joint from her nightstand and lit it. "Want a hit?" she asked seductively.

"I-I really can't," I stammered. "Y-you know I'm afraid. The monsters will come out of my head..." The word "psychosis" still wasn't in my vocabulary.

She began caressing my arm gently and slowly, saying, "Come on. Just one hit. It won't do anything."

Despite normally detesting light touch, I was powerless against her. Against my better judgment, I agreed. I would do anything she asked.

That one hit turned into two joints that we shared. Quite disinhibited, I leaned over to kiss her, but in that same instant, she playfully pulled my hand, saying, "Get up! Let's go!"

We walked along the esplanade overlooking the Hudson. There

was a knee-wall with waist-high iron bars on top. The river's current crashed against the wall, spraying us. We laughed like young school-girls. Impulsively, I climbed the wall and stood on a small ledge on the other side. The bars were wet, and my foot slipped. I grabbed the spindles on the rail as my feet dangled below and held on tightly. I was petrified, even with the effects of the marijuana, and knew that I was in trouble. "Help me, Francesca! *Help*!" I screamed in panic. "*I'm falling*!"

"I don't know what to do!" She shouted back. She was tugging at my arms, trying to drag me back up, but to no avail.

At that moment, a Coast Guard ship approached and shined a vi-brant interrogation light on me. A reassuring voice echoed though the megaphone, and a big, strong man soon scooped me onto the safety of the boat. I'm not sure why, but they pulled Francesca aboard, too.

In a Southern drawl, a Coast Guardsman said, "Looks like you girls were having yourself some fun tonight?"

I was waiting for the other shoe to drop and for him to lecture us. I had almost drowned due to sheer stupidity, *and* I reeked of mari-juana. I was so nervous, I could barely speak. Francesca must have felt something similar, because we both just nodded.

"That was the dumbest thing I've ever seen!" the man continued with a belly laugh. "Well, now that y'all safe, would y'all like to see Ellis Island at night?"

I couldn't believe it. Not only were we *not* in trouble, but we also got to ride around on their ship and see Ellis Island at night, which was pretty cool. We struck up a conversation with all the guys man-ning the ship, who were really nice. When they returned us home safely, our Southern gentleman rescuer gave us each a Coast Guard hat.

We ran like lunatics to Shelley's apartment, since our parents were most likely still there. We burst in panting and told them the whole incredible story, but our parents were convinced that we had made it all up and purchased the hats! They didn't believe us or com-ment about stinking like pot! We also raided Shelley's pantry!

While I never smoked pot again, I regained a part of my adolescent self that night. Since entering the hospital, I had felt the need to be perfect; I always had psychiatric and therapeutic eyes staring at me. Analyzing me. Waiting for me to crack or fail so consequences would be forthcoming. But, just for tonight, I was a typical adolescent, which felt invigorating!

Francesca and I remained close friends but lost touch after college. When Dad told me her father passed away many years later, I called her. She was living in Michigan, was married, and had a few kids. She sounded good, and I was happy for her.

Around this same time as the Coast Guard incident, I met my next soon-to-be best friend, Ethan Lange, who eventually became the only man that I ever dated. Ethan also attended Milton Academy, but he seemed really "normal." Admittedly, given my mental patient standards, that wasn't saying much.

One day in October, I just left school and was crossing Eight-First and Madison, lost in my own world. With a cinnamon raisin bagel and a schmear of cream cheese in one hand and my backpack in another, I stepped off the curb without looking. BAM!!! Instantly, I felt a strong hand yank me back off the street and onto the sidewalk; a car had been inches away from hitting me.

I quickly realized that my rescuer was Ethan from my English class. "Thank you!" I gasped.

"You're welcome."

As I stared at his face, I suddenly realized how handsome he was. Ethan had wavy light-blond hair, dreamy blue eyes, and strong Scandinavian features. My body felt confused. I had been vaguely attracted to him before, but now, those feelings had increased dramatically. I wasn't sure if what I was feeling was due to his having saved my life or if I actually had feelings for him. And what about Francesca?

He continued with a concerned expression, "Are you okay?"

"I'm fine," I assured him.

He took my hand and helped me to my feet. The bagel was a total loss, unfortunately. "I'm Ethan. Ethan Lange. We both attend Milton Academy. I've seen you in my English class."

I was dumbfounded. I didn't know what to say. "Eh, thanks for saving my life," was all that tumbled out of my mouth. Afterward, I kicked myself for sounding so moronic. Struggling to come up with something better, I was grateful that he plowed ahead, though I was completely unprepared for his next question.

"So, since I saved your life, does that mean you might go out with me sometime?"

With little hesitation, I enthusiastically agreed. *A date? I'm going on a date? And he doesn't think I'm weird?* "Where do you want to go?" I excitedly asked.

"How 'bout I pick you up on Saturday at six? I live in Park Slope, and there's a great Italian place around the corner from me, Angelo's!"

"Sounds good!" I was excited, but also relieved that he had suggested a Saturday-night date. Fridays were reserved for *Rocky*.

I was almost seventeen, and this was my very first date. I was unclear of the standard "dating protocol" and wasn't sure what to do. My trusty *Encyclopedia Britannica* failed to provide any useful information. I ultimately confided in my mother, who helped me pick out the perfect outfit: a sleeveless black dress that ended just below my knees. I wore my bushy golden brown hair down, and my mother scattered hairspray all over it to tame it. This smelled gross, as did the perfume she doused me in. This was a stark contrast to my usual attire of sweats and a baseball hat. Frankly, I wasn't even sure that Ethan would recognize me.

When I stepped out of my lobby, my jaw fell open. Waiting outside was a huge white limousine, with Ethan holding the door. This was over-the-top and overwhelming; I almost turned and ran away, but Ethan spotted me and motioned for me to come over. During the car ride to the restaurant, he confessed that his aunt and uncle owned the limo company, which made me feel better. I had been worried that this grand gesture was a sign that he was expecting sex, which I'd never had.

At Angelo's, we dined on fettuccine Bolognese and chatted for about two hours, swapping stories about our lives. His father and stepmother, or "monster," as he called her, were famous photographers. His father was a portrait artist, while his stepmother focused on landscapes. Eventually, as we spent more time together, I met his dad, who imparted sophisticated knowledge about cameras to me and gave me some pointers on how to use my nana's equipment. We also shared portfolios; I was in heaven. Unfortunately for Ethan, his dad was often traveling around the world for work, which was sad, as his stepmother was indeed rather nasty. She didn't like Ethan or me. I'm unclear as to why. Ethan often name-dropped the famous people who dined at his home, which I didn't find impressive. While this could have seemed cool, the tradeoff of not having his dad around struck me as much worse.

Ethan and I hit it off instantly. It was very easy to talk to him. There was no pretense between us. He indulged me by listening to my stories without interruption. Over the next few months, Ethan and I spent endless hours together. I even started bringing him to *Rocky* on Friday nights!

We also both disclosed what had brought us to Milton Academy. He met my experiences of torture at Stonyfield Psychiatric Hospital with sympathy and understanding. Ethan never judged me, and I always felt accepted around him. And my parents adored Ethan, which was another plus.

Things at Milton Academy started to look up as well. Ethan had several friends that I attached myself to; they were vicariously mine, too. He was the glue that held us together. When I would start to socially drift, he would always pull me back in by redirecting my attention to the group. My only objection to these new friends was that they smoked a sizable amount of pot. I was on two anti-psychotic medications at this point, so I rarely had "daymares" (hallucinations) anymore, but I continued to be petrified of the consequences. When he learned of my fear of the drug, Ethan graciously agreed to ditch his weed habit for me. I was very pleased and surprised.

I now had friends at Milton Academy. At various times throughout the day, we would gather on the fourth-floor stairwell with a humongous boom-box cranking out Paul Simon and Art Garfunkel tunes. Inevitably, The Wart would attempt to shut down our jam sessions. Ethan's friend, whom we affectionately called Theo the Greek, had a black Seiko watch that had a timer that ran in seconds. We would all place bets, five dollars a hand, on how long it would take The Wart to climb the stairs from the first floor to give us a stern warning. Theo the Greek usually predicted her time the best. This exercise was more amusing for us than anything else, as The Wart's warnings fell on deaf ears and there were never any consequences.

Ethan was very tolerant of me and danced around my autistic symptoms. When I didn't comprehend a social interaction, I would often become exasperated because I felt like I was being misinterpreted; I didn't understand that it was *me* who had missed a social cue or misunderstood something. Ethan's friends eventually grew frustrated with me, and one day, Lane said to Ethan, "Can she leave our fucking group, please?" Ethan stuck up for me and refused Lane's request.

In addition to social cues, I also struggled with tolerating extended social interactions. Sometimes, I would abruptly walk away from the group or out of Ethan's house without warning or explanation. In such moment, I'd simply had enough interaction and wanted to be alone.

And then, there were big blow-ups over things that seemed hugely important to me, but not to Ethan, such as wearing horizontal versus vertical stripes on his shirt. One day, Ethan innocently wore a horizontally striped Benetton shirt. To me, it "just looked wrong." In my rigid autistic mind, shirts should have vertical stripes, not horizontal ones. Like many things in my life, there wasn't a reason for this; it was just "the law." Without being able to take another's perspective, mine was the only one that mattered. The possibility of compromise was scant, and I picked a fight with him. I always wanted things done my way since there was only one correct way: mine. I made Ethan go into a clothing store and buy a new shirt. I did feel responsible, thought, so I paid for the shirt. Frankly, I think he just wanted to shut me up after listening to me anxiously perseverate on his shirt for two hours.

My autistic idiosyncrasies were annoying at best, but they could not compare to my bipolar symptoms. It would be another two years before I was given a bipolar diagnosis and five years after that I was diagnosed with Asperger's syndrome. At this point, from elementary school my diagnostic lineup included "childhood schizophrenia with autistic aloneness" and from neuropsychological testing while I was at Milton, the doctor concluded that I had "the initial stages of a schizophrenic-form illness." I was on antipsychotic medications, but not yet mood stabilizers. Therefore, despite medication, my symptoms continued to fester.

Ethan was excellent at coaching me through these episodes; my life at this point would have been grim were it not for him. He tolerated the franticness of my mania and comforted me through my depression. He was always accepting and by my side. He slept over many times while I just lay in my bed and cried about everything and nothing. That's the problem when I'm depressed: nothing is actually wrong, yet I feel horrendous. Everything in my life could be going swimmingly, but I'm crying. It doesn't make sense. Not only did Ethan earn the "bipolar-supporter star of the month," but he also never got flustered in the face of my extreme moods.

One November day in eleventh grade, I stopped sleeping again. My body felt electrified, and my brain was brimming with ideas. My newest business idea was West's Sky Dining, which involved taking an airplane to nowhere and relishing a gourmet meal. I meandered into Citibank with Ethan in tow, caressing my twelve-page typed proposal. I was looking for an investment banker. I ended up sitting across from a bald man with a calm, quiet disposition. A lustrous mahogany desk was between us. It didn't take him long to firmly state, "I'm sorry, but you must be eighteen to submit a proposal."

Flipping out I began yelling, "What? Don't you know how successful this will be? Who cares about age? It's only a number! You're going to eat your shoe when West's Sky Dining becomes a success. And you are banned from dining… banned!"

He just sat in his chair looking as calm as could be.

I stormed out, and once we were on the sidewalk, I started chewing Ethan's ear off about the atrocity that had just been committed. He tried to calm me down by explaining the banker's perspective, but I was manic and my blood was racing through my body. I needed the outside world to match my inside body.

I wanted to drive fast and feel the wind on my skin while blasting music, so I fetched my car from our apartment building's garage. All the way up the Hutchinson River Parkway, I couldn't shut up: "Maybe if I gave that stupid banker my doctor's business card, I would have more clout..." Ethan just listened. It was actually all he could do, as my verbal diarrhea didn't pause long enough for him to get a word in. With each huff, my foot hit the gas harder. I was driving fast. Really fast! By the time I got up to 110 miles per hour, the "rush" of our speed finally matched my mania, which was calming (a bit). It's a miracle that I didn't crash the car that day. However, years later, I did total two cars while manic. Fortunately, both incidents were at a much lower speed.

Once this particularly noxious episode ended and I came up for air, Ethan asked, "Why can't you shut up when you get like this?" Without my future bipolar diagnosis, neither of us knew what to call it. Ethan wasn't being obnoxious; he was honestly asking.

I knew my behavior was odd because whenever an episode ended, I was able to reflect on what a mess I had made of my life. But I couldn't explain what was happening. I didn't have the vocabulary to discuss mood instability. My experiences and feelings simply baffled me. However, I knew that things were starting to spin further and further out of control.

My psychiatrist at the time, Dr. Bernice Koch, kept increasing my anti-psychotic medications, but these old first-generation drugs did not touch my mood. Dr. Koch was short and always wore a black sweater and a black floor-length skirt. She walked hunched over and was constantly mumbling to herself. Whenever we met, she displayed zero affect and had a diluted personality; I thought she was kind of weird and spooky. In our several years of working together, I never once saw even an ounce of emotion—not even a smile—and she was always very matter-of-fact about my treatment. Basically, she was kind of useless.

A month after my failed meeting with the investment banker, I crashed from the manic episode, and Dr. Koch recommended psychological testing. I asked her if I could refuse; I was afraid that if someone knew just how crazy my thoughts and moods were, I would be committed to an insane asylum for life. She politely reminded me, "If you don't get appropriate treatment now, the next step is residential." I didn't press her to elaborate on that, and I agreed to the psychological testing.

In reviewing my records for this book, I found Dr. Shulman's report tucked into my file from Milton Academy. Like the hospital's records, it was very grim. There were comments such as, "Poor prognosis," "Continues to display increased symptoms," "Emotional labile with considerable and specific mood swings," "Diminished social connections," "Confused about sexual orientation," etc. In the report's conclusion, I read that I had "the initial stages of a schizophrenic-form illness." The treatment was to increase the anti-psychotics. Ugh! Back then, Asperger's syndrome was still not a diagnosis and most members of the psychiatric profession believed that bipolar disorder only occurred in adults, so I assume they never seriously considered it as a possible diagnosis.

Despite all of my challenges, Ethan loved and accepted me for who I was and never viewed my life as "grave." I appreciated that. Still, I never really understood the nature of our relationship. We did go on that one formal date, and we hung out together all the time, but were we casually dating? An official couple? Casual acquaintances? Good friends? I just didn't know, and I wasn't sure how to find out. Did one simply ask?

Ethan's father and step-mother owned a stunning farmhouse with a huge stone fireplace about sixty miles outside of New York City. Since his parents were never around, we would sometimes go there on the weekends. One night while we were out there, Ethan decided to move our relationship forward and answer my unasked questions about what we were.

He came up behind me and kissed my neck. Well, now I had at least part of my answer! Next, he leaned in to capture my lips. I wasn't sure how I felt about this, but I kissed him back. I felt weird doing so and a little repulsed, as if I had kissed a relative. I knew that I loved him, but was this the same as being *in* love? My heart was not aflutter like it had been with Francesca. More investigation was required. I was really confused.

We both knew that having sex was off the table. I was emotionally immature and not ready to engage in such behavior. But perhaps we could fool around. What would that even look like? I was so nervous. I didn't know what to expect. I knew Ethan would be gentle and would stop if I asked him to.

"Weird" is the best word I have to describe the experience. I was very emotionally attracted to Ethan, but physically, I felt nothing.

Despite that, we seriously dated for about three years. I still don't quite know why. Two years into our relationship, I had my first sexual experience with him. Ethan had a loving touch, and he treated me well. He knew about my hospital experiences and always respected my anxiety about being on top of me or holding my wrists down. He also understood my sensitive sensory system and was respectful when I didn't have enough "sensory points" for sex.

We dated all throughout my time at Milton Academy and into college. Ethan was tolerant of my psychiatric illness and social quirks when we were at Milton, but he grew increasingly frustrated as our relationship progressed. All of my overtures benefited *me*. I had minimal perspective-taking skills back then. And, even worse, when I started college in Pennsylvania, I ditched all of my medications. That was a New York thing! Now, it was time for a new chapter! In retrospect, I can see that the social one-sidedness of our relationship was maddening for him.

As time passed, my highs and lows grew exponentially wider and disturbing, and these were also trying for him. When high, I would call Ethan at three in the morning, demanding various things. The words flew out so quickly, I could barely take a breath. Once, I drove at breakneck speed to his dorm at Lafayette College, which was about thirty minutes away from where I lived. It was mid-semester, and I scattered travel brochures all over his bed while he slept. When he didn't rouse, I made my presence known by yelling, "Get up! We're taking a trip to St. Lucia! It's already paid for! Pack! Go!" Manic energy also unleashes ravenous sexual desire, and, let's face it, what man is going to turn that down? So, he packed, and off we went!

Unfortunately, over time, the highs and lows of my bipolar disorder became too much to handle. Ethan had dreams of his own, and he moved on. He eventually left for Morocco to follow in his father's footsteps, and our relationship ended. To this day, I've never had a better friend.

At this point, I was in my freshman year of college and was hypomanic. I lacked any kind of introspection and didn't think that anything was wrong with me. I couldn't understand why Ethan had left, but this did give me a little breathing room to figure out my sexuality. I had always known that I loved Ethan, but what does being "in love" feel like? I didn't even have fiction to draw on, because I had never been able to follow the characters' perspectives. In short, I had little understanding of sexual orientation or love. I was an avid television and movie watcher, but my genres of choice were the Surgery Channel, *ER*, and *Star Wars*. The latter two contained slight romance, but not as the main premise.

Fortunately, my parents had numerous gay friends, and since I'm not religious, I felt entitled to explore. While this, coupled with the fact that I lived in a very liberal city, somewhat buffered me from any negativity surrounding my sexual orientation, it was also the 1980s and the AIDS epidemic had recently exploded into the public consciousness. Though negative propaganda about AIDS was mostly directed at gay men, this wasn't the best time to hang a rainbow flag from my window. Then, around this time, our close family friend

Shelley was diagnosed with end-stage AIDS, and he passed away shortly after his diagnosis. Given all of this, I decided to restrict my explorations to within my own mind.

I began by dissecting the differences between Francesca and Ethan. I cared for Ethan deeply, but even when we were having sex, he didn't make my heart beat rapidly with excitement and anticipation. On the other hand, whenever Francesca sauntered into the room, her mere presence made my heart race.

I also thought back on my childhood crushes. *ER*'s Dr. Lewis, played by Sherry Stringfield; Murphy Brown, played by Candice Bergen; and Princess Leia, played by Carrie Fisher all made my heart jump in the same way that Francesca did. I'd also had a crush on my elementary school gym teacher until I found out that she was pregnant. Apparently, that had been a deal-breaker for me.

I knew that my parents would be fine with whatever sexual orientation I ultimately identified with, so that wasn't a problem. But I was perplexed and wouldn't know the answer until years later. At this point, I decided that celibacy was my best option. I had just started college, and there were bigger fish to fry.

CHAPTER 6

LILY PAD OF STABILITY

WHEN MY PARENTS dropped me at college right outside of Philadelphia, I didn't know what to expect. I brought along many tangible items, such as my beloved Macintosh II computer, which took up the entire desk, a humongous microwave, a light-blue bean-bag chair that we bought at Ames department store, and other items that provided comfort. With all of my possessions monopolizing the room, I felt calm. For just a moment, everything felt "right." I said goodbye to my parents and began to assimilate. Then, just a few minutes after I had finished unpacking, two loud, chatty girls barreled through the door with bundles of brightly colored luggage and assorted stuff in tow. They looked like twins, with bushy dyed blonde hair and ripped jeans.

"Who are you, and why are you in my room?" I demanded

"We're roomies!" one of them gleefully announced. "I'm Ellie, and this is Carrie."

"I specifically requested a single," I said.

"Oh, that's through a lottery. You're stuck with us!" Chortling, she continued, "Now move some of your stuff so we can all fit in! Can you just believe we're in college?"

I freaked out and called my mother on her car's cell phone. We talked for a while, and she calmed me down and helped me adjust to the idea of sharing a room. I guess the three beds should have tipped me off. Still, I couldn't help but think, *For God's sake, even in the psych ward, they eventually gave me my own room. They knew I couldn't handle living with others.* I could already tell that Ellie and Carrie were not understanding like Ethan and Francesca. And we would *not* be "besties."

Living with others in a postage-stamp-sized room and navigating the social world was quite overwhelming. At Milton Academy, my peers had all been struggling with their own labels and diagnoses, leaving me sheltered from the "normal" world. Due to our circumstances, my behavior was generally tolerated and excused by them. But now that I was among "normal" people, both my developmental and psychiatric deficits grew much more apparent. I felt alienated and never knew what to say. It felt like I was back in elementary school. My insides often quaked, and I longed for a Valium.

At home, except for Francesca and Ethan, my friends had all been out of convenience, such as living next door or knowing the same people. I didn't have a single friend at college, and my roommates quickly came to hate me. The resident advisor came to check on me once a day, which was nice. I assume she could tell that I was struggling. While Stonyfield Psychiatric Hospital and Milton Academy were "therapeutic" settings, new skill acquisition was skimpy. During my stint at college, I drove back home once a month to continue my work with Methuselah and Dr. Koch. Although I enjoyed our conversations, I never really learned anything and continuously ditched my medications. I lacked introspection and believed that it was not me who needed to change; In my autistic mind I thought the problem lay with the world.

After getting over the learning curve of actually finding my classes scattered across the lush green campus, academically, I was doing acceptably and continued my pre-med quest. After all, I still had business cards left! When I enrolled in college, Milton Academy had sent along a "comprehensive college plan" for me, which automatically launched relevant support services. Theoretically, I was set up for success. I had untimed tests; twice-weekly learning center support sessions, which did help with executive functioning skills; and weekly counseling, which was fairly useless. I really missed my twice-a-week chats with Methuselah.

Socially, I was floundering, and I grew rather despondent. I was tired of sitting alone in my dingy dorm room night after night while my roommates were out partying. I missed Ethan, Francesca, and Friday night *Rocky* something awful. My mother suggested that I join the same sorority she had, which had filled her social life in college. I found a flyer, attended their information session, and reminded myself to be kind. Apparently, there is a rule that if your parent participated in the same sorority, you're automatically accepted. It's called being a legacy, and I was one. I was in.

Most of the "sisters" were popular and partied every Thursday, Friday, and Saturday night. News of their hook-ups slid off their tongues the following mornings in the cafeteria. While I was now part of their group, drinking no longer interested me, and I continued to be petrified of drugs. Most of the sorority sisters were mean catty girls, and I was disheartened.

But then, one day, I met a sorority sister whom I actually bonded with. Her name was Eliza Levy. Her long, wild, curly, light-brown hair, coupled with her thick accent, practically screamed, "I'm from New York." She was very fashionable, always with a designer purse adorning her left arm and a black velvet scrunchy decorating her right wrist. Eliza and I both had a disdain for drugs, liquor, and parties, but we enjoyed tennis (the only sport I could play) and adored art. This brings me to our mutually beneficial deal: Eliza was kind and sweet but had a substantial learning disability and struggled academically. However, if I helped her write her art history papers, she would go out to Lina's Restaurant with me every Saturday night. This wasn't a date, but it was nice to spend time with someone as a friend. More importantly, as our friendship progressed, I found that she was willing to clean up many of my bipolar messes.

I still didn't have the vocabulary to label my bipolar symptoms, but I knew the signs when a hypomanic episode was approaching:

boundless energy, big ideas, and no need for sleep. My brain refuses to shut off as I plan frenetically and grow more eccentric. My desire for and proficiency with social interaction also increases. There's no rhyme or reason for how long this hypomanic stage lasts. However, when the cycle progresses, my productive thoughts and social interactions grow increasingly incoherent. What was once a passing thought or plan now becomes actionable, regardless of how ludicrous it actually is. It's as if I'm missing a reflective function in my brain and cannot anticipate consequences.

As my mania ramped up, I started sitting with the sorority sisters at breakfast and was even moderately interested in their "walk of shame" escapades. I was having fun, and I was fun to be around.

But it didn't last. I was soon swinging from hypomania into full-blown mania.

My mother is a true gourmet cook, and back in New York City, due to my parents hectic schedules we also ate out several nights a week at fancy restaurants. I knew good cooking, and the college's cafeteria didn't cut the mustard. One day, before the cafeteria's morning rush, I rearranged all the silverware and then pushed my way into the kitchen, where I was met by a heavyset Jamaican cafeteria worker sporting a hairnet. "What you doing here, girl?" she demanded.

"I don't like the way your silverware's arranged," I yelled angrily, "and I've come to make my own breakfast!"

"Put the silverware back and get your ass out of my kitchen," she said, shooing me out with a dishcloth.

Frustrated that my veggie omelet and hash browns were not going to come to fruition that morning, I drove to Sears. A few months earlier, some fool at America Express had sent me a credit card, which had no limit. "Screw the cafeteria," I ranted as I drove. "I'll make my own veggie omelet in the dorm!"

I purchased a full set of kitchen appliances, and a few days later, two burley men drove up to my dorm in a large white delivery truck and began unloading an oven/cooktop, refrigerator, and dishwasher. The resident advisor, Mary, began peppering me with questions as I guided them toward my room. Being none too pleased with my actions, she finally interfered and sternly instructed the men to return the appliances to the store. When they had left, Mary demanded of me, "What the hell were you thinking?" I wasn't sure whether this was rhetorical, so I answered, explaining exactly why I wanted the appliances.

To survive with autism, I've learned through trial and error that certain topics should only come up in my head or within my immediate family. These include things like comments about people's appearances, questions about their sex life, anything about their age, and counting the number of freckles or age spots on their hands. Lack of inhibition from mania, however, does not play well with autism. The rules dash out the window and are replaced with a lack of verbal restraint. When manic, I can't reflect on my own behavior or what rule I had broken, let alone remember that there was a rule to break.

In retrospect, I realize that as the intensity of my mania grew, people around me were pulling away. The national president of my sorority called me one day, informing me that I was no longer welcome due to my harsh remarks and erratic behavior. She also twisted the knife, adding that I was the only person in the history of their sorority who had ever been kicked out.

Exhibiting the same capricious behavior in lecture halls, I couldn't stop talking during class. And, and worst of all, paranoia was slithering back in. Once, during biochemistry, I was certain that everyone could hear my thoughts. I started hearing a muffled "radio show" and two distinct men's voices talking to each other behind me. This occurred on and off throughout the day. One day, I'd had enough of their commentary. I turned around in class and screamed at the top of my lungs, "Shut up!" The professor asked me to leave the class. In hindsight, I wonder if he thought I was talking to him.

During this time, I was relatively isolated. My roommates banished me from the dorm at night so they could sleep. Apparently, my endless barrage of verbalizations kept them awake. I spent my nights in the Anderson lecture hall, where I lay on the cold floor by myself.

It was so quiet, there was plenty of room for my thoughts. During the day, when my roommates were out, I returned to my dorm room, but ended up just staring at the books that covered my desk; my mind was racing too quickly for me to read. *Perhaps*, I thought, *I can extrapolate meaning by staring at the white space on the page.* My thoughts were also racing too much to attend class, and I stopped going to the learning center. My days mostly consisted of going to the university's Health and Counseling Center for therapy, listening to music, and running.

With heighten mania and without sleep, my illness grew increasingly frightening to both myself and others. Yet I was oblivious to how out of control I was.

The color red matched my "fast" insides, so I decided that a trip to the paint store was in order. I painted my entire dorm room scarlet red, which my roommates hated. This forced a meeting with the RA, who knew something was amiss. She ordered a trip to the Health and Counseling Center where I saw Sandra, my therapist whose calm voice kind of annoyed me.

After what felt like an endless period of time where I monopolized the conversation, Sandra told me to breathe. As I did so, she quietly added, "Alex, I need you to pause and share the conversation. I have a few questions."

Oh, here we go, I thought testily. Before she could begin, I rocketed in with, "I'm not suicidal or homicidal. I'm not hearing or seeing anything. I really feel fine. F-I-N-E, *fine!*"

"Have you taken any drugs or drank alcohol in the past twenty-four hours?" she calmly probed, ignoring my outburst.

"No. That's a stupid question. Don't you listen? I once smoked pot in high school, and that's it. And I'm done with alcohol," I snapped. I paced around Sandra's office, unable to sit. I was muttering under my breath; I couldn't hold my thoughts in. I increasingly felt trapped and bolted for the door.

Sandra's chair was close to the door, and she quickly blocked my only escape route, effectively holding me in custody. She asked me to sit down, and I tried my very best to comply. I didn't have a clue what she was thinking, but at this point, it was probably clear that I was in emotional trouble. Years later, while reading her clinical notes, I ascertained that Sandra thought I was a lunatic, though of course, she didn't say so in so many words. Her notes read: "This student is exhibiting out of control behavior…she continues to speak fast-paced without regard for the listener…She is also unable to understand my or her peer's perspectives…The writer is worried about her prognosis as she's unable to access therapy at this time…Due to her increasingly concerning presentation, HCC is making a referral to Beacon Medical Center."

Although I'd had a horrible experience at Stonyfield Psychiatric Hospital and couldn't imagine this being any different, I signed the consent forms and voluntarily admitted myself. While I had been angry at Sandra in her office, I could also feel myself growing increasingly out of control. Every thought I had felt actionable and real.

Dr. Nathan Gabelman, the head psychiatrist, met me on the unit, and we exchanged business cards. During my time at Beacon, I handed these out to everyone. For some reason, I couldn't get the song, "I'm Henry the Eighth, I Am," out of my head that day. I loudly sang the lyrics over and over again for hours while pacing up and down the halls. And for the record, I can't sing! Dr. Gabelman gave me a high dose of a sedative, and we touched base again later that day after the singing stopped.

Dr. Gabelman was a short Jewish man who was patient and kind. As with everywhere else, I had no muzzle or filter in his office. I frequently jumped out of my seat to touch the trinkets on his desk without permission and monopolized the conversation. My jibber-jabber was incoherent and jumped from one subject to another in a way that made sense to me, but not to anyone else.

After a few days, we had a frank conversation. "Alex," he said kindly, "you're nineteen years old, and you are free to sign yourself in and out of the hospital. You are an adult and can make your own decisions. That being said, I think you should stay with us for a while.

I also think you should call your parents after we talk."

"Let's talk first, and I'll think about it," I growled back.

Dr. Gabelman nodded and continued, "You have something called manic-depressive illness…" "Manic-depressive illness" is the former term for bipolar disorder.

We talked for about an hour about the highs and lows I experienced, and I revealed how I had tried to kill myself. I struggled to focus on what he was telling me, but I managed to take away that (1) it's a biological illness, and (2) I have no control over it.

I was relieved that my symptoms had a name that depicted my psychiatric experiences accurately and that there was something I could do about it. Dr. Gabelman assured me that I would need to take Lithium and Thorazine for life and that I would feel better in a few weeks, but I would also need to stay with him while the medication took effect.

Then, like a doting Jewish grandmother, he handed me the phone and said, "Let's call your parents."

I spoke with my mother, who expressed her grave concern for my wellbeing. My father wasn't home. I also called Miriam, my mother's mother, who expressed her disappointment in me. We only conversed for a few minutes, and her main comment was, "I hope you will be out before Thanksgiving. After all, what would I tell the rest of the family?" There was an evident social stigma and shame that my mental illness brought to our family.

I wished my nana were there with me. I really needed a head rub.

My family and I had thought that my adolescent hospitalization was simply a blip on the radar, but now, Dr. Gabelman had unveiled an unappealing portrait. I was mentally ill, and there was no stuffing this fact back in the box. My stay at Stonyfield Psychiatric Hospital had been brushed under the rug, but this couldn't be.

I had taken Thorazine before, and it caused brain fog that made me feel as if my thoughts were swimming through glue. This new drug, Lithium, I *hated*. My joyous mood came to a screeching halt. I couldn't access my emotions. I was subdued. Bland. Boring. My social skills were monumentally worse. I was stable, but miserable. Mania is analogous to cocaine; the highs are addictive, and falling can be disastrous.

Thankfully, I was never restrained at Beacon Medical Center. The staff were all kind. While waiting for the Lithium to kick in, they sat with me all night when I had "big ideas." No one leered; they just kept me company. They listened to my stories, and eventually, I was able to converse with them. No one looked down on me. No one called me "retarded" or "crazy." I never felt an *us* versus *them* mentality.

Just as my grandmother had hoped, I was discharged the day before Thanksgiving. Tanked up on Lithium and Thorazine, I made it home in a presentable state of mind, which my family appreciated. I talked with my parents about living off-campus, describing my dorm experiences as "tough." They didn't probe, and I didn't offer any additional information. They graciously rented me an apartment close to my school in downtown Philadelphia and bought me a new car so that I could commute; I had totaled the first one while driving too fast during a manic episode. Before the new semester started, my mother came to visit and beautifully decorated my new one-bedroom apartment in hunter green and white tones. There was even a large stone cascading water fountain whose soft sounds reminded me of Morgan's Island.

Knowing that I could never make it through med school on these powerful drugs, I reluctantly switched my major to psychology. Perhaps studying the subject in-depth would help me better understand myself. In high school, after I underwent that neuropsychological evaluation, Methuselah had reviewed the report with me. I had brought the labels of "autistic-like" and "initial stages of a schizophrenic-form illness," along to college with me. Now, Dr. Gabelman had added "manic-depressive illness" to the mix. These labels stuck to me like Krazy glue, yet I had little insight into what they actually meant.

I thought my first day in Professor Lewis's Intro to Psychology class would be easy. Day one is generally effortless, no matter the subject; most professors review the syllabus and expectations, give a quick assignment, and let us go. Instead, for three hours, Lewis dove into the history of psychology, while intermittently scattering information about the various psychiatric diagnoses we would cover that semester. His depressingly desolate descriptions, sometimes of conditions I had been diagnosed with, put me on edge. I saw his lips move in slow-motion, and phrases like "Grave," "Will not live independently," "Remain sick," and "Disturbed" echoed through my head. To this day, I'm not sure whether I actually heard these words or just imagined them. What I did experience was the sensation of his face growing larger, while the other students seemed to fade away. Feeling extremely exposed, I walked briskly out of class and didn't return. I was still somewhat delusional and thought that Professor Lewis could magically read my thoughts and understood why I dashed out. I felt exposed.

My other classes were rather bland. I spent my free time at the library researching my diagnoses. An education was what I really needed. If I knew what the diagnoses meant, I could out-think them. This faulty logic permeated my thinking for almost thirty years. Unfortunately, at the time, the information I gathered from textbooks painted a bleak picture of my future. The internet was still in its infancy, and there was no Amazon. Barnes and Noble had a generous self-help section, yet I didn't find the books there useful. I was out of luck.

From what I could tell, autism was akin to a death sentence, with patients unable to live independently. There was no distinction between levels of functioning. Bipolar disorder was a chronic rollercoaster of being in and out of hospitals. And schizophrenia, which I don't have but share some psychotic symptoms with, would condemn me to a life of group homes.

Understandably, I freaked out.

This information left me paralyzed, and so I thought it wise to stop taking my medications and going to classes.

Within a few weeks, I was like a funnel cloud spiraling out of control. At first, I felt better and was able to resume my life, though I did not go back to school. For a short period, I functioned as if I had never set foot in the library. But, unfailingly, the high grew immense.

Craving social interaction, I was often found hanging out with my apartment building's concierge or tracking down people in my mailroom and striking up one-way conversations. My chatter could go on for hours, and I drove through countless peoples' patience.

As the mania morphed into psychosis again, I became plagued by religion and began professing that I was the Messiah. I wrote a check for $100,000 to the Christ Church near my apartment. Of course, it bounced. Sleep became unnecessary, and I would quickly drive from Philadelphia to New York City twice each night, never stopping to see my parents or even to pee. This speed matched my thought process, which felt good. However, I made many careless errors, such as running out of gas on the highway at two in the morning. My inner turmoil hijacked my attention, making it all but impossible to focus on small, though practical details. Then, at some point, my mania dipped into a full-blown psychotic episode.

This is a photograph of my apartment in Philadelphia during this episode, where I spent a solid psychotic month held up by my formidable mind. I started to see the walls breathe, so I demolished my mother's beautiful furniture and decorations. I needed to take everything off the walls. These were the devil's walls. I started cutting up my textbooks and magazines, believing the papers' layout was giving me special messages.

One day, in a brief moment of clarity, I got scared and called Dr. Gabelman, asking to be readmitted. I could no longer babysit myself.

I went back on Lithium and Thorazine, and within six weeks, I had gained forty pounds from both medications. My emotions were again blunted, and my thoughts were filled with glue. But I was no longer manic nor psychotic. I was flat and bland. *Why would anyone live like this?* flashed across my mind countless times. Moreover, I was conscious that my social skills were not up to par, and I was continuously concerned about how I was perceived. When I'm psychotic, relationships are not my priority, and I can't reflect on how my behavior is affecting others. But now, I was aware that I had trashed what meager friendships I had made at school. Eventually, Eliza stopped bringing me flowers, and I lost her as a friend.

About two months into my stay, Dr. Gabelman walked into my room and announced, "You're being discharged today, but I made arrangements with Dr. Koch to transfer your outpatient care to me. Traveling to New York every month doesn't make sense. We both think you need a closer eye and more frequent visits." He had always taken good care of me, and now, I could feel his mental hug. While I hated his prescription regiment, making smarter decisions and feeling calmer did feel healthy. Before he was finished, though, he put on his serious face and added, "There's a caveat!"

I didn't like the sound of that.

"For the next thirty days, you will come to the hospital *every day* at nine a.m. to take your medication," he said. "I *really* like you, Alex, but I don't trust your judgment. Yet! My goal is to get and *keep* you better."

There was a long awkward pause after that, as I didn't know what to say. I also liked Dr. Gabelman, although I detested his diagnosis and conditions. *No more medication tinkering on my own?* I thought unhappily. *What if I gain more weight? What if I can't think anymore? What if I can never feel happy again? What if I get depressed and try to kill myself?* While all of these thoughts swam leisurely through my dulled brain, Dr. Gabelman was waiting for an answer.

With an expansive sigh, I shook his hand and said, "You've got a deal. Thanks for believing in me."

The chair of the psychology department at school graciously permitted me to audit my classes for the remainder of the semester, which decreased my stress. I repurchased my textbooks, as my originals were cut up into ribbons on my floor. I also reacquainted myself with the learning center and Sandra from the Health and Counseling Center, who promptly referred me to a local clinic. I kept the number, but never called because I didn't think I needed therapy. It was clear that Sandra was done with me; I was not what the Center had signed up for!

Despite my best efforts, though, my head was not in the game. I was on 800 mg of Thorazine, 2100 mg of Lithium, and 2.5 mg of a new drug, Xanax. The combined experience was… interesting. I could hear just fine, but my interpretation of words lagged far behind. Even when my professors were lecturing on something I was actually interested in, my ability to interpret language and extract meaning was muddled and delayed. I couldn't think quickly enough to have a coherent conversation and felt lost and confused all the time. The drugs also interrupted my memory. It was as if I couldn't hold two pieces of information together at one time. I could focus on the present, but by the time I had to say something, "the present" was two steps behind. Plus, I had ghastly tremors. Unable to eat without spoiling my clothing, I eventually hid in my apartment doing an abundance of laundry.

When my thirty days of outpatient reporting to Dr. Gabelman was just about up, he pressured me to connect with a therapist. I called Methuselah for advice, and she suggested I try the clinic that Sandra had recommended. Reluctantly, I agreed.

A few days later, I had an appointment with a social worker, Gretchen Dupree. I was trembling when I pulled into the parking lot knowing I was not on my "a-game," so I gave myself a pep-talk before going in. Not possessing optimal perspective-taking skills, I couldn't imagine what she might think of me. I wasn't manic or floridly psychotic anymore, which worked in my favor.

Gretchen was a heavyset woman in her fifties with tight, curly black hair, porcelain skin, and innumerable wrinkles around her mouth and eyes. She had a calm, soothing voice like you would expect a therapist to have, and she seemed pleasant enough. I sat lifelessly on her blue and cream couch for the first ten minutes. She was not animated like Methuselah, and I wasn't sure of my role. And strangely, she kept asking me about my childhood.

"My childhood? Uh, I guess I have a few stories," I said uncertainly. "There was the tape factory and the stinky place. I loved to take apart televisions and put them back together and build bicycles." My pace picked up as my excitement grew. "There was the time I sunk our hot tub with Mr. Bubble, bursting the pipes in our house. I took my father's car for a spin when I was about twelve. Oh, oh, oh, and my favorite was going to the supermarket and watching the bright lightbulbs click on and off, spelling P-A-T-H-M-A-R-K-D-E-L-I, first one letter at a time and then all the letters flashing at once. I definitely had some good times—"

"Hold on." She cut me off by thrusting her palm up, like she was saying "Halt!" With a serene voice, she pointed out that none of these childhood memories involved people. She wanted to explore why that was.

I tried to explain that my elementary and middle school experiences were less than stellar and that high school, although better, was not triumphant. For me, confessing that I never really had friends satisfied the *why*, but Gretchen had other ideas.

Without warning, she announced that I *must* have been horrifically abused and had just repressed those memories. This was the late 1980s, and repressed memories were the newest psychiatric rage, but I had also just met this woman! *Oh, God*, I thought. *Where is Methuselah when I really need her?*

Gretchen used her psychiatric superiority to pummel me into entertaining this possibility. Her forcefulness and lack of joyful affect scared me, and I grew increasingly troubled by her remarks. When we parted, Gretchen gave me a homework assignment to think about who may have abused me in the past. Later that night, I lay in bed, unable to complete this task. My medications made it too hard to think.

Once my thirty days of having to report to Dr. Gabelman for my medications was up, independently I discontinued all medications… again. I knew their side effects would cease, and hopefully, my ability to think would return to normal.

Within a few weeks, the side effects did indeed dissipate, but I wasn't feeling better. I was depressed. *Really* depressed. I abruptly spiraled downward and landed in a suicidal state, unable to get out of bed, shower, make meals, or put on clean clothes. Too depressed to even attempt suicide, I lay in bed all day. This is a suicide note that I wrote during that period:

THE VERTICAL SOLUTION

Surrounded by four white walls of silence, I scream a fierce roar. Entangled in my head are vines of terror intertwined with pain. Crisp walls vibrate, echoing each complex tear.

Upon the door rests a one-minute window for viewing the animal banging profusely. I wish it would open. I turn inward to a piranha sucking the poisonous blood from my wrist. There is chatter outside my ear.

Is the conversation from a village past still plaguing me today in my mental cast? I ask myself for fear of today. It is now that my reality has gone astray. What happened to my life, anyway? It has disappeared.

Cpz (Thorazine) is coming my way. Charles, possessor of the needle, I beg of you, the village is back. They are ready to attack. My brain is at war fighting a losing battle. Money and madness create war and sadness. CPZ, take me away.

I sit quietly so as not to disturb, crunched in the corner with my mind, deteriorating from birth. Ready to snap. I remember back to my friends in the corner; myself and I. Lonely and scared a war is beginning, but never has it actually stopped.

Dastard Charles, I cry, shackles to a green mattress in misery. I call "Save me from this man who has locked me in, alone with myself." I cry. Longing for my mind to come and save me. I guess I'll wait, no never. Yes, it's dismantled forever.

Evading the past, I scamper up the wall, clinging insanely to disquiet. My needs and reality separated at birth. Today, I sit in blackness alone, dark and dingy, but I call it home. The soldiers are dead, but their hearts still beat. White turns to black as different poles are reached.

Dr. Gabelman called a few times, but I didn't have the energy to talk, so I let him leave messages on my answering machine. After three calls from him in one day, we chatted. He was disappointed that I had gone off my medications and wanted me readmitted. We cut a deal: see Gretchen once, and if I were not any better, I would sign myself back in. Frankly, I already knew how this would go. My hands were tied. If I didn't agree and comply, there would be commitment papers with my name on them.

Depression is the flip side of mania, and it is exacerbated by autism. Part of a robust treatment plan for depression relies heavily on family and/or friends to shoulder the burden. I was alone, though. Ethan had left, I had long-since stopped speaking with Francesca, and Eliza was so shocked by my symptoms that she eventually backed away. My bipolar disorder and autism challenges simply turned people off.

Living on the eighth floor with wide windows, I knew I could jump and end my life, but I couldn't vacate my covers. So I lay in bed thinking about Gretchen's questions. *Was I abused?* I wondered. *Why don't my younger memories contain many people?* I just didn't know. Doubting myself, I gave it some thought.

Dr. Gabelman and I spoke again the next day. My depression continued, but I requested one more week before entering the hospital, which he graciously granted.

That week, with a touch of lucidity and now just a hair above suicidal, I called Gretchen to schedule our appointment. When the day came, I tumbled out of bed and sheepishly returned to her office, unaccompanied by my "homework." I explained that I had thought long and hard but was unable to conjure up any memories of abuse.

"There, there," she said calmly. Then, she leaned in and whispered in a sort of creepy, excited way, "I knew it! The memories are hidden down deep. Go ahead! Find them!"

My loud, angry voice bounced around the room: "I think you're wrong!"

This apparently pissed her off. She pointed to the cream-colored sofa on the other side of the room and firmly instructed, "Move over there and lie down. Take your sneakers off first, so you don't dirty my furniture. I'm going to hypnotize you."

Annoyed and irritated, I obeyed. My sensory system was heightened by lying on Gretchen's itchy couch, and I didn't know what to expect. *No commitment to this wacky woman*, I thought. *No commitment.*

Confident with her conclusion, Gretchen muttered some strange words over me. Then, she instructed me to open my eyes and started pulling out large glossy photos of brutal abuse and assault inflicted on children. She played audiotapes of people screaming. I recollect thinking, *Gabelman would* never *approve of this.*

Finally, she turned off the audio equipment and stopped flipping through the photos. "How are you feeling?" she asked. "Remember anything?"

"Nope." This was true, but I was also quite frightened of her by now. I was scared to be in her office and scared of what she would do to me next.

That night, I sprang up from a nightmare, and I reviewed the content with her the next day. In 1977, a girl named Laurie Strode was ominously chased around a hospital by Michael Myers, who was wearing a white hockey mask. The date was Halloween, and every Halloween since then, he went on a killing spree in the woods, in his home, and in the hospital.

"Will you draw it for me?" she asked.

"Of course." What I actually drew was a picture of my living room in the late seventies and me watching this scary scene on TV. The television was sucking me in, like in *Poltergeist*. This was not a real memory, but rather a memory of watching the movie *Halloween*. When I was seven, my parents let me rent the Betamax, and it gave me nightmares. I was petrified of Halloween well into my teens, and to this day, I hate the holiday.

Gretchen and I chatted for a while after this. She was now more convinced than ever that I was a trauma survivor, and she pled her case. "I can tell by how shaken you are that this memory must be true. I'm an expert on abuse. I knew I was right."

"Ah, okay?" I said apprehensively. This whole thing still didn't make sense. Turning back to the drawing, I asked, "Then why does the scene take place on TV?"

"This is such a powerful memory that you needed to remove yourself from it." With that, Gretchen instructed me to call my parents, confront them with their crimes, and break all ties. "This is the only way you will get better," she concluded.

My mind was trapped in a spinning vortex. This directive didn't make rational sense to me, but for the most part, I did what I was told. I still wasn't on my medications, I was fairly delusional, and suggestions frequently came across as commands. I could hear a muted tone of rationality within myself, asking, *Why would I listen to Gretchen? Why is she forcing me to accuse my parents of something they never did?* Unfortunately, it was not powerful enough to duel Gretchen.

With her breathing down my neck, I called my mother from Gretchen's office and (falsely) accused her of horrific abuse. She was shocked and asked many questions, but I cut the conversation short. As per Gretchen's instructions, I was excommunicating them.

We lost touch for a few years after this call, and while my parents and I are exceptionally close today, there is still some earwax that occasionally comes between us because of it.

After I hung up with my mother, Gretchen called Dr. Gabelman from outside her office. Despite the closed door between us, I could hear her tone escalate, though I couldn't make out her words. Still, the result of their conversation was clear: Dr. Gabelman wanted me voluntarily readmitted or I would face a commitment again. Gretchen drove to Beacon Medical Center while I followed behind. This was to be my fourth admission there.

Back in Gabelman's comfortable office, he lectured me about abruptly stopping my meds. I had known this conversation was coming. And how could I argue with him? Going off my meds had been a careless, but conscious decision.

Then, Gretchen and Dr. Gabelman stepped outside, but I could distinctly hear their horrendous exchange. They were yelling at each other about the etiology of my illness. One was on "team bipolar" and the other, "team abuse." Depressed, suicidal, delusional, and defenseless, I couldn't pick sides. Even though I loathed Dr. Gabelman's drugs, emotionally, I did feel better and struggled less with the cocktail. And, most importantly, I felt safe with him. Gretchen, for whom I had no respect, was vehemently opposed to readmitting me. She did not win this battle.

I spent the next two months at Beacon Medical Center, slowly stabilized, and eventually only had quiet mood swings during this time. Dr. Gabelman agreed to test my medication threshold and reduce them slightly, which I appreciated. However, the medications' side effects still overwhelmed me. Back in my groggy, flat state, I was barely able to care for myself, so I withdrew from college. This was both sad and a necessary relief.

While I was content at Beacon Medical Center and truly trusted Gabelman, my private insurance eventually reached its maximum lifetime benefit. I would need to transfer to a local community hospital about thirty minutes away that accepted Medicaid. At this point, I was unable to take care of myself. All I wanted was a hot meal and a place to sleep.

Conway Community Hospital was unremarkable, but I hated it nonetheless. All I could think about was the fact that Dr. Gabelman was gone from my life. I hated how the drugs made me feel. I hated that I was locked out of my room all day. I hated the indifferent staff. I hated that they didn't understand me and, worse yet, they didn't even try. And I hated the intermittent chemical and mechanical restraints they used. I much preferred being locked in the "quiet room."

I wasn't restrained frequently at Conway, perhaps every month or two, but it was generally for stupid infractions, such as throwing my sneaker at the TV or screaming from complete sensory overload. However, I was also restrained for grander behavior, such as bolting out the door to run away from my hallucinations or having a bizarre delusion that resulted in hitting a staff member when he came too close. None of this excuses my behavior, of course.

My entire treatment plan was utterly ineffectual. Being restrained just made me angry and taught me not to rely on hospital personnel. I felt misunderstood by the staff. Because a typical hospital protocol is taxing on the sensory system (I was locked out of my room, there was a lack of exercise and fresh air, food comingled, and I was forced to interact with people all day), I was constantly battling against myself to stay in control. If my sensory needs had been taken into consideration, I am certain that my outbursts would have diminished. Plus, my medications were changed by the unit's psychiatrist and not tweaked enough to prevent my moods from cycling, so those were not well-regulated, either.

I had no idea what I was supposed to glean from other aspects of my treatment, such as "group therapy" with other patients and my regular three-minute check-in with my psychiatrist. I did love art therapy, though. On Mondays, Wednesdays, and Fridays, from one p.m. to three p.m., the doorway to an otherwise-locked room sprung open, and a whole other galaxy awoke! I could breathe again! When I draw, write, paint, collage, or take photographs, I feel fluid. My art is very personal and transcends my disabilities. I'm not stigmatized. I'm lighter. That art room was a blessing.

I abhorred my treatment, but the occasional niceties from the nursing and mental health staff made my stay tolerable. Underneath it all, they were kind people. My third Christmas at Conway Community Hospital was especially eye-opening. One-by-one, the unit's patients left to visit their families, leaving many vacancies at the "inn." By Christmas Eve, I was the only patient left in the ward. My stay was considered long-term, and my relationship with my parents was prickly, so going back to New York City was not an option. I missed my nana.

I went to sleep and awoke to the usual smell of French toast, greasy bacon, and powered eggs on the cafeteria's cart. I sluggishly crawled to my doorway, where my eyes expanded to take in the sight that lay before me. The *entire* unit was adorned with holiday decorations, with one wall more beautiful than the next. Lights flickered, tinsel and garland shimmered, and ornaments abounded. There was even a real Christmas tree with presents! Ellen, one of the nurses, motioned for me to approach the tree. I saw that the presents beneath it were labelled with my name. They were for me! The staff had bought me a new sketch pad, drawing pencils, and watercolors, all things I could no longer afford without my parents' financial support in the wake of Gretchen's interference. Graciously thanking the staff, I invited them to my Christmas breakfast. I will always think fondly of that Christmas morning.

Not only did Conway Community Hospital take care of my psychiatric needs, but they also connected me with a social worker, Jim Webber, who helped me apply for social security income, which would give me a tiny stipend each month for living expenses. Now that I was officially "disabled," I qualified. However, like most applicants, I had to jump through a plethora of hoops with rejection after rejection. Jim helped me all the way, never once letting me get discouraged.

At that same Christmas breakfast, Griffin, another nurse, handed me an envelope that looked governmental and official. "Here, Jim wanted you to open it," he said with a smile. "It's his Christmas present to you."

"What is it?"

He playfully answered, "Open it and find out!"

"This is a letter from social security," I gasped as I tore open the envelope and pulled out the letter. My eyes raced over the page. "I'm approved?" Whipping my head around to look at the gathered staff, I screamed with glee, "What? I'm approved? Are you kidding me? This has taken a whole year, but it finally came through! Oh, thank you, Jim! Thank you, everyone! This is the best Christmas news I've had—not to say your presents weren't awesome, too." I was ecstatic and could feel my body radiating warmth.

I spent several years in and out of Conway Community Hospital—mostly in—and it is where I was living when I eventually took that fateful drive with the jug of gasoline.

CHAPTER 7

CATHARSIS

ABOUT SIX HOURS after I impulsively decided to check myself out of Conway Community Hospital and drive to Boston, I arrived at my destination: the Boston Common. The sweet scent of flowers emerging from the earth awakened my senses. I found a place to park and set out to explore. There was life brimming all around me, just like I had seen on the television. Young children were feeding newborn ducklings. People were taking photographs of the trees' new leaves. And I was simply enjoying life and soaking up my freedom.

After my jaunt in The Common, I returned to my car and started the ignition, and that's when my inability to foresee future consequences hit me like a ton of bricks. Where was I going? I didn't have a place to live. I hardly had any money. How was I going to eat? I slept in my car that night, and while I was uncomfortable, I was free and I was alive.

However, after a few days of living in my cramped car in a wealthy part of downtown Boston, the novelty of my newfound freedom was wearing thin. Returning to the hospital or my parents' apartment felt like a colossal failure that I just couldn't stomach. I was surrounded by newly renovated apartment complexes and vintage townhouses with exquisite architecture. Either of these living options suited me just fine, so I took my disheveled and slightly odoriferous body to a rental agent's office.

Jesse, the slim, perky, thirtyish-year-old rental agent, wore shiny black shoes with pointed toes, which looked quite uncomfortable. When I expressed interest in renting an apartment, she began asking questions about my employment history. I didn't put two-and-two together for why this was relevant. I proudly (and naively) explained that I hadn't been employed because, after several years, I had just been released from a mental institution. Lucky for her, I had selected her complex to lay down new roots.

As you can well imagine, I was not a desirable tenant, and after she voiced a few choice and degrading words about my being a "crazy mental case," she promptly showed me to the door.

After years of institutional living, I didn't realize how oblivious I had become to the stigma to and marginalization of people with mental illness. In the hospital setting, the tolerant professionals I knew had chosen to work with the psychiatrically ill, and the other patients were my peers. Mental illness was the norm; everyone had something.

After several similarly failed attempts to rent an equally fancy apartment, I encountered a gentleman who kindly pointed me in the direction of a pay-by-the-night room on the other side of town.

When I pulled up to this three-story complex at sunset, I internally recoiled. Inside, the seedy clerk with a greasy comb-over took my seventeen dollars and gave me the key to room 216, my new home. While it wasn't an ideal environment, I was exhausted and needed someplace to rest. I was frightened by the fact that I wasn't thriving as I had in my fantasy in the hospital's parking lot. However, I made up my mind to give this place a try.

Lugging my bag up the stairs, I then opened the door to room 216. The tiny room had four white walls, a bed with a thin plastic army-green mattress, and a dresser affixed to the wall. The walls were stained with some unknown yellowish substance; I thought it best not to investigate what it was.

As I lay down on the sheet-less bed, I could smell pot and saw tiny puffs of smoke creeping under my door. My ears ached as my body was invaded by the sounds of yelling and rap music blaring from the hall. They were loud enough that they shook the bed. I was alone and petrified. This freedom was not all it's cracked up to be, and these living quarters were a far cry from the beauty of the Boston Common. I threw my gray hooded sweatshirt over my head, curled up into a ball, and cried for hours.

By four in the morning, everything had quieted down a little, but I was still panic-stricken. I went to the payphone in the hallway and called the institution. Candace, a kind and maternal nurse, was working the overnight shift. When I told her where I was, she said, "Oh dear, Alex, this is an awful situation. Just come back, and you can be readmitted. We still have your room open for you. Just come *home.*"

Her words were the first sound of comfort I'd heard in the five days since I left. I agreed to return and began to pack all of my worldly possessions back into my brown duffle bag. However, as I grabbed my paint swatches, I recalled my "suicide trip" to New York and the words of all the people who had condemned me over the years: "You can't," "You won't," "Not with your diagnoses."

Determined not to let those words win, I decided that I couldn't just give up after a few stressful days. I called Candace back, thanked her for listening, and politely declined her offer. She respected my decision, and after talking for another hour or so, she imparted some advice about what I would need to do in order to live "on the outside."

Step one was getting a job.

Step two was finding a safe place to live.

Thanks to my social worker, Jim, I was now receiving monthly disability checks from social security, but the amount was far too little to live on the outside of the hospital and especially not in Boston proper.

I contacted my parents and let them know where I was and what my plans were for my future. After recounting a story of being so hungry that I was window-shopping at the grocery store, they kindly offered to supplement my social security checks so that I could both eat and have a roof over my head, instead of choosing one or the other. At this point, they were living in a one-bedroom apartment in New

York City, so moving in with them wasn't an option, even if I hadn't been too proud to ask.

Within a week of my call to Candace, I was applying for jobs. At first, I scoured the *Boston Globe*'s help-wanted section and applied to several biotechnology firms and laboratories as well as some high-level executive positions. They sounded interesting, and I didn't think that my lack of a degree or experience would be a turn-off in any way. I was turned down from every single job I applied to. But then, I saw an ad that spoke to me. Soon after, I had secured an interview with Hertz Rent-A-Car at Logan Airport.

As a child, I had been obsessed with cars and knew intricate details about them. My favorite activity was lining up my entire Matchbox car collection against the kitchen wall. Like my parents who parallel parked their cars, I imitated parking my Matchbox cars in a line all day long. Given my devotion to and childhood experience with cars, I thought Hertz might be a viable option. I called my parents for some advice. All of the other jobs I had applied to turned me down, so getting my Hertz interview right felt paramount.

Before the interview, I needed to submit a resume and cover letter, which my dad helped me with. He also gave me some tips for the interview itself: "Look interested the entire time. Oh, and nod if someone talks to you. And, really important, compliment the person–they like that!" He took a deep breath and added, "You _can't_ tell them that you were in a psychiatric institution. They're going to think you're crazy and won't hire you. Put on your resume that you worked for me for the last six years. List me as your contact and put down my number."

"Thanks, Dad."

On the morning of the interview, I splashed cold water on my face, put on my favorite shirt and best (only) pair of tan pants, and drove off. From blunt conversations with my father, I knew better than to wear my grungy gray sweatshirt that he always hated because it was sloppy.

At the interview, there was a large group of applicants from all across the lifespan. Mike, Hertz's recruiting director, stood at the front of the room and explained the job and benefits package. With his thick East Boston accent, pudgy hands, and colossal double chin, he pasted on a smile and basked in the glory of working for Hertz.

As my father had predicted, we were required to fill out some paperwork that included our employment history and contact information. Between my father's pearls of wisdom and my experience with Jesse, the rental agency lady, I knew to keep my mouth shut regarding my history as a mental patient.

After a perfunctory ten-minute interview, Mike enthusiastically shook my hand. "Congratulations, Alexandra," he bellowed. "You're one of the new Hertz representatives!"

I couldn't believe it. I was *actually* hired.

Mission number one, landing a job, accomplished!

Beaming with pride, I exited the office and soaked up my achievement.

I proudly called my parents to let them know that I had secured a job as an Hertz customer service representative. I could now stop receiving disability checks; I was employed! I think this was the news my parents were waiting for. Whenever I exhibited even a modicum of normalcy, they immediately went from thinking I had a disability to being certain that I was cured. I don't believe this vast denial comes from a place of malice, but rather from wanting their child not to suffer.

On my first day of Hertz orientation, my bubble of pride burst when I realized that the characters in my training group were not *that* different from my mental patient peers; basically, anyone who could fog a mirror was hired. I wanted people to see my strengths. I wanted to be viewed as "normal." This sort of cheapened the experience for me.

Hertz's training program involved learning their computer system. I picked this up instantly and actually thought I had a future with the company. The next part of training was considerably harder, though, as it involved interacting with the customers. I managed to skim by, and after a few days, I was out on the floor, renting cars.

Now, imagine this: you've just gotten off a long flight. You're hot, tired, and want to start your vacation. After waiting in a slow-moving rental line, you approach my station. I start with a simple script: "Reservation number, please." Unfortunately, after this, things go awry…

"Oh, I see you've reserved a mid-size car," I say. "Let me tell you what your options are. You can choose a Ford Taurus or a Mercury Sable. The Mercury Sable has a 3.0 V6 engine, whereas the Ford Taurus has a 3.1-liter V6 engine. However, if you wait until two p.m., there will be a Ford Taurus returning with a 3.8-liter V6 engine. This is really a better car, and even though it's four hours from now, you should really wait for it. But the wheelbase in the Mercury Sable *is* much larger and can have a better feel when driving…"

In my autistic mind, there is no "gist" to get to. Everything is—and must be—exact. The Ford Taurus that was returning had a 3.8-liter V6 engine, not just "an engine." In over-focusing on details, it is easy for me to neglect the big picture. While this can be asset in some area, customer service is not one of them. My job at the front counter lasted about three days.

After several customer complaints, Susan, the manager, sat me down and earnestly, but bluntly said, "Alex, you have promise, but no people skills."

Susan wanted to help, so she offered me a new job that was more suited to my detailed-oriented mind. After that, I was away from customers in the back room, working on computers for Hertz's gold customers. I never told my parents about this change because, although it was technically a step up, I was embarrassed. As for Susan's comments, I wasn't at all offended. In fact, I was almost relieved. Working on computers to crank out contracts for the "important business customers" seemed like a better option for me. In this job, I simply had to print out the correct contract from a list of customers renting that day and put this document in their car with the key–no social interactions required.

This was a busy Hertz location, and being successful meant having the capacity to think fast on your feet. While I enjoyed this job, the pace was stressful. I had by now connected with a local random psychiatrist who was handling my prescriptions. The psychiatric medications that I was on—Lithium, a mood stabilizer for bipolar disorder; Valium, an anti-anxiety medication; and Thorazine, an antipsychotic—dampened my spirits and slowed my thinking. The fastest way to reconnect with my past highs and be an employee rock star, I decided, was to stop taking my Lithium, since that governed my moods. So, about a month into working at Hertz, that's exactly what I did.

After ditching the pills, everything followed the same, familiar pattern. Hypomania crept in, and initially, I was able to keep up with everything that was thrown my way. In fact, at Hertz, hypomania was a godsend. I was efficient, and social interactions with my coworkers and Susan were much more manageable.

As my mania ramped up, I started using two computers at once because my mind was racing faster than one computer could handle. My fingers struck the keys at lightning speed. The pace was challenging, but I was in symbiosis with my hypomania. I started to get accolades from Susan, which felt unusual and quite lovely.

But then, within about six weeks of going off of Lithium, the hypomania turned to mania, and the dark clouds rumbled in. Judgment and perspective went astray. My arrival at work began to fluctuate. Attention to detail was almost nonexistent. What little social judgment I had failed. Wanting no part of the "important gold customers," I constantly left my station to bellow to the supervisor's office about some insignificant thing that had ticked me off. Sometimes, I would suddenly leave work in a frenzied state and run to the airport terminals, looking for flights that I could take for my important journeys. Fortunately, I couldn't afford any flights, as my credit cards were always declined.

One day, Susan had had enough. She sat me down for "the talk." No, not the sex talk. The talk about drugs.

Her chest rose and fell quickly as she began speaking in a serious tone. "Alex, I think I know what's going on," she said. I had my ideas, but I entertained her. "I know you're on cocaine, and I want to help you—"

I was angry at the very suggestion that I was on drugs, and I cut her off: "I'm not on cocaine, and there's nothing wrong with me!" With that, I dashed out of her office, slamming the door behind me.

That afternoon, I happened to have an appointment with my beloved psychiatrist, Dr. Catherine Saar. She reminded me of Audrey Hepburn, since she was very thin, always wore her brown hair swept back, and adorned her neck and wrists with fancy jewelry. Her movements were slow and graceful, which I loved. We bantered during our appointments, which was fun, but she drew the line when necessary.

I actually made it to my appointment that day. I can't even imagine what she thought when I walked through her door. Unable to sit still, I paced in a circle. My paranoia was abundant. I thought Hertz was trying to poison me, so I was going to take over the corporation and fire everyone. As I paced, I stared at the Amish quits that decorated three of her four walls. I had so many questions about these brightly colored quilts, mostly having to do with the meaning of the symmetrical patterns. I couldn't get them out of my mind. All of Dr. Saar's questions seemed unimportant in the face of my need to discharge my millions of racing thoughts. All I remember of our conversation is her two lines:

"Why did you stop taking your Lithium?"

And, "You're going to be hospitalized today. You can't leave this office."

I was furious. I knew this drill. Even back then, I could write a book on mental patient protocol, having learned my lesson several times. If I refused, Dr. Saar would commit me for seventy-two hours, maybe longer. I acquiesced.

Fortunately, the hospital only held me for a few days. They put me back on Lithium and Thorazine and signed my papers, so I could return to work. This was not a ruthless stay, and I wasn't restrained. It was just something I needed to live through.

After my discharge, I met with Susan, explained the situation, and begged for my job back. She seemed relieved that I was not taking cocaine and returned me to the back computer room for the gold customers. It took a few weeks for the Lithium to fully kick back in, and Susan very kindly let me adjust my schedule until then.

At the hospital, they had increased my dosage of Thorazine, which made me feel groggy and dampened my mood even further. While I appeared more emotionally stable and my paranoia evaporated, this increase in medication also slowed me down. I was not as successful at work as I had been before. While I still had a job, the accolades stopped, and my peers steered clear of me, likely due to my unusual behavior before my hospitalization. I felt like I was back in middle school again.

I really hate Thorazine.

After multiple paychecks at Hertz, I had saved up enough money for a security deposit and first month's rent enabling me to move out of the drug-infested, pay-by-the-night tenement where I'd been staying and into a one-room studio in a safe neighborhood in Quincy, Massachusetts. Although discharged from the institution, I was so accustomed to being institutionalized that the only logical way to function was to imitate the systems of the psychiatric hospital and incorporate them into my apartment. They provided me with a sense of organization and comfort.

I kept my environment simple. A white blanket and white pillow complimented the clean white walls of my new studio. I left the walls bare.

Each hospital I had landed in encompassed a level system. One's "level" was based upon compliance with the institution's rules. At my first hospital, I spent the majority of the first few months of my admission in the locked "quiet room," which didn't earn me any brownie points. By my last admission, I had learned how to manipulate the system and was able to leave the hospital unaccompanied. True manipulation requires proficient perspective-taking skills, which I still didn't have. However, after witnessing the interplay between cause and effect a zillion times, I learned important patterns, such as "keeping my suicidal ideation to myself" equals "independent day passes." At my apartment, I simulated the idea of privilege levels. Of course, I was on the highest level because I left "campus" each day.

I also created an activity schedule that listed options for the day when I was not at work, such as reading, writing, crafts, art projects, taking nature walks, and photography. I established a "sharps" closet, where I signed out things like my razor, scissors, and nail clippers. I purchased a whiteboard and hung it by the door to serve as my "sign-in/out" board, so the imaginary staff would know where I was. Signing in and out of my apartment felt like the first step in a chain of events that led to an activity or outing. In my mind, without this first step, the other steps could not follow. It was as if the steps were glued together.

While I was able to push myself out of my comfort zone by living independently, implementing these systems made me feel safe. Although I had physically left the institution, mentally, I remained completely institutionalized for many years. Living this new life and working was psychologically exhausting. I was still only marginally functioning, and this bothered me. When I left the institution and drove to Boston, I had expected a more fulfilling life.

To help myself adjust, about six months after I left the institution, I started engaging my neighborhood more by participating in photography seminars, going on community nature walks, and spending time at the library.

One afternoon, while on a "day pass," I walked to my local public library to borrow a book. As I entered the massive brick building with impressive columns, I saw a large pumpkin-orange sign hanging in a small vestibule that read: *Autism Support Group / Friday 7 p.m.*

At this point, I was officially diagnosed with Asperger's, and the spectrum had come to represent misery in my life, so I angrily curled my lip and wrinkled my nose as if I'd smelled something terrible. I mumbled under my breath, "Asperger's is just one more diagnostic label." I knew what my diagnoses were, but digesting and accepting them was another ball game entirely. I used to think that if I accepted these diagnoses, I would become trapped by them. So, instead, denial seemed like a pleasant place to live.

Ignoring the orange sign, I walked up the stairs and immediately headed toward the physics section. At Milton Academy, my physics teacher had taken a liking to me, and we spent many hours after school discussing various theories of how to explain almost everything in the world. Physics just made logical sense to me. On the library's wooden shelf, a large, brand-new, neon-red book titled *Principles of Quantum Mechanics* by R. Shankar jumped out at me. Ah, a good night would be had!

As I trotted back down the stairs, book in hand, I passed the autism sign again. This time, the innocuous sign had taken on a life of its own and seemed to barricade the stairs so that I couldn't flee. I repeated the pessimistic monologue that had played on a loop in my mind since I was about nine: *I hate my life. Why can't I just be normal? I hate my life. Why can't I just be normal? I hate my life. Why can't I just be normal?* These thoughts raced through in my head, becoming louder and more forceful. My pulse was now raging. The sign had turned into an obsession.

With gusto, I faced my fear and confronted this sign, even going so far as to touch it, knowing that hundreds of other people had touched the same paper and left their germs on it. After several minutes of contemplation and again reflecting on my suicide trip to New York, I thought, *Maybe I should just go to this support group. Nothing else is helping. I'm not really "making it" on my own. I'd rather die than return to the institution, so I don't have anything to lose.* That scary sign representing everything I hated about myself began to seem almost hopeful. *Maybe there are other people out there like me. Maybe they'll have the cure.* I quickly assigned a numerical value to my thoughts based upon my calculations and decided. *I'll do it! I'll go to this meeting. After all, what can it hurt?*

For as long as I can remember, I've lived my life through

mathematical calculations. Every decision in life, from what I want for dinner to what I decided to major in at college, was based upon a simple calculation. I had long-since learned that I couldn't rely on my body to give me accurate information, so as a coping mechanism, I used calculations.

Once, an institutional compadre explained that when she was selecting a dessert, she decided what she wanted based on how it made her feel. For example, "Do I *feel* like chocolate cake or ice cream?" This always confused me because my thinking is so literal. And who wants to "feel" their dessert? When I ask my body "What do I want?" the response is generally complicated. I might not get a response at all, or I'll get a strange response, such as a mental image of the laundry vent at Lenox Hill Hospital that smelled so good, I would often skip school to hang out around it. In contrast to this confusion, calculations were consistent, accurate, and reliable. Plus, I just like them.

On the night of the support group meeting, I stood in my studio and dressed in the least-offensive, non-scratchy, tags-cut-out clothing I could find. I began to think about my institutionalized life and wondered if there would be anyone at the meeting who was like me. In the institutions, the chronic long-term patients were primarily people with schizophrenia and bipolar disorder. I had read in college that people with autism often couldn't live independently, but I never met any in the institutions. So, where were they? I certainly never came across anyone like me, with a combination of autism and bipolar disorder. Granted, we're all individuals, and I did meet people who shared some similarities with me, but no one was an analogous match. I could relate to the symptoms of those who had bipolar disorder, but there was something missing, something that made me feel different. Maybe this meeting would finally bring me face-to-face with people who really "got" me.

When I was ready to leave for the autism support group, I walked to my dry-erase board and signed out, writing as my destination, "autism support meeting - back at 9 p.m." I spent a good ten minutes trying to figure out if "autism" had a capital "A." I was probably just anxious.

When I arrived at the meeting, there were about twenty adults around my age, and they all appeared to be very comfortable with each other, even enjoying themselves. I didn't know anyone, so I eavesdropped as a way of blending in. Dumbfounded at how easily these people conversed, I thought, *They must have "the answer."* However, not understanding the context of their stories made me uncomfortable, and I wanted to run.

As I started to head for the door, a tall, slender woman with a broad smile and wearing a bright-red dress noticed me. She had been buzzing about and talking excitedly with everyone. She hurried over to me as I was leaving and introduced herself: "Hi, I'm Daphne. The autism meeting is in here. Come on in." As she guided me back into the room, she started asking me questions about "my child."

"I don't have any children," I said, confused, "and I don't understand why you're asking."

Puzzled by what I was doing there, Daphne explained, "This meeting is for parents who have *children* with autism."

We came to the same conclusion: clearly, I was misplaced! We both laughed at my blunder and spoke for a bit. I was relieved to have met a friendly person who was not spooked by my autism. In fact, once she learned that I was diagnosed on the autism spectrum, Daphne asked if I would come to the next support group and talk to the parents about my experiences. This was not what I had hoped to gain from this meeting, but since I had no friends, no life, and basically nothing else to do, I agreed.

In a million years, I never would have guessed that the next support group meeting a month later would have such pronounced ramifications on my future. But it did. It truly changed my life.

Nine parents sat in a circle on hard, white, folding plastic chairs. The format was Q&A. We talked for hours, and the parents asked question after question about my experiences. I answered them all honestly—sort of. My experiences with bipolar disorder were so provocative and cruel that I didn't want to relive them in any way, so I kept them to myself. Plus, countless experiences over the years had taught me to keep my mental illness a secret for fear of being ostracized.

I had spent my whole life being judged and belittled for my differences, but at the Q&A, the parents were kind and seemed sympathetic. It was quite the opposite of what I was used to. I was also slightly hypomanic, which was helpful, and I didn't grow weary of the social interaction.

The parents asked all sorts of questions about my childhood, friends, romantic relationships, sensory system, meltdowns, and many, many other things. I answered their questions as honestly as I could. I didn't realize until years later how cathartic this meeting was for *me*. In a way, the parents helped me as much as I helped them.

This was the first time I had told my story as both a speaker and observer of myself. I listened *and* felt. I was finally in touch with all of my feelings about having autism, ranging from the pure elation of perseverations to the profound sadness of poor socialization and bullying in my childhood. Unlike in the hospital admission process, where the goal of telling my story was to obtain approval from my insurance company, I felt compassion from these parents. There were no pretenses or psychoanalytical interpretations–it just *was*. I was treated like a person, not a patient. And, surprisingly, the parents were genuinely interested in what I had to say. I felt valued, as if talking about my path might actually help someone. In this meeting, the assumption was that "I could," "I did," and despite my diagnoses, "I will continue to" thrive. That night, I went home and took down my whiteboard. I was institutionalized no longer.

At the Q&A, no subject was off-limits. I spoke positively about some of the pleasurable aspects of autism. Perseverating, or repeating a thought, behavior, or verbalization, is downright delightful. My whole body quakes with excitement, and I can feel fluids swish through me. I'm drawn to these obsessions like an addict to methamphetamines. I only have a few perseverations, but the visuals I crave are satisfying. Watching spewing fountains with finely synchronized water dances, such as outside the Bellagio in Las Vegas or the Christian Science Center in Boston, is extremely pleasurable, but it is something that people without autism can also enjoy. Collecting old cameras seems fairly reasonable. But obsessing over the Massachusetts General Hospital cafeteria's three-tiered "tray-taker-awayer" is something I cannot explain or share with others. Still, if my autistic life just consisted of pleasurable perseverations, I would lift my glass in a toast. However, my faulty social skills, rigid thinking, and disorganization also hitch a ride.

Yes, there are fantastic aspects of autism and bipolar disorder, but there's also a scary, dark side, especially when one is institutionalized. When I threw a tantrum at home well past my toddler years, there were coping strategies I employed, such as going to the playground and using the swing set or wrapping myself up like a burrito in my thick, heavy down blanket. However, in the hospitals, when I lost control, I didn't have access to this toolbox of interventions. Revealing this dark side, I spoke to the parents' group of enduring restraints, being locked in a timeout space, and withstanding aversive therapy.

The idea behind aversive therapy is that if you pair a behavior with an adverse reaction (for example, a mouse getting a shock after hitting a specific bar), the subject will no longer seek specific stimuli or engage in a particular behavior. Since the age of ten, I had braved various types of aversive therapy both in school and the institutions. They ranged from being shoved in my elementary school's coat closet to being strapped down with leather restraints to the dreaded "Army bag." Even worse, though, were the "chemical restraints," such as Haldol or Thorazine. When these were injected into me, I couldn't talk or walk and breathing was a laborious process. The staff would just inject me, then plop me down and lock me in the quiet room. I hope the seemingly malevolent clinicians and teachers were doing what they genuinely thought was best for me, but I have my doubts.

Aversive therapy was employed when I was either manic or

psychotic and I couldn't contain myself physically or emotionally. However, it was also used when I was experiencing extreme sensory dysregulation due to my autism and didn't have access to my toolbox of coping strategies. In those cases, I may have been running around the unit, stripping, screaming, or making other noises and simply *appeared* to be out of control to the staff. In reality, I was trying to regain control of myself and my senses.

As an autistic teenager without introspection, I had often struggled to understand why the adults were so mean. I couldn't connect my actions with their reactions and was repeatedly angered and held grudges about my treatment. Feeling vulnerable, I rarely spoke with the staff for fear that something I would say might trigger an explosion in them.

Aversive therapy was just part of my life's story, and I had never lamented it before. It just *was*. In fact, I often felt that I had brought these consequences on myself. In order to emotionally survive, I needed to believe the hospital staff's intentions were good. After all, why else would someone want to hurt me?

But now, as I spoke to the parents' group, I watched their faces contort in a way that informed me this type of "treatment" was not okay. Over the years, I had learned that it was sometimes necessary to borrow others' perspectives until I could internalize them as my own. In this instance, I borrowed the parents' reactions and began to process just how inhumane my treatment had been. It was an eye-opener.

I still lacked the innate ability to automatically read nonverbal cues, which are essential in understanding what other people are feeling and thinking, but I had by now learned a few tricks to get by. One of the most valuable was creating a system to inform me that another person was experiencing an emotion or giving me nonverbal clues of some kind.

I did this by taking a mental photograph of a person's neutral face the first time I met them and put it on a grid. When their face contorted in more than two standard deviations—such as a big smile where the corners of the mouth move away from the center, the cheekbones rise, and the corners of the eyes squint—I knew some emotion was occurring. Guessing what that emotion was became easier over time, but I continued to struggle to understand what people were thinking. And, when manic or depressed, I wasn't invested in translating facial expressions.

Then, in my early twenties, I found a technique that was immeasurably helpful that dealt with something called "microexpressions." I watched a documentary on microexpressions that are universal and convey the same seven emotions: anger, fear, sadness, disgust, surprise, contempt, and happiness. The theory is that people's true feelings are expressed in the 0.04 to 0.5 seconds before they conceal them and instead express their more socially acceptable emotions. For example, Betty asks Jane to go see a movie that Jane finds boring. Jane will make an anger microexpression (her true emotion) before she smiles and says enthusiastically, "Yes, let's go see that movie," which is the more socially acceptable emotion, so as not to hurt Betty's feelings.

Finally, I could reliably predict what emotion people were feeling! But this still left me uncertain as to what degree and, more importantly, *why* the person was experiencing this emotion. So, like a sleuth, I would look for clues to help solve this mystery. I studied people feverishly, which was enormously helpful now that I had a scientific system to help me identify and label emotions. Not only did I surveil people in public locations, such as Harvard Square, but I also scoured television, as the camera angle often captured faces. Explaining this technique to the parents' group was, I believe, instrumental for them.

Despite my new and growing toolbox of techniques, my social skills were still rough, and I struggled to read subtle social cues, which is where most meaning in conversation is made. And, I had no friends with whom to practice. I was continually, yet unintentionally, offending people. I saw their faces contort and knew that I had said or done something to piss them off, but I could never ascertain exactly what. It was endlessly frustrating.

My fourth-grade teacher had once snapped at me, "You're so stupid. Why don't you just get *it*?" It was the *"it"* in social interactions that no one had ever explained to me. "Why did you do it?" is incomprehensible, whereas "Why did you tell me that I looked fat today?" makes it clear what the otherwise unspoken *"it"* is.

Similarly, it drives me crazy when people don't bind their references. "Let's go to *her* house" is confusing, whereas "Let's go to *Sally's* house" is crystal clear. The lack of binding leaves those with social disabilities in a constant compromised position.

At the parents' group, I explained this predicament in detail. I hoped that they would come away from our meeting with some helpful tools for interacting with their children and that their children would benefit from my own experiences.

As we were talking about understanding other peoples' thoughts and emotions, Allison, a mom with beautiful waist-length blonde hair and wearing a pink sweater, asked kindly and gently, "What about your emotions? Do you feel the way we feel?"

I really wasn't sure what she was asking. I honestly hadn't contemplated whether my feelings were the same as others'. Besides, how would I even know, when I still struggled to understand what others were feeling in the first place?

Before learning perspective-taking, which came later in life, I struggled with unobvious empathy. I was capable of sympathizing with others, but only to a degree. I could make the leap to guess that if someone had experienced a similar situation to me, they would have a similar reaction. Of course, this didn't take into account that all people are different and may have different reactions to similar things. However, if I had not previously experienced something myself, my emotions usually registered as blank, and I couldn't make the leap to sympathy. Of course, this doesn't mean that I don't feel things very deeply. I have a profound love for my children, nature, bridges, photography, and fountains. I do <u>have</u> a rich inner life. But lacking perspective-taking skills may be why a person with autism would be perceived as socially odd, egocentric, pathological, or emotionless.

Before I perfected perspective-taking, my basic emotions were intact. For example, I could recognize in myself feelings such as happiness, sadness, anger, and envy. More complex emotions, though, especially those that are relationship-based and hence involve more perspective-taking, were compromised. I never really experienced jealousy. Guilt and embarrassment were quite muted. If I wanted a new car and my neighbor had one, I didn't care that he had a new car. I wasn't jealous; I just wanted a new car, too.

Rarely was I embarrassed, even though, when one has bipolar disorder, there are frequent reasons to be. For example, once, during a manic/psychotic episode when I was in college, I was walking around a dangerous section of Philadelphia one night, convinced I was a mosquito. I believed that I was invisible and tried to suck blood from a police officer's arm. After he tried to reason with me, I mouthed off. He was none too amused, put me in the back of his police car, and took me to the emergency room for a psych consult, which resulted in restraints. I should have been embarrassed when this episode ended and I regained lucidity, but I wasn't until years later after learning perspective taking.

Shame and guilt were other emotions that were compromised. Shame arises from how we believe we are perceived by others and may result in thinking we are fundamentally flawed (I am wrong) whereas guilt involves making a judgement that is against your moral compass resulting in others perceiving you in a particular light (I've done something wrong.) Both provide feedback and help change future actions. And it simply was not in my repertoire for many years. When I was about eight, I decided that I wanted a bigger and better bathtub. We had a hot tub in the solarium, which I thought would do. Taking my Mr. Bubble pink liquid soap out of my shower, I ran to the solarium, turned on the hot tub jets, and poured a small amount in. It made some bubbles, but they weren't satisfying enough. I was looking for the bubble bath motherload. My slippery hands grabbed the Mr. Bubble container and squeezed with gusto. Soon, about half the container was gone. Suddenly, bubbles rolled out of the hot tub, exploding onto the brick pavers that surrounded it. The bubbles quickly grew waist high. Now, *this* was what I was looking for!

I jumped into the hot tub with glee and thrashed around like a superhero. After a few minutes of fun, I looked around and realized that I couldn't see anymore. The bubbles had taken over the room. I felt my way out of the hot tub and took my naked little body to my mother, who was beyond furious. This is where guilt should have joined the party, but it didn't. Not only was there a mess, but I had also inadvertently broken the hot tub and destroyed the sand between the pavers.

My mother's forehead squished together, creating creases as she yelled. This configuration of expressions registered as angry, but I wasn't sure if she was mad at me or the broken hot tub. I simply grabbed a towel and sauntered to my room to get dressed.

"Did your emotions affect your schooling? It must have been hard with friends," another parent commented after I addressed Allison's question as best I could.

I was honest with them about never having many friends growing up. In addition to others viewing me as "weird" or "annoying," I saw people as serving a function, not as emotional companions. When I did reach out, it was for selfish reasons. Only my own needs mattered.

I told them the story of my third-grade classmate Jimmy, who sat at the oblong purple table next to me. That April, his mother died. After he returned from his mother's funeral, I (unintentionally) tormented this poor boy for weeks by whispering, "Is your mother dead?" His face would melt in both a frightening and inviting way, like in a horror movie. He would tear up, and his face would contort with an emotion that I can now guess was sadness. Why did I do this? Because every time I asked this question and glistening tears welled up from the corners of his eyes, I could somewhat see the reflection of the windowpanes in his tears, which I thought was really cool. Because I was unable to take his perspective, all I knew is that when Jimmy cried, I could see the windowpanes from a different angle. Now that

I have perspective-taking skills, I realize that this was horribly cruel, and I feel terrible about the whole incident. People with autism are often thought to be un-empathetic and self-centered, but when you lack the ability to take another's perspective, you _are_ the center of the universe.

One might think that years of "therapeutic intervention" in the psychiatric system would have been a prime venue for learning perspective-taking. However, in reality, inpatient settings are not a venue for learning missed developmental skills. In fact, in most institutions are simply holding pens, I was forced to socialize, which only ramped up my anxiety. They called it "staying in the milieu," and doing so gained one points on the level system, earning passes for temporary leave away from the hospital. I called it "throwing me to the wolves." Unable to flee, this requirement actually had the opposite effect and forced me to live in my head even more.

I covered these topics and many more that night with the parents' support group. Honestly, we could have chatted all night. This type of conversation came easily to me because it all revolved around me and my own experiences. I didn't have to take perspective.

Finally, Daphne ended the meeting well after its official close time. The parents thanked me and let me know that they valued what I had to say. It was the first time ever that I felt my experiences had significant meaning and might help someone else.

One of the parents in the audience, Erin, pulled me aside after my talk. She told me about her three-year-old daughter with autism, Harper, and wanted to know if I could help her. I was uncomfortable with the suggestion and explained that I really didn't know anything about childhood development, psychology, or education. All I had was my own experience. Yet Erin was persistent, and we talked while walking out to the parking lot together. "I don't care if this is not your background," she said. "I think you could help Harper! Please, just visit her new school. Please..."

After listening to her pleas, I responded, "I need you to know that I don't know anything beyond my own experiences. I think you should hire a professional."

But she calmly insisted, "Please, just visit!"

I thought about it and reluctantly agreed, though with the caveat that I was uncomfortable with this arrangement. On the other hand, it's not like I was busy with anything other than work.

A few days later, Erin set up an observation for me with Kristen Laurent, the director of the Little Red Schoolhouse, the special education preschool that Harper attended.

On my appointed "observation day," I felt nervous and jittery inside. I kept ruminating about being a fraud, even though I had been upfront and completely honest about the fact that I knew nothing about education. I stood in front of my shiny silver mirror that morning and tried on outfit after outfit. I knew that my preferred attire of shorts and a t-shirt were not appropriate, but I struggled to find something in my wardrobe that was "business casual," as I could hear my father saying in my head. My closet consisted of several yellow, black, and white Hertz uniforms and some other raggedy comfort clothes. I finally decided on the tan khaki pants that I wore to the Hertz interview and a white turtleneck. This was comfortable and seemed good enough.

When I arrived, I sat in the parking lot for several minutes, frozen with anxiety. My stomach was churning, and now I had gas. I was sweating, and my chest was tight. *What will I find inside?* I wondered. I panicked. I threw down a Valium and eventually mustered up the courage to exit my car. As I walked up to the school's doors, I ruminated, *What am I going to see?* I didn't know what to expect and secretly prayed that Harper's education was in sharp contrast to my own. I was petrified that there would be restraints and quiet room spaces, which would almost certainly cause unpleasant flashbacks for me.

As soon as I walked through the doors, my fears vanished. The building was nothing like I expected. It was bright and cheery. It had clean walls. Vibrant colors abounded. And the staff actually seemed fond of the students. One helpful staff member with an ample smile ushered me to Kristen's office.

Kristen was tiny, maybe four-foot-nine, with long, wild, dirty-blonde hair and rimless glasses. Her bright fuchsia t-shirt seemed to scream "Hello!" Everything about her seemed quite energetic. Her voice was boisterous as she greeted me. "You must be Alex. I've heard a lot about you!"

I was a little scared. Where did she get her information? My hospital records? *No*, I thought to myself, *that's too farfetched*. Anyway, I had been out of the hospital for about a year now. She had clearly spoken with Erin, who had arranged this visit. A little stiff with nerves, I answered, "Yes, I'm Alex. Nice to meet you." My dad's lessons echoed through my mind. I could hear his voice saying, *Shake her hand*. I obediently extended my hand, even as I searched for something else to say, but my mind was blank.

Thankfully, she was chatty, which turned down the pressure valve. "Erin told me that you have autism. Boy, your observations would be really helpful. You seem so high functioning, too. That's great!"

I didn't feel "high functioning." What did that mean, anyway? Yes, I now rented an apartment, lived on my own, had a job, and drove, but I had also spent the better part of six years institutionalized. Could she not see that?

Kristen went on to ask me very personal questions, mostly relating to what it felt like to have social skills deficits and be autistic. Initially, I felt naked, but things warmed up as the day progressed. As we toured the school, she disclosed what seemed like specific information about various students' symptoms and asked for my advice.

And I did have some suggestions. For example, there was a six-year-old boy named Lucas who was quite autistic. When I observed his class of five students and two adults, they were having "circle time." Lucas was unable to sit still and kept jumping up. His teacher grew angry and frustrated with him and kept redirecting him back to the hard stool in the circle, which he seemed to dislike. I suggested that there were several easy options to resolve this issue.

Lucas might have tactile defensiveness, and the hard chair might be aversive to him. I knew that *I* had hated the hard wooden chairs at school when I was growing up. So, I suggested bringing a beanbag chair from the book corner into the circle area and having him sit on that instead. Another option was to let him stand behind the chair. And yet another option was to let him be a part of the activity by standing with the teacher and holding the prompts.

I ended with the caveat that these suggestions were based upon my own life experiences and not some educational guru's wisdom. I honestly didn't understand why no one seemed to care that I knew nothing about education and helping preschoolers with autism.

As we toured the school, I was pleasantly surprised at how amazing it was. There were about thirty students between the ages of three and seven, all with significant autism and a few with mental health concerns. I immediately fell in love. The school was idyllic. The staff were providing *real* learning opportunities. The kids were treated kindly. The educators were obviously fond of their students. It was an eerily weird feeling.

When I watched the students, I kind of "got them." While I was much older and less impaired, I could relate to them. Their autism was much more profound than mine, but in my head, I was able to formulate hypotheses about their behaviors and relationships to each other and the world. I didn't know if I was right or wrong, but I knew that I belonged here.

When the loud piercing bell rang, signaling that the school day was over, the students and staff vacated the building. However, Kristen invited me to her office, and we talked for hours, mostly about autism. I didn't disclose my mental illness, as this seemed too risky. When it was finally time to leave, I asked Kristen if I could come back and volunteer. I wanted to shadow her, doing individual therapy with these kids and working in the classrooms.

She agreed, and after a month or so, she offered me a job as a teaching assistant. In this position, I helped support students by doing everything from changing diapers to using augmentative communication systems to teach students how to communicate. In the early

1990's this was done by trading pictures of objects for the objects themselves—for example, a photo of a cup of juice for actual juice.

I threw away my scratchy Hertz uniform. I finally had a career! This position afforded me the opportunity to work with diverse students who displayed a variety of complex profiles. The other staff actually asked for my advice and valued my opinion. I would always preface my responses with, "I'm not an educator," but secretly, I felt important. The team accepted me, even with all of my quirks, such as not wearing shoes or socks, usually only wearing shorts even in the New England winters, and insisting that the school's toy closet be organized in a specific way.

After a few successful months of working at the Little Red Schoolhouse, I started to feel great again. I was ecstatic with my new position, but this feeling was a smidgen more magnificent than it should have been. When life is going well and the Lithium is working, I feel balanced and start to doubt that there is anything fundamentally wrong with me. I toss the drugs, failing to notice their contribution. This is exactly what I did now.

As the weeks progressed, I began waking up with a twinkle in my eye a little earlier than usual. I struggled to shut off my mind at bedtime and gradually stopped sleeping– a classic sign of an impending bipolar episode. My stupendous mind raced around the clock, which felt immensely pleasurable. I had ideas. Big ideas! Papering my apartment's walls, I detailed all of my big plans in thick red, blue, and green Sharpie markers. The ideas sprang from my head faster than I could write: building a college for people with disabilities, running for the Massachusetts state senate, building a cable-stayed bridge from Alaska to Russia, landing a job at NASA…

But while I had big schemes, their execution fell short. What I really needed to do was lasso my thoughts and rein them in, but this was impossible. On Mondays, Wednesdays, and Fridays, I organized the school's toy closet alphabetically by the toys' names. Tuesdays and Thursdays were categorical. Mostly, it was just a shamble. Nevertheless, everything seemed to make sense to me. Nothing was bizarre. I had no regrets. As my mania became more intense, work grew less manageable.

Bipolar disorder not only encompasses an elevated or sad mood, but also often swoops into anger and irritability. During this episode, I struggled to engage in work friendships with the other adults in my classroom and often would often make flippant remarks, causing considerable tension. Additionally, I now felt that I was "the autism guru" and became belligerent if my peers didn't follow my suggestions. I refused to listen to anyone else's directions and implemented interventions that I thought were correct.

Noah, a beautiful, non-verbal, African American six-year-old in our class, would bite his hands until chunks of thick, raw flesh were ripped off, leaving him bloody. Verbal coaching was ineffective. With the best of intentions, I decided to put my thick, tan leather gloves on his hands and duct-tape them to his shirt to protect his skin. I didn't know what else to do. To this day, I feel bad about this. The other adults frowned upon my intervention, letting me know in blunt and unkind ways of their judgment.

As my behavior became more erratic, my attendance also became spotty. I started developing psychotic features and becoming paranoid. I thought the school was conspiring against me. During my sleepless nights, I devised plans for how to take over the Little Red Schoolhouse. While I had thrown away my Lithium and Thorazine, I kept the Valium because I liked the stillness that it brought when my body felt somewhat out of control. Unsurprisingly, I went through a lot of it around this time.

When I ran out of Valium, it was time to go see Dr. Saar for a refill. I had little insight into just how "high" I was when I walked into Dr. Saar's office looking like a disheveled mess.

"Okay, what do we have here?" Dr. Saar asked, a trace of annoyance in her voice.

I raced through my words. "I'm great! No problems here! Just need a new 'script for Valium. And, I always mean to ask you: *what's* going on here, on your walls? What do these quilts mean?" I gestured frantically at the Amish quilts on her walls.

"Please sit down," Dr. Saar said calmly.

"No, I'm fine! I don't need to sit!"

"At least for a moment," she directed, her tone firm.

Exasperated, I acquiesced.

Dr. Saar looked concerned, and she spoke slowly and with intention, "When was the last time you took your Lithium and slept?"

"Lithium? Umm, let's see. Maybe a month ago? I don't know. Time doesn't matter! Don't you value my opinion? I don't need Lithium!"

"What about sleep?" she pressed.

"I don't remember. I stopped sleeping five, maybe six, days ago. I don't really need sleep! I'm perfect. Just need a refill on my Valium. That's why I'm here. Oh, and let me tell you about my big ideas…"

Dr. Saar was having none of it, though. She pulled the psychiatrist card, and I was back in the hospital. I left a message for Kristen saying that I had some "health problems" I needed to tend to and that I wouldn't be at work for a few days. At Hertz, I had learned to call bipolar disorder "health problems." People would shy away from the subject then without asking any follow-up questions. Sure enough, Kristen never pressed me for more details.

Back on Lithium, Thorazine, and Valium, I was again groggy, but functioning. Kristen graciously accepted me back to the Little Red Schoolhouse. Upon my return to work, my colleagues asked kind, concerned questions, such as, "Are you feeling okay?" This was unfamiliar to me, but I appreciated it. Walking into my classroom, I realized what a mess I had left it in and spent many hours putting everything back in its place. There was also a shared materials closet, which I had trashed before my hospitalization. It, too, returned to a spotless condition.

During the year and a half that I worked at the Little Red Schoolhouse, I had three manic episodes resulting in hospitalizations, and I was always permitted to take "health breaks" to refocus my mind when that happened. I slowly came to realize that my colleagues genuinely cared about me.

Foremost among them was Kristen, who was instrumental in diminishing my differences and replacing them with new functional skills. The hours we spent together evolved into a long, marvelous friendship both inside and outside of work.

After work, we often hit the Ninety-Nine Restaurant to indulge in burgers and buffalo wings. Then, to further unwind, we would drive back to Kristen's place, where we would play doubles Tetris for hours. We both loved the video game, though she always kicked my butt. Kristen was quite understanding about my autism and gave me a free pass to leave when I'd had enough social interaction for the day. No explanation was needed.

As we grew closer, our conversations began to extend throughout the weekends, with in-person visits and phone calls. We talked about our students and our own experiences growing up. I learned a great deal about her, but I still did not disclose some of my rockier parts of my childhood and my mental illness. I was too afraid to lose this rare real friend.

I had initially attended the autism support meeting to help myself, but it proved to be the beginning of an unintended career that has spanned decades and enabled me to help hundreds of children with autism spectrum disorders and countless with mental illness. It led me to meet wonderful people and make lifelong friends. That one meeting literally changed my life.

CHAPTER 8

THE EXECUTIVE WHO LEFT HER DESK

VARIOUS PROFESSIONALS WERE employed at the Little Red Schoolhouse, and due to its petite size, everyone was a snug fit. We all knew each other well. Everyone knew that I had autism, but I kept my bipolar disorder a closely guarded secret. The students we worked with were generally preschool age and mostly non-verbal, so I became the resident "expert" on autism, regardless of how loudly I protested that I wasn't.

There were three people with whom I regularly shared lunch and dialogued about autism theories: Sadie, the speech-language pathologist; Stacey, the speech intern; and Aaron, the psychologist. I called them "the trio."

One day, as I was walking down the hall, Sadie playfully grabbed my arm and pulled me into her office. Aaron and Stacey were there as well. "Sit down. We have cartoon for you," Sadie said in her thick German accent. "Here, read! Read!" When I had finished, Aaron asked, "Where will Sally look for the red ball?"

This task seemed reasonably straightforward. "Of course Sally would look in the box!" I said. This, I thought, was obvious.

Straightaway, the trio began giggling like school kids. "I told you!" Sadie said to Aaron.

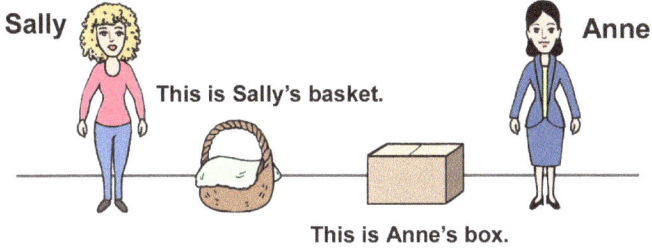

Sally

Anne

This is Sally's basket.

This is Anne's box.

Sally puts her red ball ...

into her basket.

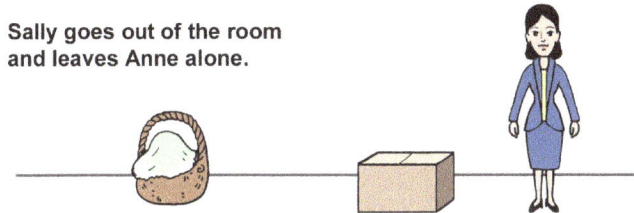

Sally goes out of the room and leaves Anne alone.

Anne takes the ball out of the basket ...

and puts it in the box.

When Sally comes back ...

she wants to play with the ball.

Where will Sally look for her ball?

135

"You're right!" Stacey said.

"What? What? Why are you laughing?" I asked. I wanted to know what the joke was.

"You bombed the test!" Sadie exclaimed. Barely containing herself, she added, "That was the wrong answer!"

I scoured the cartoon, but couldn't ascertain why my answer was incorrect. I felt dumb. My aneurism exploded. I recoiled as my mind shot straight to my third-grade teacher's assessment that I was "retarded." Obviously, I was missing something.

Created by Simon Baron-Cohen, Alan Leslie and Uta Frith, this now-famous 'false-belief' cartoon is called the Sally-Anne test, and it measures a person's ability to take another's perspective. To know that Sally would look for the ball in the basket, the test-taker needs to be able to take the perspectives of both Anne and Sally. They would need to understand that Sally was not in the room when Anne moved the ball and, hence, conclude that Sally would not have this knowledge of where the ball really was.

In hindsight, I'm not surprised that I "bombed" this test, since I still had a fragile ability to take another's perspective. The idea that people had thoughts that were different than mine and that my opinion was not the *only* opinion was baffling. I was missing a critical skill that makes us human: innate perspective-taking. Without knowing that I was missing this skill, others most likely presumed that I was rather arrogant. This caused me problems my whole life. Struggling to make and, more importantly, keep friends and the numerous difficulties I encountered with patients and staff in the hospitals were direct repercussions of this lack.

Sadie comforted me in my despair. Obviously, it was only a silly cartoon and not the first time I had failed something. When an explanation is provided, I generally "get it." Understanding this cartoon, however, was arduous. In order to comprehend it, I needed to hold both Anne's and Sally's perspectives in my mind simultaneously, which proved to be mentally exhausting. Slowly, I realized that the problem wasn't with the test; it was with my thinking.

I didn't immediately understand perspective-taking from this, but now I knew intellectually that others had perspectives and that they may even be different than mine. A ripple effect occurred within me as I processed this information throughout the day. To maintain mental stability, we all create paradigms to make sense of the world around us. A deluge of confusion and anxiety came crashing in when I realized that my paradigm was possibly wrong.

I only had part of the puzzle, though. I understood what was wrong but did not yet possess the skills to gauge others' perspectives. I also started to reflect on how perspective-taking deficits intertwined with my disabilities. Bipolar disorder was a known quantity, but until now, I had never appreciated how insufferable I became to others when I was manic or psychotic. Although I was dubbed the resident autism "expert" at the Little Red Schoolhouse, I had insufficient information about the disorder itself. For the first time, the Sally-Anne test had shown me what perspective-taking was and that it was often skewed in people with autism.

Later that day, as I leaned against the cold white brick corner wall in Sadie's office, I started to cry. She affectionately embraced me against her pink cashmere sweater. I could smell her fancy perfume. In a soft, kind voice, she said, "Come to dinner tonight. My apartment." How could I refuse?

Sadie lived in a beautiful brownstone on the outskirts of Boston. Walking through the door, I was surprised to see that Stacey and Aaron were also there.

"We're unsettled about the way things ended today," Aaron said. "You were so upset. We want to help, and the best way we know how is to teach you perspective-taking." He was a brilliant "absent-minded professor" type who wore round wire-rimmed spectacles and always had raggedy, windblown shoulder-length hair.

I was shocked and touched by the trio's generosity. Aaron confessed to me years later that they had anticipated just a single lesson, but this project ultimately spanned three years, with informal and formal lessons and conversations on the internet. I'm perpetually grateful to the trio for teaching me how to take perspective.

We reviewed the Sally-Anne test multiple times that night, and when it ended, I headed straight to Staples, where I purchased several multicolored notebooks. In these, I started journaling what I thought and felt and the connections between events. This would prove to be ground zero of a ten-year journey. I had both the time and patience to spend a decade analyzing the process of deconstructing my mind and observing the developmental stages I passed through as I gained ground. As Ely Fuller said, "I'm experiencing the bizarre miracle of reincarnation, more lucidly than at birth in the same lifetime." While this process began by targeting my residual autism symptoms, what I also found were underlying executive functioning deficits that were related to traits of bipolar disorder.

After two months of journaling, I had an "ah-ha" moment. I realized, *I don't know what others are thinking and feeling. And, importantly, what their perceptions are of me.* To find out, I started recording my own thought processes. But something was missing. Then, it hit me. In Stonyfield Psychiatric Hospital, when sitting on Josephine outside the nurses' station, I read about something called the "Johari Window." It is a psychological technique that helps people better understand themselves and their relations to others in a group. In simplified terms, it goes something like this:

This is what we know.
This is what we know we don't know.
And this is what we don't know, we don't know.

Conceptually realizing that I fundamentally didn't understand others' thoughts was scary and depressing, but it was something that I now knew that I didn't know. I now understood that there was a knowledge base that I was unaware of and didn't know how to access.

I felt paralyzed.

I realize that the paradigm I had lived within was incorrect. The best metaphor I can find to explain this conundrum is of drawing a picture of an alien. I was proficient at drawing the outline, but that's all I thought there was. It didn't even occur to me that there was an inside to be drawn. Now that I knew there *was* something to draw within the outer lines, I didn't have a clue what the interior of an alien looked like. What was I supposed to draw?

I continued to experience the world, but for the first time, I knew that my interpretations were not always correct. Yet, I didn't have a replacement paradigm. I knew that people had their own thoughts and beliefs that might be different from mine, but I had no way of filling in the blanks.

Faced with this monumental discovery, my mind began to fracture. I didn't need this stress. I never asked for that cartoon. Frustrated and anxious all the time, I began calling in sick to work. Feeling better was my only goal. I contemplated going off my meds since I knew it would alter my mood, but which mood I ended up with was a crapshoot. I made a hasty decision, threw away my meds, and went back to work after a few days.

A few weeks later, I had my monthly visit with Dr. Saar, my psychiatrist. She always offered me honesty and directness without regard for my reception. With gusto, I blew through her door, talking at breakneck speed, and exuding magnificence. She called me on it straightaway, and I confessed, "I feel horrible. I can't sleep. I'm hallucinating. The floor people are back. People are looking in my curtains. I keep hearing a muffled radio playing. I'm ecstatic, but I also want to die. There are some moments when I can't stand being with myself, and at other times, I feel elated. What's wrong with me? Oh, and I went off my meds three weeks ago."

She sighed. "I think you're having a 'mixed episode,' where you're depressed and manic simultaneously or in rapid succession. I don't know how to get this through your thick head. You *can't* go off your meds every time you feel better or want to change your mood. Lithium especially is like plasma for you. You need it to survive. I have to be honest: you're a hell of a frustrating patient to treat. Tell me what *I* can do to help you. I'm not going to hospitalize you this time, but we need to find an answer that works for both of us."

In that instant, I had another "ah-ha" moment. Dr. Saar was *frustrated*. I was able to put myself in her shoes and *feel* how frustrated she was with me, and I didn't even blame her. After a long talk about my revelation of having limited perspective-taking skills, she suggested some coping strategies and wrote me a new prescription for Lithium, Valium, and Thorazine, which I reluctantly agreed to ingest.

I did indeed take my pills, and within a few weeks, I felt regulated but still anxious. And dull.

I was sitting on my smooth navy-colored denim couch writing in my lemon-yellow notebook one day, contemplating this infuriating project. *How am I supposed to know what's not known to me if I don't even know I don't know it?* I thought. In a thick black Sharpie marker, I wrote on the cover of every notebook, "Scrap this project." Then, I put them away out of sight so that I wouldn't have to lay eyes on them again.

The next morning, after getting some sleep, I was a little more optimistic. While the Little Red Schoolhouse's trio continued their lessons, which were invaluable, it was becoming clear to me that this undertaking required a consistent and higher level of formal education than what I possessed. So, I set sail to educate myself.

I applied to Vermont College's weekend program to finish the degree I had started ten years earlier in Pennsylvania. Whether through accumulated good karma or sheer luck, I had found a college where I could create my own course of study, and I focused on the executive functioning and perspective-taking aspects of neuroscience. To augment my formal education, I made use of the Massachusetts Institute of Technology's impressive collection of books and articles on these subjects. Finally, before returning to conventional higher education, I opted to partake in neuropsychological testing, hoping to shed light on what specifically was wrong with *my* brain. Between my formal education, research, and neuropsychological testing, I compiled a bank of knowledge on how typical and atypical brains function, resulting in an expansive common vocabulary that I could use to speak with neuroscientists and psychologists around the world. I was determined!

Before my education at Vermont College, reading the results of my neuropsychological test was like reading a foreign language. Comprehending the "conclusion section" was relatively easy as it was written in layman's terms, but the other twenty-three pages of test results and statistics threw me. I took the report to my faithful Dr. Saar, and over the course of several weeks, she helped me digest it. I must have read the conclusion a thousand times: "[In sum], Alexandra struggles with the following areas of executive functioning: joint and shifting attention, non-literal thinking, planning/organizing, sorting relevant from irrelevant, inhibiting impulses, rule acquisition, cognitive flexibility/set-shifting, problem solving, and inference." This was a tall list, but at least now, my life's challenges made sense, and my disorders sprang open. Prior to my formal education, I understood the symptoms of my disabilities only from my perspective. I now grasped the fundamental organic mechanisms underpinning them. Now, I felt exposed.

One day, as I was going over my report with Dr. Saar, it all suddenly seemed like too much. "Dr. Saar, please help me," I said. "My lily pad of stability can't hold on for much longer. I knew my brain wasn't playing with a full deck, but I didn't realize so many cards were muddled or omitted. That report is horrid. I'm so disabled. I'm a mental patient. *A mental patient!*"

"Stop right there," she commanded. "First of all, you've left the institution, so we're not going back to your self-proclaimed 'mental patient identity.' I don't have the energy for that, nor does it serve a purpose. Second, nothing has changed. You're a really good person, Alex. You're still the same person you were before the testing. The only benefit of the testing was to enlighten us for how best to help." She always knew just what to say.

After all my years of institutional living, I had learned the labels for my disabilities, but no one had ever explained their foundations or the causes of my symptoms. I had been institutionalized to get better, yet without extensive executive functioning training, I never could have healed.

Even before my classes at Vermont College started, I purchased several neuroscience textbooks that I intended to add to my syllabi. I reclaimed my discarded notebooks and massive Post-It notes from my spare bedroom (at this point, I had moved into a larger apartment). It was late August, and the Little Red Schoolhouse was on break. As I sat on my soft blue couch, the textbooks I had purchased seemed to call my name. I filled my days by devouring knowledge from Russell Barkley, Chris Jarrold, Paul and Patricia Churchland, and many others. Each book provided some clarity on the neuropsychologist's report. I still didn't like the information it contained, but at least I now understood its meaning.

In light of the fact that I was missing a plethora of executive functioning skills, I decided to start there. Executive functioning involves an ensemble of skills, including many of those listed in the conclusion of my testing report. This group of skills is analogous to the orchestra's conductor, who needs to assemble multiple components to direct a complex symphony. A person may be a fine cellist in isolation, but it requires a leader to organize each instrument so that they play simultaneously or sequentially, but always harmoniously. For people with executive dysfunction, the individual skills (instruments, in this metaphor) may or may not be intact, but either way, they are unable to function effectively as a whole. The music isn't playing any kind of recognizable song, and it certainly isn't harmonious.

Everyone uses executive function skills every day. They arrive at work on time (organization) and complete daily tasks to meet deadlines (prioritizing). If their boss or spouse asks for something to be done differently, they generally comply (flexibility). They read information and retain the meaning (memory). When frustrated, they speak rationally and don't act out or raise their voice (inhibition and control). We all exhibit varying degrees of executive functioning skills as we maneuver through life.

As a child, my executive functioning skills were atrocious; I couldn't plan or organize anything. My Trapper Keeper, despite the little white reinforcing disks that my parents bought, was always filled with pages that had at least one torn punched hole. Eventually, they would fall out. I never knew where my homework had run off to. I must have gone through thirteen sets of house keys a year, even though they were roped around my neck with a shoelace. And, to be honest, I had a temper. I would often overreact to situations.

My executive deficits impacted my social skills, as well. Some mornings, I would knock on my neighbor's door at 5:30 a.m. to ask if I could play with her toys. Her mother, Mrs. Evans, always sporting curlers and a hair net, would shoo me away, saying, "Don't come back until nine!" As I sprinted down her lush lawn, I could hear her continued bellowing, "And make sure you've eaten breakfast. I'm not running a diner, you know. *And* fix your clothes! They're always inside-out and backward!"

Academically, I found multiple-choice exams extremely difficult, especially when they had questions like, "Pick the best choice…" or "Which one of these answers is *not* true?" I struggled with the process of elimination. I could usually think of logical reasons to pick *each* of the choices, but I couldn't narrow them down to the "best" one. They all seemed relevant.

When I first started my journaling project with the trio, the content of my journal had been a mess. Everything seemed relevant. With no logical reason for entries, they were sloppy in terms of content. In writing this memoir, I literally had to cut and tape each entry to my wall in order to develop cohesive chapters. Using this method, my apartment was covered in journal entries and sticky notes of my realizations. I should have just signed my paycheck over to Staples! However, by organizing this information visually and kinesthetically, I was better equipped to create a cohesive project.

One of the more salient observations that I made through journaling was how the speed of my thoughts and what thoughts were in the forefront of my mind at any given moment were dictated by my autism and mood. In hypomanic states, my organizational output is considerably improved; I can't explain why, but this extra burst of energy is noteworthy. However, when I'm manic, my thoughts and actions lack a caboose and just run away while still only loosely associated. No longer is there a beginning, middle and end thought. Thinking about a new invention might trigger twenty other thoughts that only marginally relate to the original. When I'm depressed, I struggle to link two ideas together. But with autism, I have unalterable rigid rules. These mandates prevent me from knowing what to do and think in the face of uncertainty or ambiguity, which causes an influx of anxiety.

I continued to feverishly journal my thoughts and emotions, and I shared my revelations with the trio and Dr. Saar. Between my neuropsychological testing, academic knowledge, research, and introspection, I was compiling an abundance of insights. However, I still struggled to verbalize my thoughts. I often knew the concept for what I wanted to covey but strained to explain it. Like Temple Grandin, a famous author and speaker with autism, I think in pictures, not words. So, conversations were often grueling.

One night, around eleven p.m., a lightbulb went off. I needed to draw it, so back I went to the "all-night" Staples for more colored markers.

I understood my thoughts, reasoning, and actions in my own visual language, but to forward this project, I would need to translate this information so that the trio could comprehend. My words explained my thinking, but to really "get it," I had to elucidate this information visually. I began to put together a series of exercises and art pieces to explain my world.

This was the first exercise that I put together to help bridge their world and mine: *Within these words, there are several important sentences, but only one sentence is the most important. Please take up to ten seconds to determine what the most important sentence is. And... Go!*

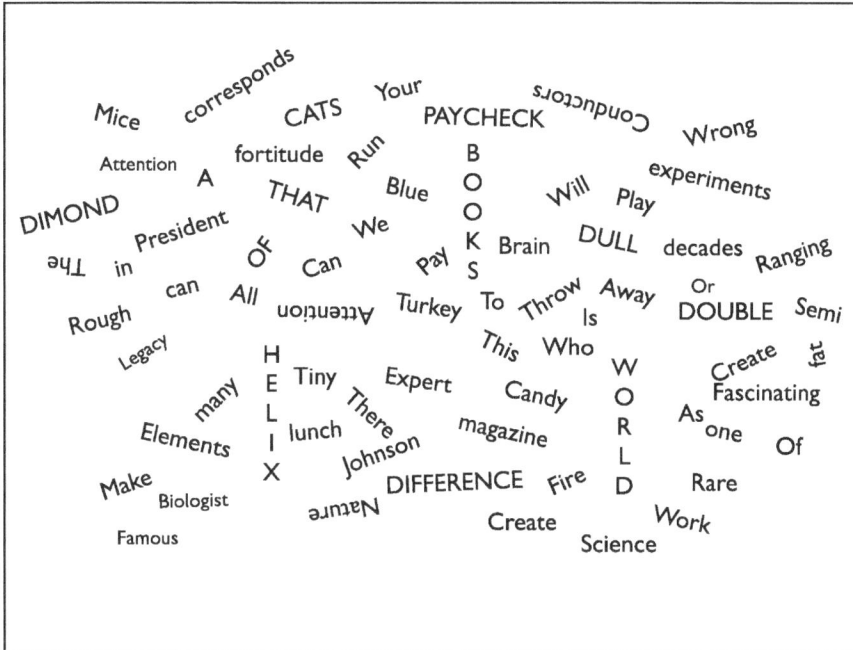

Give up? Now turn the page and try this exercise again....

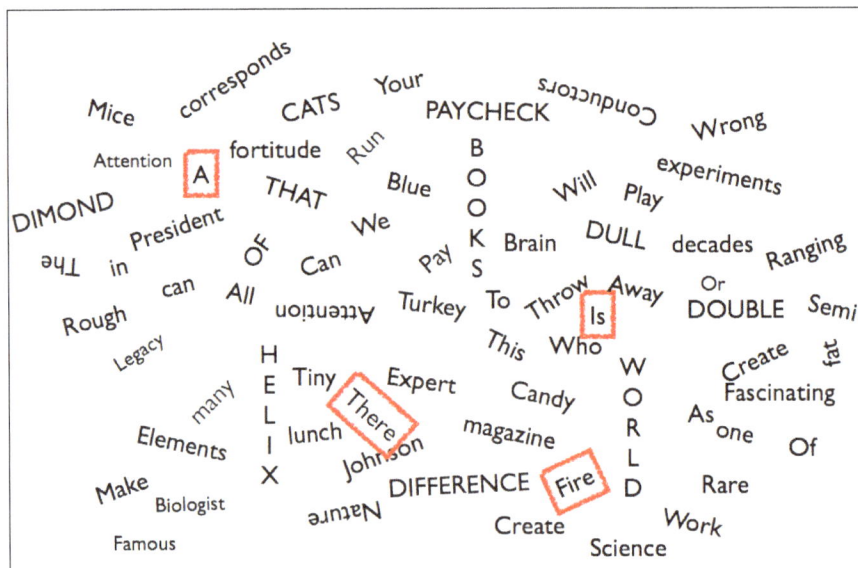

Were you correct? How many seconds did it take to figure out the answer?

The primary difference between the two images are the red boxes around a few of the words. They don't provide any contextual clues as to the meaning of the message. They simply serve to distinguish and categorize one part of the information from another. In essence, they make *relevant* stimuli stand out from *irrelevant* stimuli, which helps you figure out the message being conveyed.

I showed this exercise to the trio the next time I saw them. "I did it! I finally figured out a way to explain how my brain operates!" I was so overjoyed to share this connection. "Do you get it? Do you understand what my brain isn't doing?" I asked.

"Go on," Aaron said. He wanted me to articulate it.

"These red boxes are virtually absent in my brain, which makes it extremely difficult to focus on tasks and prioritize importance. When I'm looking at something or interacting with someone, in my brain, there is nothing that says, 'Hey, pay attention to this. It's important!' When I walk into a room, the ceiling tiles are literally equally as important as the people. When all stimuli carry the same weight and everything in your world seems relevant, the concepts of attention and organization are thrown right out the window. To fully navigate the world, every second of the day, my brain must make two categories: 'pay attention to this now' and 'don't pay attention to everything else.'" I was out of breath.

"I get it. This makes sense," Stacey said. "Breathe. Breathe, Alex."

"I can't!" Gasping, I continued, "There's more. Not only is the information absorbed equally, but it also feels like it's stored in either an idiosyncratically chunked or random order. I've never been able to determine why some information is organized together, whereas other information seems haphazard in my mind. Regardless, the main problem with either storage system is that I can never store the gist or essence of the experience or information. Instead, the entire activity, with every component, whether relevant or not, is stored. And that makes decisions exceptionally hard."

"We've talked about storing information before," Stacey said. "If I understand correctly, this is why you always give boundless details, both at school and at Sadie's house, right?"

I'd been speaking so quickly, I needed to grab my asthma inhaler. After a few puffs, I nodded and continued, "Yes, yes, yes. Unfortunately, the storage lacks a filing system. My brain is like a thirteen-year-old's bedroom where everything just gets thrown on the floor. Disorganized information entering the brain leads to disorganized information upon recall. It's the details versus the Gestalt that comes up when I try to access it. When I need to recollect something, not only is it an ineffective search because I'm looking through *all* of my brain, but also, when I do find the information I'm searching for, the entire story is elucidated with every detail. And sometimes, information fragments hitch a ride into other files. I feel like I don't have simple answers."

Sadie pushed a tall glass of cold water toward me. "Drink, Alex, drink." I flopped on Sadie's couch and drank, as instructed.

"Write this down, Alex, in a place you'll remember it!" Stacey joked.

No longer breathless, I continued, "Okay, but one more thing. And this is important! Sadie, remember when you had long hair and you annoyingly cut it short and I got upset about it?"

"You don't like my haircut? You're saying not nice things." Sadie's temper was beginning to flicker.

"Hold on! Hold on! Don't get mad! Because all information is stored as a packaged chuck, each time I return to that information or location, I expect it to be exactly the same. When a change occurs, it's as if a whole new model is created. Sadie #1 had long hair, so the only logical solution was to create Sadie #2. When someone alters their appearance or physical location, the information is incongruent. I can't handle it. It's an atrocity. I'm confused when people use phrases like 'the same,' 'similar,' or 'kind of.' The word 'same' implies a carbon copy. And if something is not an exact copy, the only alternative is 'different.'"

This is why Venn diagrams were so hard for me to understand in elementary school.

Today, I can use my imagination to hypothesize what might have happened to cause such a change. For example, when I see someone with a new haircut, I can put a picture of their old face and hair on one side of the diagram and their new hair on the other. In the overlapping center, I can now visualize the old hair being cut off and create a realistic story about what happened. Nevertheless, even with all the knowledge I've gained over the years and how far I've come with my autism "training," I'm still vaguely disconcerted when these slight changes occur. My inclination is still to cling to Model #1.

Later that week, I woke up with another insight. Calling the trio, I requested an emergency meeting. I couldn't sit on this! At lightning speed, I assembled these drawings representing the next concept that expounded my mind.

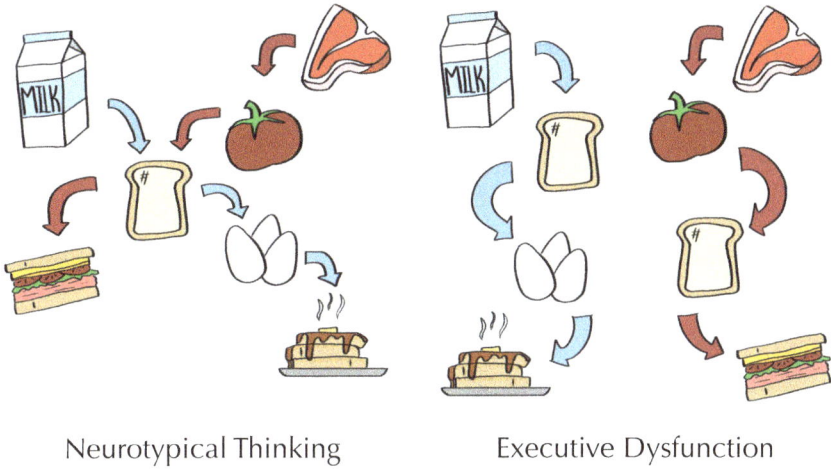

Neurotypical Thinking   Executive Dysfunction

Once everyone was assembled, I dove right in. "I understand generalization!" I announced. "When I was a child, there was a rule in the town's library against eating and drinking. But, when I went to my school's library, I wasn't able to generalize the concept of 'library.' I ate and drank there until the librarian told me not to. I never learned *the reason behind the rule* and therefore didn't generalize anything, which was not only pivotal for executive functioning, but also crucial for social skills."

I explained the two pictographs I had made that denoted how information is processed and stored. In frame one (neurotypical thinking), the ingredients are all separately known quantities that can be combined in different ways to make various meals. In contrast, in frame two (executive dysfunction), the ingredients are all stored separately. The problem comes in when something like "hamburger bread" is not available; the person with executive dysfunction may not be able to generalize that the sliced white bread she had for breakfast could be used as an adequate substitute. For me, with autism, information is processed and stored as a whole sequence; the hamburger bun is simply a different product than the white toast for breakfast. With the components glued together like this, I was emotionally a slave to my mind, causing many rigid behaviors.

The neuropsychological testing elucidated these points: "Answers [Alex] provided were idiosyncratic and highly unusual indicating an overall disorganized thinking pattern. For example, when asked the question, 'What is similar between an apple and an orange?' the client answered, 'They are both found in the same aisle in the grocery store.'"

Not long after my testing, Kristen and I were hanging out after school one day when I said, "Kristen, can I ask you a question?"

"Sure."

"What is similar between an apple and an orange?" As with the Sally-Anne test, it really ate at me that my answer had been wrong, yet I couldn't ascertain how or why.

"What do you think?" she asked in response.

"Well, I know that the right answer *is not* that they're both found in the same aisle in the grocery store, but I don't know what the correct answer is."

My question prompted a philosophical discussion that lasted for hours and ultimately pulled Kristen into the ongoing work of teaching me perspective-taking. We discussed how my answer was correct, just not vigorous. I finally understood the more appropriate and logical answer: they're both fruit.

Desperate and embarrassed, I perseverated on the fruit conundrum for quite some time, ruminating not on the wrong answer, but how to reach the correct one. To understand how my answer had been incorrect, I needed to pull up a Venn diagram in my mind. While the trio had perfected the concept of using Venn diagrams, my use of them was infantile. Frantically, I searched my apartment for two objects to compare and practiced Venn diagramming until three in the morning.

"Stop right there," I suddenly said aloud. "Holy shit. This is epic!" After several hours of practice switching my attention between two objects, my understanding of metaphors, irony, and jokes opened up.

In third grade, Andrew, my desk mate, had loudly announced after a big math test, "This test was a breeze!" In response, I firmly held my paper down so that it wouldn't blow away. Now, years later, I finally understood that he wasn't talking about wind.

Before Venn diagrams became a daily vocabulary word, my thinking was concrete and rigid. In eleventh grade, my teacher announced one day that we were taking a spontaneous field trip to the Intrepid Sea, Air, and Space Museum on the West Side of New York. My ears were filled with boisterous cheers of "Yes!" "All right! No class!" and "Way to go, Mr. Joe!" None of these sentiments passed my lips. It was third period, and this was science class, not field trip time. This was not pleasurable. It was not exciting. I felt no exhilaration. It was a nightmare. This proposal was out of my routine, unfamiliar, unpredictable, and, well, just plain wrong. I refused to leave my seat, and as a consequence, I had to stay back and complete work. I was thrilled. However, if I had been able to use a Venn diagram back then, I could have compared learning science in the classroom with learning science outside the classroom and realized that the concept of "learning science" would remain in the overlapping center and still occur. The location was irrelevant.

Fortunately, I now had this skill, and in using it, I stumbled onto this new developmental phase. Jokes fell into place for me for the first time. Take the classic riddle, "What's black and white and red [read] all over?" Hearing the punchline, "a newspaper," causes laughter because surprise results occur when an anticipated outcome actually has another meaning or answer.

While being able to comprehend metaphors, irony, and jokes brought me pleasure, the best part was the relief of some of my vast anxiety. Before I was able to divide my attention, I struggled to make future predictions. When my sensory system declared an emergency, I couldn't tell whether it was a false alarm or the real deal. Have you ever become enraged, but then calmed down quickly? In my world, there was nothing to calm down to. When in one state, I couldn't quickly access a different state. Being able to hold only one state in my conscious experience also wreaked havoc with my depression. Life is much easier now that I can entertain that there might be another state that I'm not currently accessing. This could never have occurred without mastering divided attention.

To make a future prediction, I must ascertain what the present situation is and plan for the future. In essence, I need to be able to hold two options in my mind simultaneously and shift between them, determining the best course of action. At Vermont College, I learned that the state has five seasons: winter, summer, fall, spring, and "mud season." Mud season occurs when the days toggle between snow and sun, causing the land to erode, forming large puddles of mud.

One Sunday in April, I was on a dirt road near campus, and my car became stuck in the mud. At first, I panicked. *What should I do?* I thought. Vermont is not my home, and this was my first "mud season." I envisioned my car sinking further and further down, as I didn't know how deep this puddle went. I felt trapped! Taking a deep breath, I mentally reviewed the situation and created eight possible solutions. Of the eight, I used a pro and con list to narrow down the solutions to three. Then, a frontrunner emerged: call a tow truck!

This technique may not be spontaneous, but it is effective.

I was now the proud owner of a mind that could entertain that there is more than one possible outcome or solution. Over time, I became notably less rigid in my thinking. Barbara Griggati Harrison once said, "Fantasies are more than substitutes for unpleasant reality. They are also dress rehearsals, plans. All acts performed in the world begin in the imagination."

At this point, I had learned how to (1) determine what was similar from a group of items, (2) divide my attention, and (3) make future predictions. This was all fine and good, but inferring other peoples' thoughts and feelings was a whole different ball game and a skill I still actively sought. Inference is the ability to make educated predictions based on context clues in the environment. It's a significant component of executive functioning.

For example, in one of our lessons, Kristen posed a pictorial scenario: "You walk down the street and see a boy on the ground. His knee is bleeding, and there's a bike on the ground next to him. What happened?" You have to "read the room" to deduce that the boy fell off his bike and scraped his knee. However, with disordered inference skills, it's simply impossible to fill in the blanks because the only state that exists is what *I* currently see. Surmising a "before" and "after" requires inference. I endured many such "what if" exercises with the trio and Kristen to acquire this skill.

At Vermont College, I received services from Delilah at the learning support center to help me with organization, rigid thinking, and emotional support. She was a strikingly beautiful woman with soft skin, a petite frame, and long, straight, brown hair. She had a soothing voice and was exceptionally kind to me. She was relatively "crunchy" and always wore loose, flowing clothing. Delilah championed environmental causes and taught me about eating healthy. Enjoying meat way too much, I didn't subscribe to all of her ideas, but at least now I could ascertain and respect her perspective—and keep my comments to myself! Delilah was also a great storyteller. She knew about the trio and jumped on board, extending their lessons when I met with her in Vermont. I explained where we were in the process, and her novel ideas quickly took flight.

One day, we were talking about inference, and I whined, "I know *theoretically* what inference is. I just don't possess it!"

"Well, why would you need inference?" she asked.

I had never really thought about it before, but because my neuropsychological testing said I was devoid of these skills, I knew they were important. I answered, "Well, when I encounter a situation where I don't know something, I don't know where to look for the missing information."

I thought about this for a few more minutes and then drew a quick pictograph to help her understand my way of thinking:

Try this. Read aloud the below information in the box: box 1, then 2, then 3, and then 4.

MEAT	CHEESE
(Box 1)	(Box 2)
CHEESE	?
(Box 3)	(Box 4)

"Meat… cheese…. cheese…" she said slowly.

Excited, I pressed, "Now what does box four say?"

"Meat?" she asked slowly.

"You're wrong. It's a question mark!" I announced. "I'm just kidding! You *inferred* from frames one through three that the correct answer is actually 'meat.' This wasn't a trick! You were right! Most neurotypical people would say 'meat.' But for people with autism, if you had said anything other than 'question mark,' you'd be incorrect. After all, that *is* what box four says. Think about how remarkable this is. In three simple frames, non-autistic people have learned a pattern and applied old knowledge to a new context."

While I had figured out how to explain *my* problems with inference, it took me about a year of onerous exercises and journaling to master it. The trio, Kristen, and Delilah gave me endless "what if" scenarios, such as the boy who fell off his bike. With some work, I got these. The key was filling in the blanks between the frames, pulling from my own mental knowledge. For scenarios that consisted of activities that I encountered in the real world, it was relatively easy, since I had real-life knowledge to draw upon.

More difficult, though, were abstract exercises, like recognizing a very rudimentary drawing of an apple. I struggled with not knowing what came between the most basic drawing and a realistic image. So, I did what I do best: I feverishly drew each step of the progression from a basic line drawing of an apple to a more realistic colored drawing, with each stage in between. Holding a pencil and drawing by hand locked the concept of abstraction in place and helped me generalize other scenarios through this multisensory approach.

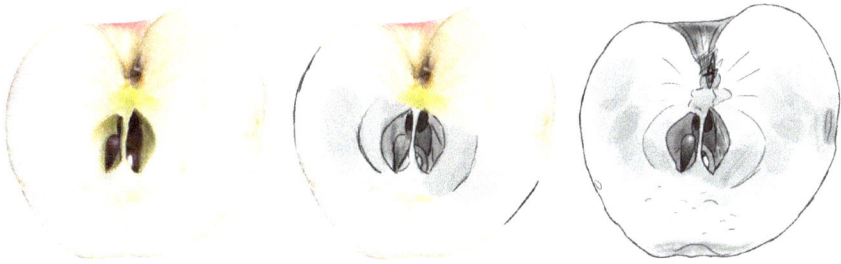

Ultimately, I came to understand inference, though the skill initially manifested in a rather frightening way.

In the midst of all these lessons, I vacationed in the south of France with my family. While there, we visited the Pont du Gard, a massive stunning aqueduct that is one-hundred-and-sixty feet tall and thirty-one miles long. I was slightly manic and electrified by the bridge (I often perseverate on bridges), so I ran up the walkway, which was permitted. Arriving at the top and discovering that there were no guardrails, I immediately started to walk along the ledge, as I had the one time I smoked pot in New York City with Francesca. Like a bolt of lightning, I suddenly envisioned myself falling and then lying dead in the quarry below. My heart pounding, I pulled myself back from the edge, opting instead to see the sights from the bridge's center. I had held two images simultaneously, made a future prediction, and chose a better option. When I returned to the hotel, I thought long and hard about all the ways I could avoid danger with this new tool.

After that, I became vigilant about warding off potential dangers. Everything I did now involved inferring risk. My deductive reasoning skills were unleashed. My anxiety heightened, and a profound depression fell upon me, surrounding my world with darkness. My mind was fracturing again, so when I returned home, I called Dr. Saar after several months of not seeing her.

We chatted for some time, and I explained my project of learning perspective-taking and executive functioning skills. She expressed both her admiration and concern, adding, "Let's get together. Why don't you come in tomorrow at three?"

I was a little scared that she would hospitalize me, but since that was no longer the norm for me and I didn't know where else to turn, I knocked on her door at precisely three p.m. the next day. I hadn't even been able to shower and was a disheveled mess, dressed in the same gross stained sweatshirt that I'd been wearing for two weeks.

Dr. Saar didn't even say hello; she just jumped right in: "How bad is the depression?"

"It's pretty bad. I can't help it, but I think about killing myself all the time. Everywhere I look, I see danger. Please don't hospitalize me. I swear I won't kill myself. I promise."

Fortunately, she agreed, but she insisted that I visit her three times a week for the time being. And she gave me an assignment: shower!

As the months passed, I became less fearful and depressed. I began living a fuller, though appropriately cautious life.

CHAPTER 9

MINDBLINDNESS

SIMON BARON-COHEN, A psychologist who pioneered work on autism, wrote, "Imagine what your world would be like if you were aware of physical things but were blind to the existence of mental things. I mean, of course, blind to things like thoughts, beliefs, knowledge, desires, and intentions [pretending, guessing, imagining, dreaming, deceiving, appreciating, cooperating, tolerating, giving, and inferring], which for most of us self-evidently underlies behavior…In saying that an individual has a Theory of Mind, we mean that the individual imputes mental states to himself and others." (Baron-Cohen, 1997).

If I'd had a modicum of executive functioning and perspective-taking skills while growing up, life would have been monumentally less complicated. As a child, my toys were important to me. In this regard, I wasn't different from other kids. On many weekends, I would wake up at five a.m., dash to the dining room, and plop down on the floor with my face hugging the bulky white shag rug. There, I would line up my *Star Wars* action figures and Matchbox cars in front of two mirrors that sat at a ninety-degree angle from each other. Watching these objects project into infinity was tantalizing, like a roaring visual whirlwind. Unable to contain myself, I would mutter, "Deep breath. Exhale. Breathe in. Out. Ahh… It doesn't get any better than this!"

My mindblindness precluded the ability to input others' mental states, which also meant that my toys never "sprang to life." They were always just objects. Typically, at some point in infancy, perspective-taking begins and ignites briskly, culminating in proficient and naturalistic imagination and interpersonal relations.

Like many people on the autism spectrum, I was a whiz at memorizing data. But, at some point between late elementary school and junior high, academics progress from memorizing basic facts to manipulating the data, resulting in more robust knowledge, higher-order thinking, and conceptualizations. With minimal perspective-taking abilities and lacking the proficiency to manipulate data, I fell behind both interpersonally and somewhat with specific academic skills.

Manipulating data requires being able to create two categories: what's important and what can be discarded. To determine the most important information, one needs to be able to decipher what's "paramount" in any given moment. This, in turn, involves "reading the room," "analyzing the facts," and "drawing conclusions." In my case, I was doubly impaired, as both mania and the rigidity of autism impact what's "paramount." For me, only my opinion and skewed schema are valid.

By junior high, just figuring out what the *most important* part of an assignment was left me anxious.

Then, in seventh grade, a lightbulb went off.

As I was flipping my books over one day, I noticed a pattern: a unique identification number was listed on the back of every book. I thought, *What the hell is this? It must be important!*

To confirm my suspicions, I asked Mrs. Simpson, the school librarian, who resembled Whoopi Goldberg, what those numbers meant. She joyously explained what ISBNs were and why they were so important. "A unique code?" I echoed. I was impressed as well as relieved. After that, I consistently copied down the relevant book's ISBN in the upper-right-hand corner of my notes.

One day in math, I had just finished taking a quiz and was writing the ISBN of my math textbook on the test paper. Joey Palquesi leaned over and whispered, "Hey, what did you get for number two?"

I concealed my paper with my hand and snapped back, "It's none of your dammed business!" I had cracked the code and wanted it to shine on my paper.

Although math came naturally, science was my first love, but that began to give me trouble in junior high, too. In October, we began the unit on the scientific method. After reviewing the concept, I felt the vibrations of my heart racing. As Mr. Mores passed around our assignment, I took several deep breaths to calm myself; I could hear my nose whistle a bit.

As I gnawed on my yellow number-two pencil and squirmed in my seat, my teacher patted me on the back, asking, "Alex, what's wrong? Why haven't you begun the assignment?" I was generally a good student, so my resistance was uncharacteristic.

Frustrated, I replied, "I can't do this." I flipped over the paper. "It's impossible. How would I know the outcome if I don't first do the assignment?"

"Use your imagination," he said cavalierly while walking away. But back then, I didn't have a robust imagination. I tried to explain that I couldn't *predict* what the outcome would be because I didn't *see* it, but that conversation went by the wayside. With both bipolar disorder and autism, it was always hard to explain my perspective. I could never understand others' perspective, so I had nothing to compare mine to.

The following week, Mr. Mores paraded around the classroom handing back our assignments. The only thing written on mine was my name, the textbook's ISBN, and a big fat "0" in red ink. I was devastated.

After science was English, which I detested even more. Unable to input mental states to characters or understand the gestalt of a story made English oppressive. And, frankly, unlike science, I didn't care.

One particular writing assignment in seventh grade sticks out in my memory. Mrs. Gibbs asked us to write a three-page essay on a famous person of our choice. This seemed reasonable. I picked Erwin Schrodinger, a Noble Prize-winning physicist whom I admired. Two weeks later, barely able to contain myself, I proudly presented my ten-page paper. *This is surely "A"-quality work*, I told myself.

Mrs. Gibbs handed the paper back to me four times with the angry command, "Condense the content!" But I couldn't. How could I know what was most important and what could be cut? And, more importantly, how could I predict Mrs. Gibb's reaction?

Rocky perspective-taking skills continued to haunt me in college. At this point, perspective-taking was the linchpin of my work with the trio, Delilah, and Kristen, which coincided with finishing my undergraduate degree at Vermont College. The December before graduation, my advisor called me to her office and informed me that I was short a literature course, preventing me from graduating in the spring. After several conversations, lots of talks with and prayers to the universe, documentation of my disability, and input from Delilah, my advisor made a "special dispensation" for me. For my English literature requirement, I could read auto/biographies of scientists and write essays that were not limited to three pages. This worked for me!

Many of these biographies included photos of the scientists, and I tried to meld their backstory with their face. In theory, I should have been able to draw connections between their facial expressions and their backstories. And I did… sort of.

By now, I was able to tell when I missed a cue. There was something sour in my gut whenever this happened. In this case, I didn't always know the label for the facial expressions of the scientists I was reading about. I realized that the number of expressions I had memorized was not plentiful or sufficient; I needed more. Many more.

So, I snuggled on my soft blue couch and buried my nose in the latest issues of *Seventeen*, *Time*, *Entertainment Weekly*, and several other magazines so that I could stockpile expressions. As faces flew off the pages, I memorized every aspect I could and amalgamated the backstories that I read, although I never really found them interesting. I was now filled with even more facial information to help me interpret expressions and emotions.

Interestingly, though my depressions and manias continued to rumble, when I wasn't experiencing significant symptoms, I became increasingly aware of how my bipolar behavior and/or actions affected others. I was starting to predict how others might view me. My study of faces was paying off in unexpected ways.

However, life doesn't always provide someone's backstory. Sometimes, you need to dig deeper. In real life, you need to ask probing questions to unlock the whole story. But how does one do that?

From reading scholarly articles on neuroscience and education, I discovered that a person's backstory and their emotions often go hand-in-hand. If I knew the gist of someone's backstory, I could now better guess the emotion they were displaying. But if I just knew the feeling, guessing their backstory was infinitely harder. Once I had identified the emotion they were experiencing, I tried to deduce a plausible scenario that would cause that emotion—in other words, inputting mental states. This ultimately enabled me to change my behavior to reflect or modify a desired outcome.

For example, during one admission to a psychiatric hospital in 2012, Mary, my nurse, visited me on their Josephine (every hospital seemed to have such a designated chair). She was wearing *a face*. Not her regular face. What was it? Grouchy? Angry? Frustrated? Happy? No, that last one didn't seem right. She began talking to me. My brain raced for an answer. *Okay, Alex, why is she here?* I snagged it from the sky. *She's angry.* But why? *Because I was cutting paper snowflakes, and she's upset about the paper scraps I left all over the floor around Josephine.* I apologized and picked them up. Crisis adverted!

Back when Delilah, Kristen, and the trio were teaching me how to take perspective, there wasn't a textbook or curriculum for them to draw from. We simply played games—lots of them. Kristen and Aaron picked most of them. They were generally simple childhood games, such as picture sequencing, emotional bingo, and the like. We developed an array of exercises, some of which opened the door to higher-order skills while others fell short. Nevertheless, bigger and better prizes now awaited!

I was a willing student and worked feverishly to document and discuss my introspective thoughts. As I began increasingly invested, I started picking the games we played. Predicting what people were feeling and thinking with relative accuracy was my goal. And, even more importantly, adjusting my responses. Of utmost importance was the connection between executive functioning skills and Theory of Mind skills. I knew that until I perfected my executive functioning skills, I would never be able to take others' perspectives. It was the passport. Now, I was primed and ready to go!

And then, I cracked the code.

I frantically ripped Post-It notes off my wall to make room for new ones. I needed to document the key executive functioning skills, which would enable all other breakthroughs. These skills were: *divided attention* (I see that Mommy sees the airplane); *shifting attention* (deciding whether I want ice cream or a hamburger by imagining both); *non-literal thinking* (my toy car represents a real car); *deductive reasoning* (all ice cream is cold. I'm eating vanilla ice cream. Therefore, the ice cream I'm eating is cold.); *planning and organizing* (figuring out how I will obtain ice cream); *regulating emotions* (what I do when I discover that there's no more ice cream); *flexibility* (realizing that I can eat the hamburger instead); and *self-monitoring* (realizing that I feel frustrated, so I take a few deep breaths instead of having an outburst).

Once I mastered these executive functioning skills, perspective-taking skills soon followed, like dominos set up in a line. The learning process wasn't exactly automatic, but it felt brisker and much less agonizing. Also, the aforementioned skills were not learned in any particular order or for any reason. But once I possessed them, my world finally felt a little more settled.

Divided attention is a component of executive functioning that permits us to shift our attention, to share a moment with another person, or to coordinate one's attention with a partner. It was the first major skill that I acquired and I felt triumphant. Divided attention begins in infancy, generally around age one, when babies learn to point. For example, when an infant says, "Mama, uh, uh," while pointing to an airplane in the sky or visually follows the mother pointing to a new toy on the ground, he learns new information. These actions teach the infant that others are a source of information.

One late-September day, the trio came over to my apartment for lunch. With enthusiasm Stacey immediately pulled a twelve-foot-long brown string out of her bag.

This is going to be interesting! I thought.

Stacey muttered something to Aaron in private, and then, she put one end of the string by her eye while Aaron held the other end. Stacey looked at various items in my apartment, and Aaron moved the other end of the string accordingly, following her gaze. The two were grinning.

Finally, Sadie prompted me, asking, "Where is Stacey looking? Look at her eye and trace the string."

After a few rounds of this new game, I understood that her eyes were a source of information, a clue as to what she was thinking. It had never occurred to me before that people's eyes had value beyond sight.

While I mastered most of the games we played, some lessons didn't automatically generalize, which was incredibly frustrating and almost caused me to give up until one day when Sadie made a magical, important call. She didn't even wait for me to say hello before exclaiming, "Come to my house tonight. I have a surprise for you!"

"Uhhh, okay. What time?" I asked nervously.

"Six. Stay for dinner." With that, Sadie hung up without even saying goodbye.

That evening at Sadie's house, I was complaining about getting frustrated with this project. I was grateful to the trio for their help and commitment, and I had come so far, but I was starting to feel like I was running up against a brick wall.

The trio lapsed into silence for a few minutes, thinking, and then Sadie snapped her fingers and announced, "I got it! I got it!" She smiled at me and explained, "I've been thinking all day. We'll act Sally-Anne out. We'll do it twice. Once, Alex is Sally, and next, she's

Anne. The cartoon will come to life!"

"I'm game!" I said.

We started by having Stacey hide a fortune cookie behind the curtains while I was in the room. Then, I left the room and was not privy to Stacey moving the cookie behind a wine bottle, which obstructed the cookie from my view.

"Come back, Alex," Stacey bellowed from the living room.

When I came back in, I went straight for the curtain. Since I had by now studied numerous perspective-taking tasks, I was not surprised to discover that the cookie was gone. However, I wasn't sure who had taken the cookie or where I could find it.

Next, the trio requested that I trade places with Stacey. Now, I hid and *moved* the cookie. The *coup de grâce* had been unleashed. When Stacey returned and asked me, "Where will I look for the cookie?" a light bulb went off in my head.

When it had been my turn to look for the cookie, walls prevented me from seeing Stacey, who was moving the cookie. The same thing had happened to her when it was my turn to move the cookie. This exercise solidified my understanding that others had perspectives and experiences that might be different than mine and that I might not even fathom. The Berlin Wall had crumbled! I finally understood why having a Theory of Mind is essential, as it:

- *Allows us to make sense of and rationalize what we observe (for example, stealing food to feed a starving family, etc.).*
- *Allows us to understand the intention behind a "white lie."*
- *Gives us powerful leverage to understand, make sense of, and predict the behavior of others.*
- *Helps us understand lying, deception, and fraud so that we aren't taken advantage of.*
- *Gives us a deeper and richer understanding of connections between people, events, or theories.*
- *Lets us decide what's relevant versus what is extraneous information.*

- *Assists us when determining whether the other person understands us, needs more information, or does not understand what we're saying.*
- *And, "in identifying a person as 'kind' you are not just labeling her, you are making an implicit prediction which will guide behavior in a prediction which will guide the manner in which you interact with her." (M. Bennett, 1993)*

A Theory of Mind is important because:

if a person rams into your car, it's important to know whether they're pissed or hit a patch of ice!
(No known author)

Soon, observations and realizations started flooding in. One day, while driving in Concord, Massachusetts, I was annoyed while waiting for a pedestrian to cross the street. *I'm in the car, and I should have priority,* I thought. The next day, the situation was reversed, and I was annoyed again, but this time, at the car. Then, I did it! I held two perspectives at once! I could be both the driver *and* the pedestrian. With this profound realization, I was now aware that people might experience temporary states. When one has bipolar disorder, states are often temporary, which I knew from personal experience. However, I could now internalize that others' states may shift as well. I realized that someone who is angry in the morning may feel differently in the afternoon.

At our next appointment, I burst through Dr. Saar's door. I was so proud and excited to share this newfound knowledge. Once I had disclosed my insight, a meager smile crept out in Dr. Saar's composed fashion. I smiled back. "Let's review the executive function section of my testing again. I'm *so* close to mastery," I said.

She agreed.

"[Alex] often became fixated on details, which then prevented her from grasping the purpose of a task. For example, on a task that required the subject to arrange cartoon-like pictures in a logical order, she focused on irrelevant details of the picture and was unable to complete the task. Of particular note, there was evidence of 'savant-like' abilities. For example, she had marked difficulty understanding the directions on Trails B, a test that requires one to alternate between numbers and letters in a connect-the-dot format. When the test was turned over to reveal the target numbers and letters, she instantly exclaimed, 'Where's the 'M'? I can't do it because there's no 'M.'"

While I now had a plethora of social knowledge, I knew that there must be more I wasn't accessing or digesting. When I asked myself, *What is this person thinking or feeling?* I was now able to provide a broad social spectrum of possible answers. However, the number of conjectures was immense, as I never *really* understood what information to keep and what to ignore. There were a few loose ends that were required to finish this project, most notably *inference, ascertaining relevance*, and *imagination*. Relevance seemed like the next logical step.

Socially, I never knew which follow-up questions were more or less relevant. Therefore, the trio introduced me to the work of Sperber and Wilson, who study the search for relevance. They theorize that interactions occur by "Paying attention to the actual words a speaker uses, but also focusing on what we think was the gist of what he or she wanted to say or wanted us to understand." Sperber and Wilson (1986) call this a "search for relevance."

"The listener assumes that the meaning of an utterance will be relevant to the speaker's current intentions. Thus, when the cop shouts, 'Drop it!' a robber is not left in a state of doubt over the ambiguity of the term 'it.'" (Baron-Cohen, 1997). However, for mindblind people, that assumption is not always present. Using words with multiple meanings, such as "it," "they," "later," "over there," or "the other day" is extremely confusing. Secretly, I wish these words were removed from the dictionary. Sometimes, analyzing them is such an arduous task, it makes conversations not worth the effort.

One of my more "memorable" childhood moments took place at a fancy restaurant in New York City. I was about eight. My parents and their friends were eating slowly and conversing, which I loathed. "Fancy" restaurants generally meant that I needed to wear itchy clothes, the noise volume always pecked at my ears, and a roast beef sandwich on a bulky roll with Heinz ketchup was generally not a menu item. My mother and I were bench mates, and throughout dinner, she kept craning her neck toward me like an angry swan. Her face kept contorting, and I imagined her hissing. I speculated that she was mad. But why? Or at who? The waitress? Me? I couldn't figure it out and needed a signal to connect the dots. When she was on her very last nerve, she grabbed my wrist under the table. I felt her long, red, painted nails digging in my wrist as she whispered in my ear, "Stop it! Stop it! Stop it! You're making an ass out of yourself." Again, there was that "it" that I didn't understand. To this day, I still don't know what I did wrong that evening.

As an adult, with an expanded food pallet, and working on relevance, Kristen and I dined at a swanky new restaurant on Boston's Wharf. As we stepped inside, my eyes abruptly rose to the coffered ceiling, and I froze our conversation mid-sentence. It was stunning. As we were escorted to our seats, Kristen playfully pinched the back of my neck, saying, "Look down. I'm more important than the ceiling."

In that moment, I created a new rule: "People first, objects second!" Got it! With this new rule in place, I started paying more attention to the "essence" of people instead of trivial details, like the number of letters in their name.

I learned relevance mostly by playing process-of-elimination and logic games such as *Guess Who*; Pico, Fermi, Bagel; cryptograms; hearts; and chess. Each of these games required me to keep multiple strategies in mind simultaneously. I also read mystery novels that were aimed at very young readers. The point was not the reading level, but the challenge of the mysteries.

Next, I needed to integrate the concept of "relevance" into social interaction, for which I now had a wobbly framework. Before nailing perspective-taking, I had relied on rote skill acquisition as my fallback for all interactions. Now, I was starting to get it!

However, with every new skill that I mastered, I still felt that there was more that I didn't know, I didn't know. I felt cheated in a way. I decided it was time to embark upon my next journey: into imagination. *What does an imagination feel like?* I wondered. *What function does it serve?*

I posed this question to the trio, and they set out to show me. I thought the brightly colored games and drawing activities they came up with to help with my imagination were juvenile, but I went along with it all because they were so kind to me. Plus, I really did want to experience a true imagination. I didn't realize that imagination would prove to be a springboard for many other things. How could I, when I couldn't imagine it? After all of their propaganda, I just knew that I wanted an imagination, too! Fortunately, I had gotten a head start through my schoolwork and academic reading.

We started this work on my imagination when I was about mid-way through college. The Little Red Schoolhouse had closed its doors about a year and a half earlier, and we had all gone our separate ways professionally. This meant that I saw the trio less frequently. Fortunately, we communicated via the internet regularly and occasionally shared a meal. My perspective-taking, deductive reasoning, and inferring skills, among others, were now in pretty good shape. The trio felt I was primed for imagination.

One Saturday in April, the trio invited me to Sadie's house. Our last visit had been over a month ago, so this felt nice and familiar. Plus, there was Chinese takeout!

As I sat at the table with my wonton soup and Yu Hsiang chicken, Sadie commanded in her warm, endearing style, "You imagine a river. Now draw."

This seemed simple enough. I drew the Ipswich River, which was the last river I had visited. Piece of cake!

"Now, put a mallard duck in."

Clearly, I had been a little too cocky. My throat immediately closed. There had not been a mallard duck in the Ipswich River the last time I was there. When my mind experiences incongruence, I mentally twitch. In my brain, there are truths and lies, but never a half-truth or a white lie. The truth and the lie have separate attributes, and they can't comingle. I feel sick when I need to exercise my cerebrum in this manner. Yet, I wanted this knowledge so badly and appreciated the trio's time (and the Chinese food). Feeling dejected, I said, "I don't think I can do this," and put my head down on the table.

"Yes you can! Now, you draw a duck," Sadie replied, sounding slightly annoyed.

On a separate piece of paper, I drew a mallard duck.

"No!" Her temper flared. "You draw a duck *in* the river."

Aaron, the psychologist, jumped in, providing a metaphorical life raft. "Let's try this: everyone draws their own animal on their own paper," he suggested.

Stacey drew a bat. Sadie made a bird. Aaron created a bear. When that was done, Aaron suggested that we cut out our pictures and glue them onto the Ipswich River. As the glue slowly dried, I tentatively began to accept this picture and the concept underlying it.

We continued with this concept, creating new pictures by cutting and pasting two cars together to create a new car. My imagination steadily took flight using this "cut and paste" method. Still, I didn't see why this was fun.

But as my proficiency grew, I eventually found that I could simply *use my imagination*! Learning to "fill in the blanks" seemed like the pinnacle of imaginative thing for me. And, as with all the other new skills I learned, there were developmental stages that slowly unlocked this skill base over time.

The trio began briefly revisiting the concept of switching or shifting my attention so that I could hold both a representation of an object and the real object in my mind simultaneously. When dealing with imagination, one must be proficient at switching between a real and pretend object, such as the these two cars. For example, in order to imagine a tire, one must be able to both look at a real tire and visualize this object as a circle *and* look at a circle and imagine it is a tire. This type of switching attention helps build imagination skills.

We engaged in many switching activities, but the one that struck me the most was playing two games at once and shifting between the two. This was effective because both games required opposing strategies. We also worked on switching tasks from a sensory perspective, by having me hold hot, then cold, items in rapid secession.

Switching my attention proved to be useful beyond engaging with juvenile toys. I could now think about the possible outcome of an event. Switching, or imagining, unleashed possibilities I never even knew were conceivable; I now knew what I didn't know, I didn't know. If I became overstimulated, I could now imagine the result of a coping skill, such as being calm as a result of diaphragmatic breathing. In essence, I *imagined* it.

Heading off future challenging possibilities was useful all around. With my bipolar disorder, my coping strategies were rarely successful because I couldn't *see* or *feel* myself in a different state. When an episode struck and depression or hypomania engulfed my world, I was unable to envision another state of being. The other state simply did not exist—or I could not access it. Plus, when I was manic, my brain was so irrational that suggestions often fell upon deaf ears. Introspection didn't occur, nor did the ability to imagine what might be helpful. Unwanted comments from my therapeutic team ricocheted off my armor, as they felt untruthful and unimaginable. I couldn't switch my attention and take their perspective, especially when they told me what mood state I appeared to be in. Dr. Saar would say things like, "You're talking really quickly, and your ideas are far-fetched," but the only perspective I could take was mine. Now, the exercises having to do with switching my attention and imagination were key to teaching me perspective-taking as well as using better coping strategies.

Without an imagination for defense, literal thinking dug deep roots. In the past, I couldn't switch my attention between two states. I wasn't able to imagine any other possibility than the one that my mind had created. Therefore, there was only one "right" state.

In second grade, I was hanging out with Eric Anderson, my neighbor from across the street and a fellow lover of Legos. We were playing in his basement when Denis, his portly dad, came down the stairs heavily panting with a massive box wrapped in brown paper. "This is for you," he said, gently tossing the mystery box toward Eric. I could hear the rattling inside but couldn't quite place the noise. Like feral cats, we ripped open the box. It was the new "Space Lego" set! We were thrilled, and building commenced immediately.

Like me, Eric had no desire to play with the Legos. Our enjoyment came from building them. As I sifted through the pile, I found the pieces for the astronaut Lego man and proudly showed Eric. This figure consisted of five parts: the legs/feet, the body/arms, the oxygen tank, the head, and the space helmet, which had to be assembled in that order. In a stern voice, Eric bellowed, "Don't take the oxygen tank off his back, or *you'll die*!"

Terrified, I jammed that astronaut into my pocket at lightning speed. We shared toys all the time, so I felt entitled to take it. Plus, if my life depended on the state of this Lego astronaut, I wanted to oversee him myself.

Each day, for protection, I gingerly moved the astronaut into my new clothes. This continued for about two years until one day, during English, my fourth-grade teacher, Mr. Meaner, caught me fidgeting with my Lego space man under my desk and confiscated him.

I flipped out. Crying hysterically, I threw myself onto the ground, ranting about the situation. "Be careful! Watch his oxygen tank! Don't touch the— Nooooooo!" I screamed.

Mr. Meaner had ripped the Lego man's head and oxygen tank off.

I frantically thrashed around and gasped for breath. After about five minutes, I was feeling pretty lightheaded (and stupid), so I sat down at my desk. Mr. Meaner kept the Lego astronaut until the end of the year. Luckily, I didn't die.

Around this same time, my literal thinking was also affected by the Tylenol scare of 1982. The common household drug had been tampered with in the factory and laced with a lethal substance, potassium cyanide, causing several deaths. This presented a problem for me. How could I *ever* know if Tylenol was safe?

Being a child, I soon caught a cold and ended up with a fever. My mother wanted to give me Tylenol, but I refused. She tried to reassure and rationalize with an irrational mind. After a two-hour tussle, I gruffly demanded, "What inexplicable evidence do you have that this pill before me is not poisoned?"

"Come on, Alex. It's late. Just take the pill. It will make you feel better, I promise." As any mom would, she tried to shove it in my mouth, but my lips were ironclad. Walking out of the room, she exclaimed, "Fine, be sick!"

In retrospect, any of these incidents could have been learning opportunities for me, but back then, Asperger's syndrome wasn't even a diagnosis. There were certainly no viable treatment options. I'm so fortunate that in the mid-1990's the trio, Delilah, and Kristen were so willing to help me build my skills over the course of many years. There wasn't a curriculum to follow. We created it. We utilized ordinary children's games, which was extremely effective. If I could go back in time and play these same games as a child, but with therapeutic intent, my childhood may have been easier.

Tapping into non-literal thinking was a game-changer and helped propel me into the next level of sophistication. As the months passed, my mind grew while playing these ordinary, yet well-thought-out games. Some activities included filling in the blanks, such as *Mad*

Libs, songs with lyrics that don't belong, cutting out parts of photographs and drawing in the missing pieces, and journaling with the prompt, "What if..." All of these silly exercises were a useful part of our overall program.

"What if" scenarios were hardest for me because they involve perspective-taking, inferring, and imagination, all tied together. One night, I was lying in bed and talking to Kristen on the phone. She posed the question, "You're walking in the woods one day, and you come across a man lying on the ground, not moving, with an unopened parachute pack on his back, and an airplane flying above. What happened?"

"Crap! I don't know!" I snapped. I wasn't in the learning mood.

"Come on, Alex, think. What happened?" I couldn't figure it out, though, and she eventually spoon-fed me the answer.

The following Sunday morning, we met for breakfast at Abe's Diner, where I went every week, usually by myself. I always had the same thing: a delectable veggie omelet, an English muffin with grape jelly, and ketchup-laden home fries. On this particular morning, Kristen deconstructed the parachute exercise by using "wh- questions," some of which were obvious. Others required a leap.

Where? The woods.

Who? A man with a parachute.

What? The parachute didn't open.

When? This wasn't stated and likely didn't matter.

Now, the hard one, *why*?

Having dissected the entire incident, I finally inferred the answer and with lightning speed the words flew out of my mouth. "He fell out of a plane! His parachute didn't open! He's on the ground! And now he's dead! I got it! I really got it!" I squealed with glee.

We ran through several other scenarios like this. Kristen also brought along colorful cards with drawings depicting assorted storylines. I was intrigued as they sprang from her bag. There were about five cards per storyline, each illuminating a different stage. Kristen started with all five cards in a story as a baseline, but then quickly hid one card. Then another. Each time she removed a card, Kristen requested that I narrate the gist of the story. I analyzed each card while filling in the blanks, eventually forging robust stories. I really got it! I was inferring! I had an imagination!

After years of practice, today, I'm fairly proficient at "reading the room" and using inference from our "wh- questions." I also learned numerous other lessons along the way. I was making progress, gaining skills, and having fun.

I could now understand that the guy on the ground with an unopened parachute was not real but rather *represented* either a real or fictional person. Understanding this was ground zero for developing social skills and "gut instincts."

My skills continued to develop as more sophisticated concepts were presented to my mind. Shortly after the "wh- question" activities with Kristen, Vermont College was holding a soiree that included dinner and dancing. Everyone was expected to attend. I claimed to be coming down with the flu so I could get out of it, but earlier in the day, I had an appointment with Delilah.

When I walked into her office, she said, "Let's stretch," I thought she meant some kind of physical yoga exercise, but she continued, "We'll be at the soiree tonight. My husband, Henry, will be there with me. What do you think he looks like?"

Dumbfounded, I answered that I didn't know. I tried to scope out her office for a picture so I could cheat. There were no photos.

She held out a piece of paper. "Let's draw him!" she said. As we worked through this task, she prompted me by asking binary questions such as, "Does he have brown or blond hair?" "Does he have a beard, or is he clean-shaven?" "Does he have brown or blue eyes?"

I thought this was kind of stupid, but I did see the point. The challenge initially aggravated me, but as we worked through it, I became curious. My "sniffles" would need to go away. After all, how could I duck out now? I would have to meet Henry at the soiree.

When I met him, I finally understood the phrase, "You don't look anything like I thought you would!"

Oh, and I survived the soiree.

Learning perspective-taking was arduous at first, but as I progressed through the concepts, they became more solid in my mind. Plus, I was now actually having fun. One major door that I struggled to unlock was taking various pieces of information and using them to make future predictions. I finally managed to accomplish and conquer this skill while running an errand.

My town's library had an impressive collection of children's toys that residents could borrow, and I frequently commandeered their materials for the children I worked with at my private consulting practice, which I opened after the Little Red Schoolhouse closed and while I was still attending college. One Sunday in May, late in the afternoon, I was driving home from the grocery store when I noticed a shiny red rectangular puzzle piece on the floor of my car. Earlier in the week, I had returned the puzzle this piece belonged to. Apparently, this piece had fallen out. I turned the car around and headed to the library.

The problem was that, at this hour, the library wasn't open. Remembering that they had a metal slot to put books in, I figured I could just deposit the puzzle piece in there. Before I could even finish that thought, I slammed on the mental breaks. "Hold it!" I shrieked in my car. I imagined the librarian finding the puzzle piece the next morning. In a whirlwind, I blurted loudly, "She wasn't with me when I used the puzzle or found the piece. She doesn't have the same mentalistic knowledge as me. She may not even know it's a puzzle piece. She may throw it out, thinking it's trash. The next person to borrow the puzzle will feel sad." I did a happy dance behind the wheel of my car. This puzzle piece incident triggered a cascade of inferential thinking that culminated with proficient imagination.

Around the same time, I received an email from Delilah with a link to an article that would change my life. It was about sleep, as she knew that sleeping was a challenge for me. Based on Dr. Saar's orders, if I wanted to stay out of the hospital, I needed to take the prescribed doses of my medication *every day* and get enough sleep. Since decreased sleep is a sign of an impending manic episode and my medication generally helped me sleep, I complied. However, even with my meds, when an impending manic episode is on my doorstep, I struggled to get enough sleep and now was often sleeping only two hours a night. So, I mentioned this to Delilah, hoping she might have some tips. This article she sent was clearly from the realm of academia, but I comprehended most of it. When I came across a word that I didn't understand, I simply looked it up online.

As I continued to read, my mind was suddenly yanked away from the article. *Holy cow!* I thought. *I finally understand why I don't grasp literature.* When reading fiction, if I come across something that I can't discern, there's no way to look up the information. In a fictional story, when John takes his son to the cattle ranch, I'm left with gaping holes: "Who is John?" "Who is his son?" "Which cattle ranch did they go to?" "How did they get there?" What is the purpose of their visit?" I just have so many questions. At that very instant, I realized that my imagination is where I "look up" the missing information. The characters are not real people, but rather, a composite of values, opinions, stereotypes, and ideas. They are the bat, bird, and bear on the Ipswich River. In grade school, teachers always said, "Use your imagination!" Now, I knew what they meant.

Finally, I was able to put all of the executive functioning skills that I had learned together, yielding the door to social skills. Learning social interaction requires constant interpretation and continuous integration of information, which is obtained from contextual and non-verbal cues. In other words, when one interacts with another person, unconsciously, their antennae are always raised, taking in information from the environment around them and monitoring their partner's body language for clues on how to act and what to say. With all of this information, one can shift and re-shift their priorities like a dance, even within one small interaction. I finally got it!

When I reread my journals as part of writing this book, I found two entries from the period of these lessons circled in red. I've summarized them below because I think they highlight how far I had come in lifting the mindblindness veil.

Entry 1: *On April 19, 1995, not possessing perspective-taking skills or imagination, I watched as the news showed pictures of the Oklahoma City bombing. I was awestruck by the explosion itself. I videotaped the next broadcast and watched the aftermath over and over again, noticing more pyrotechnical details each time. Because I was not taking anyone's emotions into account, this was a captivating event, although I never considered its impact on others.*

Entry 2: *On August 13, 1997, two years later, I now possessed perspective-taking skills and imagination. I was again watching the news on television when reporters announced that Princess Diana had died. With sadness in my heart, my immediate thought was, "Those boys just lost their mom."*

It's amazing to see the difference that learning Theory of Mind had on my initial reactions to these two horrific events. By the time of the second entry, I was able to take the perspective of others, I had a vivid imagination, and I had a strong desire for friendship with reciprocity.

Overall, I would say that learning to take perspective, gaining inference, and developing an imagination were positive experiences with superlative results. However, they were not without a price. Divided attention provided a starting point for proficient, innate social skills and imagination. However, by dividing my attention, I was also able to see both good and bad things about a given situation.

Until this point, I had known that my institutional treatment was not stellar, but I did not attribute any of it to malice. Now, I did. And I was angry. Really angry. Using my newfound skills, I verbalized my frustration and anger in therapy and drew pictures. Many pictures.

Overall, I'm thrilled with the mastery of skills that I now possess. I am eternally grateful to those who helped me, and I've made it my life's work to pay it forward. I took my cue from Eleanor Roosevelt, who said, "When you cease to make a contribution, you begin to die." And so, that's just what I did: I contributed.

PAYING IT FORWARD

I WAS TWENTY-SEVEN years old, had finished my work with the trio, was completing college, and didn't feel well. This had been going on for about a month. I didn't feel like I was going to throw up. I didn't have diarrhea. My throat didn't hurt. My ears weren't painful. My nose wasn't running. I felt stupid going to the doctor. I mean, what would I even say beyond, "I don't feel well"? Not knowing where else to turn, I called Dr. Saar, who ran through the same list of questions I just answered. She knew that I'm not a complainer and recommended I see my primary care doctor, Dr. Robinson, who was also perplexed by my vague symptoms. She decided to run some labs and would contact me when she knew something. A week or so later, her receptionist scheduled a follow-up appointment.

"Hi, Alex," Dr. Robinson said with a disconcerting smile when I entered her office. "Please, sit down." She gestured to the chair in front of her desk. I hate it when people instruct me to sit. It never ends well. Her chair made a little swishing noise as I sat, which I found kind of distracting.

"Should I be worried?" I asked.

"Some of your labs that came back were concerning. I think your Lithium is impacting your kidneys, which is likely why you don't feel well but can't pinpoint the cause."

"So what does that mean?"

She hesitated, inching her words forward with a slow, somber tone. "To prevent further damage, you're going to need to discontinue Lithium."

My jaw hit the floor. My emotions swirled. I felt elated, joyful, delighted, ecstatic, exhilarated... But in the same instant, this turned to fear, panic, dread, terror, and fright. A headache swept over me. For eight years, I'd evaded and skirted using Lithium, with disastrous results whenever I stopped taking it. Now that it was deemed harmful and not an option, I was frantic. Knowing what an "unmedicated me" looks like, what was I to do?

Dr. Robinson continued, "I'll call your psychiatrist, and we'll figure out the best course of treatment for you. Here's the name of a nephrologist. Please set up an appointment for a consult as soon as you can. I'm sorry, Alex." Her voice was pained and sincere.

I thanked her, left, and threw back a Valium in the car.

Dr. Saar agreed that this complication required a creative solution. The dilemma was that I had tried every mood stabilizer on the market with only moderate results. When I was compliant, Lithium worked brilliantly. After careful research, we concurred that I could dabble in alternative treatments, such as high doses of vitamins, supplements, minerals, and acupuncture while continuing on Thorazine and Valium. There was no other option. Although Valium is not a mood stabilizer, when mania blows my way, it certainly helps decrease the exuberance. Equally important, in larger doses, it makes me somewhat sleepy, which protects me against mania, as manic episodes can be brought on by a prolonged lack of sleep.

After stopping the Lithium, I always felt like I was waiting for the other shoe to drop. One day, I decided to take inventory of myself. Overall, I was doing reasonably well. It's not uncommon for people to go years between mood episodes, so this wasn't too unexpected. My mood was mostly quiet with just "baby swings," and although I still had the residue of autism, learning executive functioning skills, compensatory strategies, and perspective-taking had improved my overall function. With my mood stable and new skills under my belt,

I now felt poised to take my next steps in life.

Unfortunately, the Little Red Schoolhouse, where I had been so comfortable, closed its doors due to bankruptcy. Before learning these valuable skills, this situation would have devastated me. I had been comfortable at work, where I was with the same people doing the same things all the time. Everything was predictable, and nothing changed. Now, with my newly acquired skills, I was able to face this drastic change. I looked forward to my new adventures, wherever my path may lead.

The Little Red Schoolhouse was a private special education school. With its closure, the students now needed to transition to new schools, which were often back in their home school districts, where appropriate, effective programming either did not exist or was not as robust as it needed to be. Several special education administrators responsible for overseeing the students' programming contacted me, requesting help. They asked me to consult, specifically to design the students' education plans. This ranged from small items, like selecting paint colors, to more significant components, such as developing curriculum and interviewing staff, all while providing ongoing support to the students' teams. I was flattered and excited. I loved this idea, and it tapped right into my strengths. It wasn't full-time work, but this happy accident birthed a career path beyond my imagination.

I put out some feelers to gain supplemental income and connected with Ellen Akenson, a colleague I knew from the Children's Developmental Disabilities Center (CDDC), the group who had run that autism parents' meeting I attended all those years ago. She informed me that they actually had a job opening. We reconnected, and I interviewed for and got the job.

Ellen was a short middle-aged woman with curly afro-style dark-brown hair and a strong New York accent. She had a wild laugh like a hyena… and I say that fondly. Ellen was passionate about the CDDC's work and would accept nothing less than stellar performance from her employees and colleagues. I always appreciated Ellen's candor. She was very direct and never discrete with her feedback. I idolized her. Mostly, I loved that Ellen had the same expectations for me as she did everyone else and that she was blunt when necessary. For example, once a month, there was a large companywide meeting with the executive director. On two occasions, with nostrils flaring, Ellen reminded me not to read during the director's speech... and to wear shoes. Seeing her point, I apologized to the director later.

Even as I worked full time at the CDDC, my consulting practice continued to grow. Plus, I was finishing my undergraduate degree. I was stressed and knew that something had to give. I felt like an enormous hippopotamus being squeezed into a girdle. I couldn't eliminate school; I was too close to the finish line. Consulting was my passion, yet I did enjoy the CDDC. How could I combine these?

I spoke with my parents, and they helped me turn my ideas into a working proposal. My idea was for the CDDC to open a consulting division, which I would run. I would transfer all of my private consultation clients, plus any future referrals, to this new division. And, I would work only on commission. The only caveat was that the agency would provide a small office, phone, and access to the copy machine. There would be no risk to the organization.

I set up a meeting with the higher-ups at the CDDC's parent company to pitch my vision. My dad insisted that I "look the part," so I pulled out my scratchy black funeral suit, which lay crinkled in the back of my closet with my uncomfortable shoes. He even offered to pay the dry-cleaning bill. I came to this meeting prepared with spreadsheets and projected revenue statements.

After what I thought was a stellar presentation, their faces didn't glow as I expected. I couldn't figure out what I had done wrong. They asked me to wait outside for a few minutes, which I did.

When they called me back in, Patrice, one of the managers, said in a matter-of-fact tone, "Alex, thank you for this information. The idea seems well thought out, and there appears to be a need for this service. We like the idea. However, we believe you are incompetent in running anything and would never make this division successful."

I felt a stab in my heart. As I turned toward the door, "You can't,"

"You won't," "Not with your diagnoses," danced through my head. But then, I regained my composure.

Fuming with anger and impulsivity, I turned around and announced, "Screw you. I'm going expand my consulting practice and make it a success!" I grabbed a blank piece of paper, scribbled on it, and pushed it across the table toward them. "Consider this is my two weeks' notice!"

Okay, so that's not exactly what happened. That's just my fantasy ending to this story. In reality, I politely gave them my two weeks' notice.

I created legitimate business cards and stationery and hung my shingle out. I was both invigorated and frightened by the prospect of owning my own business, but I wanted to at least give it a try.

Shortly after leaving the CDDC, I graduated from college. Consulting, lecturing, and advocating captured the majority of my time. Inundated with children and school districts, within three months, I was working sixteen-plus hours a day in a hypomanic state without Lithium onboard. However, as fall crept in, I took a tumble, and while I wasn't really depressed, I was far from hypomanic, and my number of productive hours slumped. I felt overwhelmed.

I flew down to Florida, where my parents had retired, to talk with them. At Mario's Restaurant in Boca Raton, we feasted on antipasti and rigatoni arribada while we sat in a quiet corner to have our "meeting." Before we had even started, a cascade of tears crawled down my face. I told them that having so many clients was exhausting, but I loved the kids, families, and districts. I didn't know what to do.

"So hire a staff!" my father said, as if it were the obvious thing in the world.

"Are you kidding? I can't afford that."

"Al, you can't afford *not* to," he sighed.

My mother chimed in, "Don't worry about the finances. We'll back you." She's always been so supportive and practical.

Hiring a staff was not something I had expected or even planned to do. It seemed like a big undertaking. Yet, I reluctantly agreed. I found three skilled clinicians and put them to work. That turned the pressure valve down somewhat, so I could focus my attention on my own clients and running the business side of things. I had absolutely no experience with this part of the job, and while I came to enjoy it, my affinity for clinical work remained paramount. While I had consulted for several years, with these changes underway, in 1997, I formally renamed the business, and Ravenwood's doors were officially opened!

Kristen and I had started dating around the time I enrolled at Vermont College, and when the Little Red Schoolhouse closed its doors, she was hired by the Bauer School to teach an intensive special needs classroom. Bauer was located pretty far away from me, and so each day for about a year, I did my best to woo her away from Bauer and consult with me. I missed our professional comradery and after-work Buffalo wings.

Turning up the charm one day, I pressed, "Come on, Kristen, it would be awesome to work together again, wouldn't it? We could brainstorm interventions and analyze the kids like we used to. Remember how much fun that was?"

"Oh, you're killing me, Al," she chuckled. "I really want to, but I talked with my parents, and they think I shouldn't give up my safe teaching job."

"But this is an opportunity to help hundreds of kids, not just the few in your classroom," I said. "Plus, we'd be our own bosses."

Her face changed. It somehow both softened and brightened, but I didn't really know what she was thinking until her lips moved. "I have no idea what I'm going to tell my parents or how I'm going to leave the kids in Bauer, but… you've got a deal! I'll join you! We did have fun at the Little Red Schoolhouse!"

Kristen gave her notice at work, and we were officially business partners.

Our consulting work exploded, and for many years, Ravenwood spun off and housed several successful, if eclectic, divisions providing therapy primarily to students with autism. Our first spin-off division consisted of one-on-one therapy for young children, aiming to increase their skill sets in areas such as language, sensory processing, and cognitive development. We used a combination of evidenced-based traditional and non-traditional methods, along with exercises from my own experiences, many of which Kristen and the trio had taught me. We applied with the state of Massachusetts to be a licensed service provider so that families could access Ravenwood's services, regardless of their income.

As we added more programs and services, I was increasingly responsible for the business's accounting and finance, human resources, and advertising and marketing. With phones ringing off the hook, I hired additional staff and supervisors. I had to.

Ravenwood was still based out of my cramped apartment in Cambridge, Massachusetts. All five staff members arrived at different times throughout the day and manned their petite work stations in my kitchen. While everyone wanted a "real" office, at this point, I couldn't afford to have a genuine office space *and* pay the staff, so I opted for the latter.

To provide constructive feedback, the staff often videotaped their sessions. Then, all of us would pile onto my king-sized bed (which felt small with all of our bodies on it), as my bedroom housed the only VCR. There, we ate popcorn and engaged in deep clinical discussions.

Eventually, my apartment grew to be unmanageable as a workspace. The thought of hiring more people and renting a "real" office made me nervous. It meant taking on more risk. I was scared of failing and jeopardizing all of the staff's employment.

I had another serious conversation with my parents and explained my dilemma. With each, "Yeah, but…," they stopped me. Exasperated, my father finally said, "Are you playing around, or are you going to be a real businesswoman?" I burst into tears. As always, he and my mom were right. In stern but loving voices, they both pushed me to take the plunge. So, I did.

Renting a 2,500-square-foot office space enabled me to hire additional staff. This was a huge relief, especially since we were now approved by the state to provide services. And I was *thrilled* to have my house back!

Within two years, Ravenwood was in steady competition with other, larger agencies that had been around for more than fifty years. Our secret lay in providing top-notch therapy while also engaging parents, extended families, and school districts. The districts loved us because their students were making effective progress while their teachers also received relevant training.

At this point, our staff consisted of fourteen people. I had been off of Lithium for several years now and generally felt good. But then, the hypomania edged back in. Grandiose ideas were flying. My mind was spinning. I wanted to expand Ravenwood. Kristen was on board.

A few of our consulting kids required summer placement so that they could receive therapeutic programming when school was out, so we created it. Jessica Berry was a jovial woman with a huge heart who emanated positivity. She started working at Ravenwood almost from its inception, and we spent countless hours focusing on the kids both on and off the clock. She not only supervised our home- and school-based therapists, but also helped design the summer camp. Jessica was a truly loyal employee who eventually grew to become my best friend. We always just "got" each other without pretenses getting in the way.

In a little over a year, we launched Ravenwood Day Camp, offering a seven-week pragmatic (social skills) summer program. At its height, it educated about 130 campers each summer. We hired forty-five staff members and rented out a public elementary school building to house all of them. Each group of campers was led either by professional educators or speech-language pathologists and assisted by vivacious college students majoring in related fields.

The methods we used weren't exactly rocket science, but back then, there wasn't a pragmatic curriculum that we could draw upon. As with most things, we had to invent it. Most of the curriculum resembled the games I had played to learn executive functioning and perspective-taking skills. Every summer, counselors received a beefy binder listing activities and exercises that were tabbed by skillset, such as "eye contact," "friendly hello," or "reading expressions." Of utmost importance was providing naturalist teaching opportunities. Nothing was done by rote memorization. For example, when the kids got off the bus in the morning, the adults sang energetic camp songs at the school's entrance. Campers were expected to give counselors and directors a high five *with* eye contact. For those campers who were uncomfortable with eye contact, we showed them where to look on a person's face to "fake it," such as on the bridge of the nose.

Campers engaged in intensive, structured, direct learning through organized lessons and cooperative games. Every minute of their day was devoted to executive functioning and social skills training, from their morning greeting to conversation cards (or "cheat sheets") during lunch. To emulate traditional summer activities, campers also went swimming, played in sprinklers, had their faces painted, made carnivals, and had water balloon fights. It was vital to Kristen and me that the kids had fun. Campers made monumental progress, and this program ran successfully for several years. Each year, after school recommenced in September, the campers' school districts would inevitably call, requesting school consultations.

In 2005, as Ravenwood Day Camp came to a close for the summer, so did my exhilarating mood. My mind had betrayed me again, but this time, it was bigger. I was despondent. I hit such a low point that I lost my grip. The depression engulfed me, and I couldn't imagine another state, despite my training with the trio. Insufferable to myself and others, I was teetering on the edge of despair. Work felt oppressive, and I slipped away. Ever since I was fourteen, late summer had always ushered in mood instability. However, for many years, the alternative medications held me steady and my moods were generally unremarkable. I had even stopped seeing Dr. Saar; my primary care doctor handled my Valium prescription (I had stopped Thorizine years ago due to a dangerous side effect.) Heeding Dr. Saar's warnings against anti-depressants and fearing they would bring out the ravenous mania in me, I never even considered them as an option.

Morbidly depressed and out of ideas, I was too embarrassed to call Dr. Saar, so I just sat morosely at home.

Jessica, who was a gentle, nurturing soul, kept a sullen me company in my living room on my comfortable crimson sectional. I rested my head on her soft, snuggly lap and long lustrous brown hair as she wiped away my tears and covered me with a silky blanket.

I was overwhelmed and suicidal. When trapped in a profound bipolar depression, I rarely can formulate a plan to get me out. None of my perspective-taking intervention made a dent. Within a week, I single-handedly decided to say *au revoir* to our home-based, camp and consulting divisions, leaving little left of the business. I also (unintentionally) pissed off the Department of Public Health by writing an obnoxious letter about long-standing grievances I had with them. To make matters worse, I sent copies of it to all of our families.

This was an incredibly stupid decision. Once the letters were sent, while I felt short-term relief, but I also recognized that this was political suicide. One of the higher-ups at the Department of Public Health, who I respected and looked up to, reamed me out like a naughty child. I was both embarrassed and appreciative. She was a colleague, and while I didn't like what she had to say, I appreciated her candor and feedback. This conversation helped make a smooth transition for our students. Exiting these divisions was done systematically over the course of about one year to aid in the children's transitions.

Kristen continued to consult with Ravenwood, but toward the end of this period, she took a job in a public school. Worst of all, I impulsively fired Jessica, my best friend, for absolutely no just cause. None of these departures was conducted professionally. I simply needed to get everything off my plate. Quickly. I thought that if everything were gone, I would feel better. However, work was a causality in this war against my mood. Fundamentally, the problem was my mood, not my business. To this day, I feel horrible for these decisions. I can't change the past, but thankfully, I have learned from my mistakes and my parents have helped put systems in place to prevent this sort of thing from happening again. My disabilities can never impact Ravenwood, its staff, the students' programming, or the services we provide again.

Without a pause after my depression came to a spontaneous end, an effervescent hypomania fluttered in. One day, I just began to feel more vivacious, like I was coming back. My mind was swirling with ideas again.

I contacted a few of the summer camp parents. Over coffee, I listened to how their children were doing and what their current needs were. I thought about the work I had done with the trio and all of the large, bright-yellow Post-It notes I had used to build my skills. I mentally started writing the parents' words and their needs on new large Post-It notes. Hearing of their children's struggles made me want to jump into action immediately.

Then, it hit me. I wanted to open a new division of Ravenwood: a therapeutic day school. It would be the complete antithesis of my own educational and psychiatric treatment. It would actually be helpful and kind. This would soon become my new obsession.

As the other divisions of my business were winding down, I connected with the right person at the Department of Education. She sent me the private school application, and forgoing sleep, I spent all of Saturday and Sunday filling it out. The culmination was an approximately 250-page document. Early Monday morning, I waited outside the Department of Education for three hours until it opened so that I could personally drop the application off.

Back at home, I waited. And waited. And waited.

About a month later, the Department of Education reviewed Ravenwood's application for a new day school and conducted a site visit of my existing office space, which I had converted into a classroom, sensory area, and some offices. Our Department of Education liaison, Clair, said it was the best and most thorough application they ever received. And just like that, I had an approved and accredited school. I still have the initial approval letter. I wish I could show it to my third-grade teacher who had called me "retarded."

It was time to again hang my shingle out, think through what this school would be like, and hire licensed teachers and clinical staff. Sitting back on my caramel-colored leather pondering chair, I had a good think. Although I had worked at the Little Red Schoolhouse, that had been for very young kids, and the focus had not been on academics. Hoping for a firestorm for ideas, I read the approval letter over and over again.

Suddenly, I jumped out of my chair, gesturing and yelling, "What was I thinking? What the hell am I, crazy? I don't know anything about starting or running an entire school. And I know nothing about academic education!"

I grabbed a pencil and paper and asked myself, *Okay, so what do I know? What do I know? What do I know? I know... nothing!* I fetched some potato chips to distract myself. *Okay, calm down. Clearly, the Department of Education saw something in my application that suggested that my school proposal had merit.*

I started scribbling down everything that I didn't find useful about my own educational experiences. I wrote feverishly, tearing through page after page. I could produce a novel on what *not* to do. "Okay, this is a start..." I declared.

I knew that our school would have a delicate balance of competitive academics and therapeutics. Maybe advanced placement academics? Maybe taking state assessments? Maybe attending college while at Ravenwood? Hey, we could have a science laboratory where we grow genetically modified corn...

Recognizing my own shortcomings and what I could realistically do, I interviewed staff to fill in the gaps. I had a lot of big ideas and needed the help of people with their feet firmly planted on the ground to implement them. I used to simply hire people that I liked, but I'd learned over the years that it's also important to hire people with specific needed skill sets.

I conducted every interview in the exact same way, regardless of what position the person was applying for. Their words meant nothing to me. Language is just a tangled jumble of noise in my head. I needed to *see* how they thought and how they made decisions when a curveball was thrown their way. I needed to be sure that they could leave their world and find their way into our students' worlds. I needed a non-verbal interview format to inform my decisions. So, I invented one.

For the interviews, I took eight-to-ten people who were applying for various positions into a large room with a twelve-foot-long gymnastics beam placed low to the ground. "Please take off your shoes, and get in a line on the balance beam," I instructed. "The goal is for everyone to switch places, so that the line is completely reversed. Also, you can't get off the beam." Without providing any other information, I then bellowed, "Go!" I carefully watched who made a plausible plan, who was giving directions, who lead and who followed, who was encouraging the team and who was inaudible. When a strategy didn't work, who created a new one? Was there anyone who came up with a novel idea? And, who actually stayed on the beam? Believe it or not, this exercise produced an excellent crop of people for my team. When speaking with our school's principal about this book project, she recalled her Ravenwood interview. It was a "*unique* hiring process," she said with a smile.

From the janitor to the chief financial officer, everyone at Ravenwood Day School had equal value in my eyes. Our admissions director, Sophia, confessed that she enjoyed working with me because I saw everyone this way. My mother had taught me that everyone has a place in this world. I knew that if I wove this fabric of equality into my organization, the staff would work cooperatively and create a sense of community that would enable us all to help the students. This attitude pervades the school to this day.

My mind thinks big. Really big. "Astronomically colossal" might be more accurate. I've always had huge ideas and never cared what others thought about them or me. This was different, though. I needed to learn to work cooperatively. I'm a great visionary, but my disabilities, at times, impact my capacity to work collectively. I've been told that I need to involve others more and listen to their opinions. Unfortunately, my autism still impacts me and can make listening to and involving others a challenge. When I have an idea, it takes me down one trajectory, and I become fixated. It's often hard to shift gears to make room for others' input. Like Sadie's hair, my idea is complete, and adding outside input—whether good, bad, or indifferent—fundamentally changes the idea. In retrospect, I will confess that many staff members have come to me over the years with their own ideas, only to be shot down if those ideas didn't fit into *my* big picture.

Additionally, when manic, I struggle to listen to others' perspectives, including how "far-reaching" my ideas might be or how unrealistic they are to implement. And, when depressed, I sometimes have trouble doing the most basic, yet necessary, components of my job. Continuously refining my social skills remains important, so I often try to reflect upon my daily interactions.

We started with just one student. Now, sixteen years later, we have eighty students between the ages of seven and twenty-two, with seventy-eight staff members. The school grew very systematically. We began by accepting just elementary students, as referrals indicated that this population had the highest demand. With my head constantly spinning with new big ideas, I wanted to immediately expand and ran these thoughts by my mother. Her words glued my feet to the ground: "Just stick with what you know."

Having years of experience with therapeutic curriculum, both through consulting and at Ravenwood Day Camp, I was comfortable in that arena and felt secure that we were all set there. However, when it came to genuine academics, I had to settle down and do my research. As enrollment began to increase, I met with several textbook distributors and started to get the lay of the land. Then, I stumbled onto the Department of Education's website, where they had actual frameworks for goals of what our students should learn each year. That was certainly helpful! Regardless, I met with our teacher, and we picked good textbooks and hands-on curriculum.

In addition to our therapeutic curriculum, we wanted to expose students to traditional and expected skills, like friendly greetings (because this is an expected norm) and how to use textbooks (because students need to learn from them, even though it can be tricky with executive dysfunction). Later in life, having these skills would serve the students well.

Like the Little Red Schoolhouse before it, Ravenwood Day School is an accredited private special education school serving students who are funded by the student's home school district. When a student is struggling in their current placement (whether socially, behaviorally, or emotionally), the student's team, which includes the district, family, and others, may decide that a private placement would better serve the student's needs. Once that determination has been made, the district sends a referral to schools like ours, and our admissions team assesses whether our school can best help a student and, equally importantly, their family.

Our team is comprised of a principal, mentor teachers/case managers, special and regular education teachers, counselors, psychologists, occupational therapists, speech-language pathologists, transition specialists, board-certified behavior analysts, a nurse, reading and math specialists; and administrative staff. This conglomeration of professionals works integratively so that curriculum overlaps, yielding generalization of skills. Like many with autism, when I was taught a skill in one location as a child, it didn't always generalize to another location, like in my previous example of not eating in the school's library. By integrating therapies with academics, all lessons become applicable in all locations and with all people.

In addition, generalization is taught for specific skills. Take the concept of joint attention. At first, during an individual therapy session, a student may learn why it's important to make eye contact and also where to look on a person's face during conversation. Later, it's expected that this learned skill will be applied throughout the day with other adults.

All students receive special services in the classroom, such as help with social skills, coping and sensory processing skills, and emotional regulation. Some students get additional individual or small-group support with these skills, as needed. Also, when the clinicians are not actively teaching, they may work side-by-side with the teachers in the classrooms to shore up individual students' skills and support generalization.

Behind the scenes, these interdisciplinary teams have countless brainstorming sessions on how to best support the students. When students have "blips," such as making derogatory remarks to peers, destroying a room, or simply emanating disruptive high-pitched squealing noises, these interdisciplinary teams come together and try to figure out why they are happening and, of equal importance, how to meet the student's need(s) so that more appropriate skills are taught or made available. Due to my own experiences, I never want a child to suffer or be misunderstood again. Creating these teams to help analyze students through multiple lenses yields a complete diagnostic and therapeutic intervention picture. Seeing the positive outcomes, I often wonder what my life would have been like if Stonyfield Psychiatric Hospital had sought to understand me in the same way.

When Ravenwood Day School first opened its doors, admissions was my responsibility. Sophia tagged along to grow into this role and would often ask, "How do you figure out the kids so quickly? It's like you find one sentence or test score buried in a report and say to me, 'This kid has spark. We can help him!' How do you know?"

My secret lies in the fact that I can relate to others who share similar struggles to mine. When I review a potential student's neuropsychological assessment, I can visualize where the wobbly wall studs are and, based upon my professional and personal experiences, create a hypothetical intervention plan. Next, I meet the student.

Like the staff interview process, our student intakes are unconventional, as well. I need to meet students by going into *their* world; after all, that's how Mr. O'Sullivan and my nana broke through to me. Our world is easy for us, but when most of our students arrive, they're not capable of fully accessing it. To ascertain if Ravenwood can help a student, it's my job to meet the student where they are. Sometimes visits occur at school and sometimes not. I've conducted interviews in the park, on a swing, in a student's bedroom, while playing videogames…whatever it takes. Honestly, I can glean information anywhere, but if I push too hard, too fast, I will lose the student's trust and creditability.

Ellis was a shy fifth grader whom I met at his home. I conducted his intake interview over discussions about *Star Wars's* Han Solo, his favorite action figure. As I scanned the room, I noticed that all of the buttons on the remote controls had been chewed off. I asked about this, and his mother explained, "He ate them." It seemed like oral motor interventions ought to be part of his plan so that his family could have their remotes back. Ellis spent about six years with our multidisciplinary team. He just completed college and, last I heard, has a girlfriend.

Today, Sophia has her own team to make these determinations. As part of the admissions process, we have the students spend several days in their proposed classroom to ascertain whether our methods will help the student flourish and if there is a strong peer match. Given my own elementary school experiences, it is paramount to me that students make genuine connections. Each classroom is a delicate balance, and we need to look at each student both individually and in a group to make an admission determination. After one trial visit, a middle schooler, Aarav, reported to his mom, "At my old school, all the other kids are yellow and I'm blue. Here, we're not the same, but we are all green!" Kids know right away.

Many students come to Ravenwood with scarce skills and challenges that range from mild to extensive. Our admissions process is designed to see which students, with the right interventions, will ultimately benefit from our programming.

Even after their interview, we try to meet students where they are. This might mean that, for the first six months, we address coping strategies, social skills, and emotional regulation before even touching a multimodal academic lesson. For us, the clock isn't ticking. What's most important is the depth of skill achieved and how permanently it is affixed. Once students have progressed past this initial stage, rigorous academics can begin. This philosophy stems from my own training with Kristen and the trio. The executive functioning skills that we started with were very, very basic, and I often spent months learning one simple skill. However, without those foundations, I never would have succeeded. Stacking skills one on top of another like a tower of blocks is only effective if the groundwork is solid. Otherwise, the skills just topple.

One student's mother once sent a note to the school, reading:

Thank you to the middle school staff for coaxing a scared child out from behind a palm tree in the lobby, and for sitting with me and Richard on the stairs for months before he was ready to enter class. Your willingness to offer counseling to a child on the floor, on the stairs, on the couches, in the parking lot...wherever he needed it, was a testament to your compassion and commitment. You helped him build confidence and quiet his anxieties every day... Thank you for building a school where students can fall down and get back up again and again and again. You demonstrate grace, teach resilience, and show dignity to children who have often not previously been blessed with those lessons...

When I read this note, I thought back to when Ravenwood was just a pipe dream. Since then, I have worked hard to ensure that all of my old, ineffectual educational and psychiatric experiences were the anthesis of what the students experience. This note from Richard's mother is evidence that I am doing my best to prevent other children from going through what I did.

Ravenwood's wheelhouse is students like me: those who are cognitively capable but often have dual diagnoses. They generally have an autism spectrum diagnosis as well as something like bipolar disorder, attention deficit/hyperactivity disorder, thought disorder, anxiety disorder, obsessive-compulsive disorder, learning disabilities, etc. Despite their varied profiles, all students share pragmatic, sensory regulation, and executive functioning challenges. These were the core deficits that I worked on with Kristen and the trio. Our guiding principle is that treating the whole student facilitates healing. Ravenwood Day School's staff chips away what is no longer necessary or effective and replaces these dysfunctional skills or behaviors with a more functional arsenal. In other words, the same approach that Kristen and the trio took with me to great success.

One of my all-time favorite students was Sal, who equally made me proud and broke my heart. To this day, I've never encountered another student who felt so much like a carbon copy of my younger self. Sal was a fifth grader with vivid blue eyes. He was adorable, brilliant, and exuberant. He had autism and a mood disorder and took frequent walking breaks, cuddling his "squishy." He arrived at Ravenwood virtually devoid of coping strategies. There was a lot of howling, collapsing, and flailing. Flopping outside my door, Sal would holler up a storm about what, to us, seemed like minuscule infractions. To him, these were monumental issues. For several months, the staff took turns sitting next to Sal, just being quiet. But then, one day, after a screaming episode, something broke through. He put his head on my shoulder. I felt like I had turned into my nana just by holding his pain. "You okay, bud?" I whispered.

"I think so," he replied in a calm voice. He pulled himself up off the ground.

"Ready to go back to class?"

"Yeah…"

His constantly shifting emotions left Sal in a storm without coping strategies. He had no ability to process the emotions and sensations he physically felt. This reminded me so much of my younger self becoming overstimulated at Stonyfield Psychiatric Hospital. I felt deeply sad for Sal. Unlike me, math was a trigger; it was hard for him. He often became frustrated, and the shift between "calm" and "exasperated" frequently caused an outburst, during which, he would scream and clutch his "squishy." To fill in Sal's missing skills, our staff carefully and systematically desensitized him to the storm of shifting emotions by engaging in activities that provoked minuscule frustrations, such as putting his "squishy" at the end of his desk, instead of in his arms. We eventually worked up to presenting new math concepts without extensive previewing.

I got this idea from working with an art therapist, Brian Kaplan, in the early 1990s. He helped systematically desensitize me to some stimuli, such as paint on my hands, which used to make me want to scream. The very texture of this substance was equivalent to nails on a chalkboard to me. We started by dipping my pinky finger in watercolors and then moved on to acrylics until my whole hands and arms was engulfed. Each stage brought on tremendous agonizing anxiety, but once I learned coping strategies, this awful stimuli simply didn't bother me any longer.

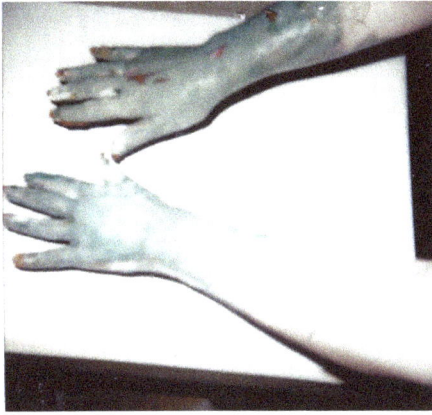

Sometimes Ravenwood Day School's students do have what some would classify as "behavior problems." I hate that word. It hits home for me, since that was a label I carried throughout my entire childhood, adolescence, and young adulthood. Moreover, it gets at the wrong issues and asks the wrong questions. Instead of "How can we correct this behavior?" we should instead be asking, "What obstacle is this student facing?"

When students struggle at Ravenwood, there are several chairs outside my office—though they're not maroon or scratchy like Josephine—where staff and students can simply sit and process what they are experiencing. Once the student is calm, a staff member often conducts a "social autopsy," helping the student understand where the situation went awry and, more importantly, identifying a better solution for the future. I thoroughly enjoy listening to staff talk with students as they suggest systems and skills. Their deliberate word choices and calming presence while discussing the incident makes me proud. After the "social autopsy," we expect increased self-regulation from the student, as evidenced by using a more controlled voice and body language. Rarely, and I mean *rarely*, do we need to "strong arm" a student, and that only occurs for dangerous behavior, such as impulsively bolting toward moving cars. When this does occur, I'm triggered and flash back to my days of being restrained, even though I know it's to keep the student safe. I have to use many learned cognitive-behavioral strategies to keep my emotions in the past where they belong.

What made all the difference in my life was custom interventions to teach absent or disordered skills, such as all of the executive functioning and social skills training I got from Kristen and the trio, and we try to replicate this at Ravenwood. We teach useful skills in a kind and humane way so that the students can successfully figure out how to negotiate roadblocks and integrate back into the world. From the start, it was important to me that Ravenwood uses an approach and philosophy in which students are viewed as having *potential* and where the staff understands that these are children who, like myself growing up, are not willfully misbehaving. Rather, they're missing important developmental skills that prevent effective functioning in the world. These kids operate in the only paradigm they know, and they function as best they can, given the cards they were dealt.

Let's not paint too rosy of a picture, though; they *are* kids. We do have the occasional inappropriate texting, pulling of the fire alarm, or graffiti in the bathroom.

Anticipating bumps in the road based upon our knowledge of the students is challenging, but never impossible. We do take categorical stereotypes and prepare interventions "just in case." Students with autism and related disorders may become dysregulated, meaning they may have a really big reaction to what should be a small event, emotion, or sensation. As a precaution, students have age-appropriate sensory breaks built into their schedules until they display not needing them. Elementary students may use things like crash pads, which are like extra-thick gym mats, indoor swings, the rock wall, or a ball pit. Our older students may walk around outside, talk with staff, or play basketball. This would have been exceptionally helpful for me as a child.

When I was growing up, my faulty sensory system would often crumble, especially when faced with transitions and changes. With such a limited imagination and poor executive functioning skills, such as divided attention, I couldn't forecast and envision what lay ahead, nor effectively cope with the anxiety that this produced. Acutely aware of this fact, I try to do as much previewing as possible for our students.

Our original school building was small, dumpy, and overcrowded. Our lease was up in 2010, so after some careful planning, I threw Ravenwood's students a curveball: we were moving! It was across the parking lot from our current school, I gave the students a year's notice, and the construction of this enormous 40,000-square-foot building took place over a period of several months. I was so excited to work with one of our talented staff members to design the space to better reflect what we were trying to teach the students. For example, in addition to external windows, there are sizeable internal windows, so students know that they are connected to the school's population at large.

To help our anxious and rigid kids, every Friday was "Hard Hat Friday." Each student received their own neon-yellow hard hat and walked around the construction site, slinking around metal columns where walls would be built. Every week, Ravenwood's administration met with contractors to get an update on their progress so that this would be safe. Charlie, one particularly anxious student, joined our meetings and took pertinent notes to share with the students, staff, and families. On move-in day, students lined up like ants, carrying their desks to their new classrooms.

During construction, I was struck by another idea to help the students adjust. It came to me during our administrator's meeting, and I suddenly burst out, "Sarah, I've got a great idea! Let's have the kids design the playground. They can vote on components, and we can put together a comprehensive whole with the winning parts!" And so, that's exactly what we did. Our playground is a paradise, with plenty of equipment to slide, spin, climb, run, and tether on. Plus, the students are proud of it. After all, it was *their* creation.

While the younger students were focused on the playground and designing cut-outs for their lockers, the older students were concentrating on their new schedules. With the new year beginning and Ravenwood Day School having access to more traditional "school-like" equipment, such as a science laboratory, a 3D printer, and a laundry room, Ravenwood stepped up its academics a bit.

For our older students, we partnered with local colleges and universities so that our students could dual-enroll at Ravenwood while also taking college courses. Although many of our students are academically proficient because these skills come naturally to them, they often lack proficiency in basic life skills, such as knowing what to do when ill, not being taken advantage of, taking medications and calling in refills, money management, cooking, laundry, self-advocating, personal hygiene, and dealing with sexuality. Therapeutic interventions in these areas round out their plates. Providing support as students move from school to adult life involves more than just academics. Taking the life skills course is paramount for success. While life skills may seem inherent, for the majority of our students, they aren't. Direct instruction and practice for generalization is the preferred approach. This is one reason why we have a mock living room, a full kitchen, laundry facilities, employment internships and job shadowing, and community outings, where we provide opportunities for learning and generalization.

In addition to academics and functional skills, all of Ravenwood's students between the ages of eighteen and twenty-two partake in internships throughout the year. Even if a student's desire is to solely focus on college, at some point, this student will join the workforce, requiring a new set of skills. Ravenwood wants to ensure that all students leave with these skills. Our students need to practice in real work environments. Not only will they gain experience, but should a challenge arise, the student can also process and learn skills for next time. If necessary, our staff can also facilitate between employer and student.

This facilitation would have been beneficial to me growing up. In eleventh grade, I got a job at the South Street Seaport on the Lower East Side of Manhattan scooping ice cream. When people asked for sprinkles, my eyes danced, as I could envision the assorted colors creating a pattern in my head. After scooping their requested flavor, I would drizzle the sprinkles over the top… and then, dig my hand into their ice cream and adjust each individual sprinkle so that it mimicked the pattern in my head. I couldn't fathom why the customers took offense at my handling their ice cream; in my mind, I was improving the outcome. After several reprimands from my boss without changing my ways, I was fired. Having job coaches is an important component of a good program for students with autism.

Ravenwood has welcomed numerous students through its doors over the years, each with a unique and interesting tale. Sal gained a plethora of skills and aptitudes while at Ravenwood. Eventually, he was ready to return to his public high school, where he thrived and received his diploma. When he departed our school, Sal was our commencement speaker. The second he began, muffled tears ran down my face.

"The progress I have made over the years has been nothing less than tremendous," he said. "I have been taught how to better navigate this world socially and emotionally, discover my academic potential, and embrace my unique gifts. Along with my family, we will be forever grateful to Ravenwood for giving me a place to heal, grow, and realize that being *me* is very special!" He continued, "And now, it is time to move on to a new chapter in my life, and with me, I will bring a treasure trove of wonderful memories, renewed self-confidence, and a whole bagful of coping strategies. This Square Peg is more than ready to rock the Round Holes! Who would have dreamed that this little ten-year-old boy who walked through those doors carrying a stuffed animal and a broken spirit would exit five years later a healthy, happy, and confident teenager!"

I'm eternity grateful for the opportunity to get to know Sal. He inspired me to never give up and reaffirmed exactly why I wanted to open a school for brave students like him.

CHAPTER 11

THE TIES THAT BIND US

IT IS A misapprehension that people with autism or mental illness can't form meaningful romantic relationships or have sexual desires. In fact, mania often results in increased social and sexual cravings. Personally, I know many people diagnosed with autism (and some who *should* have a diagnosis) that date and marry.

As with any kind of relationship, there are added complications when things like autism or bipolar disorder hitch a ride, but these relationships can absolutely still be viable. In my own relationships, prior to learning perspective-taking, there were no equitable "workarounds" for the non-affected person. My relationships always rested on whatever state I was in mentally, sensorially, or socially. Unfortunately, when experiencing symptoms of bipolar disorder, this continues today.

Shortly before Kristen and I became business partners, we also fell in love. Eventually, we married. In retrospect, I realize that I idolized Kristen; she always protected me. She was enmeshed in the autism field and had a great deal of knowledge about the disorder, which helped our relationship. She understood that my quirky needs were not of my own volition; they were not requests, but rather, must-haves. She "got" me.

Socially, she was my periscope. When an autism symptom arose, such as missing a cue at a family party or becoming overstimulated while visiting neighbors, Kristen always guided me to a safer space and created an excuse for me to depart or explain away my social faux pas by kindly jumping in and saying, "What she means is..." For me, being socially overstimulated brings about anxiety. People's faces contort faster than I can process, words jumble, and I quake inside. When manic, instead of internalizing these symptoms, I often externalize them by becoming slightly angry, interrupting others, trying to control the conversation, or simply being rude. While I've tried to eliminate them for many years, these reactions are not in my control. I can't talk sense into myself. It's not a choice mania makes.

I still use the "one hundred sensory points a day rule" that I started in junior high, which often doesn't leave much room for sexual relations. In adulthood, with my extra responsibilities, my points are gobbled up rather quickly. At night, instead of cuddling with my wife, I frequently needed space. When severely overdrawn on my sensory budget, I feel like a thousand ants are crawling across my skin. Whenever this happened, Kristen kindly used the Wilbarger brushing protocol for sensory integration, which involves scrubbing my skin with a small special surgical brush to shoo away the overwhelming screaming itch. Once the brushing ritual was complete, I would wrap myself up like a mummy in my soft white Egyptian cotton blanket, sink into bed, and close my eyes for the night.

To be honest, for me, it's not my autism that roadblocks romantic relationships. Those quandaries can be solved. It's the bipolar disorder that implodes connections. When depression descends, in my mind, every flaw in my body is magnified. I'm ugly and unlovable. That tiny pimple on my left cheek encompasses my whole face, as if I'm sixteen again. Any overture of kindness from others is interpreted as pity. I have no desire for intimacy. My one hundred sensory points are devoured as depression suffocates me. While my partners felt helpless at such times, for me, depression symptoms have always been much more manageable than mania.

Mania feels like a golden light that shines on me through a rainstorm. I'm alive, very alive, despite what social cues around me are attempting to convey. Throughout my body, I can feel my blood rushing. I crave intimacy. My sexual antenna is raised, and while I never physically cheated on my wife, I did have several emotionally intimate relationships that would have been impossible in a non-manic state. Ever since my bipolar disorder blew in around age ten, when a manic episode occurs, my one hundred sensory points multiply to infinity. When mania's biological shift occurs, there is no sensory point ceiling, and to this day, I can't explain why.

Despite my disabilities, I managed to have a few romantic partners in my life. First, there was Ethan, whom I wholeheartedly believe could have been the love of my life if I were straight and consistently medicated and if we had more honest dialogues about imposing my expectations on him. But above all, we would have needed to address how my bipolar disorder left him serving as an emotional janitor, constantly cleaning up my messes. This is a tall order, but we might have had a shot as a lasting couple.

When Ethan broke up with me during my freshman year of college, I thought relationships were only for other people. But then, something magical happened. At Conway Community Hospital, a year or so before I left, I met the most beautiful girl I'd ever laid eyes on—except, of course, Francesca. Kate was about thirty years old, five-foot-six, and thin, with a straight, ash-blonde bob that slightly curled under her chin. And, long before it was commonplace, she wore a tiny, sexy diamond stud in her nose. "Soft," "delicate," and "graceful" are adjectives I would use to describe Kate. In all the years I spent at Conway Community Hospital, I never encountered a fellow patient who set my heart aflutter the way Francesca had. Until now.

I was smitten with her, which increased my social desire and skills. Kate and I became fast friends. Having now been in several different institutions, I was becoming an expert on them, and I saw the same kinds of phenomena occur over and over again. People who would *never* mingle on the "outside" become fast friends on the "inside."

In all six hospitals I'd been in, the patients were kind and forgiving, regardless of my behavior or verbal outbursts. Kate was no exception. Her social skills *far* exceeded mine, and she was ultra-tolerant of my bipolar disorder. One day, feeling blue, I lay on my bed, snuggled under the covers and struggling to move. She entered. Wordless, she sat on my bed, gently lifted my head into her lap, and stroked my hair, just like my nana had. While depression prevailed, I felt nurtured.

Our friendship endured through my depressions and manias. Back then, except for the art room and an occasional group therapy session, there was little to do on most psychiatric wards, despite what the brochures said. Kate and I spent hours talking about everything. No topic was off-limits. I learned all about her post-traumatic stress disorder from her mother dying when she was five and her brother raping her. While I had a very different story, I could relate to some of the stressors in her life. Conversation came naturally. As Jerry Seinfeld said, "There were no awkward pauses." She was brutally honest when I made a social blunder, and I appreciated her truthfulness.

After I had not exhibited a sensory outburst in forty-three days (a record), Kate and I both filled out requests for day passes, which were granted. I wasn't depressed, but slightly manic and, as always, a little autistic.

It was January in Pennsylvania when we decided to drive my car to Philadelphia, the closest large city with shops and restaurants, which was about thirty minutes away. While driving south on Interstate 476, we hit a huge "Nor'easter" snowstorm. My car slid into the median and sank in the snow. Our doors were wedged against the packed snow, and we were trapped! For a moment, we sat there, pensively contemplating our fate. Then, we both came to the same conclusion at the same time: climb out of the sunroof!

Fortunately, the police were patrolling the dangerous roads, and one came by mere minutes later. Kate and I were waving and yelling "Help!" from the roof, so it wasn't hard to miss us.

"What are you doing out in this storm?" the police officer bellowed brusquely.

"We're just on our way to Philly," Kate said.

"Not tonight. Road's closed." He pulled us off the top of my car, adding, "Get in my car, and I'll take you to the Holiday Inn." Soon, we sped off in the back of the police car, sirens blaring.

Fortunately, I had a credit card that my parents had given me in case of emergencies and for gas. *I'm pretty sure this counts as an emergency*, I thought to myself as we checked in. The counter clerk informed us that they had only one room left and that it had a single king-size bed. Pushing my credit card toward her, I said exuberantly, "We'll take it!"

The hotel had an indoor heated pool, and Kate and I had plenty of time to kill. After letting the hospital know about our adventure, we turned our attention to the pool. Since we didn't have bathing suits, we decided to take off our pants and swim in our shirts and under-wear. Alone in the pool, we were having a blast splashing each other when suddenly, Kate approached me and kissed me on the mouth.

I already knew that Kate was a lesbian, but I had no idea that she was interested in *me*. I had always felt the sexual tension between us but never brought it up, let alone imagined it would come to fruition.

Kate's lips were soft and sweet, very different from Ethan's. It was the only thing I had to compare to. *Does she like me?* I wondered. *What should I do now?* I was confused and didn't know what the protocol was, so I decided to kiss her back. This was the longest and most tender kiss that I've ever experienced, even to this day.

We went back up to our room and shucked off our wet clothes. Kate took the lead, and we made love. This was my first experience with lesbianism.

While Kate and I only shared that one night, I fell in love with her right then and still think fondly of our time together. Kate left Conway Community Hospital shortly after this event, and I left a little over a year after her. Once she left, we lost touch, but I elect to remember the good times and our one night together. I was happy that she made it out of the institution.

In the spring of 1994, after my depression and frustration with my institutional life led me to take that frightful drive with the gasoline jug, after I saw the Boston Common on TV, after I impulsively left Conway Community Hospital and headed to Boston, I met Kristen, my now ex-wife. In honor of Kristen's privacy, I'll only disclose the information that is relevant to my story.

I met Kristen after speaking at the parents' support group. I was twenty-four years old at the time. She and I spent countless hours together both in and out of school. She always had flawless social skills, and she constantly pulled me into conversations. *Always.*

As the years progressed, we grew closer and began vacationing together. Kristen appeared to be straight, and it never even occurred to me that she might be gay or bisexual. So far as I was concerned, we were just best friends. Then, when I was twenty-seven, we drove to Ogunquit, Maine, to see a concert together. I was slightly manic and ingested far, far, *far* too much alcohol at the concert. Alcohol and mania don't mix well, as both decrease inhibitions. I'm not sure why, but I made advances on Kristen that night, just like Kate had with me. We became a couple that night and married seven years later in 2004, when it became legal. We were together for seventeen years in total.

While the first half of our marriage was enjoyable, the second half was harrowing at best. Like many couples, what we wanted out of our lives changed, and we grew apart over time. Once my severe bipolar episodes returned, I could no longer hide that diagnosis. The cat was out of the bag. After that, things went downhill fast.

Throughout it all, I missed Kate terribly. Not only had we shared a physical interaction, but we were also emotionally wed. With Kristen, I never felt the way I had with Kate, Francesca, or even Ethan. We were simply not deeply connected emotionally, though we did enjoy the same activities and share a close comradery. All during our friendship and marriage, Kristen and I never spoke of our emotional lives. I had been more emotionally intimate with Francesca, so I knew what I was missing. Sometimes I wondered, *If I had kissed Francesca, would we have ended up together? What would kissing her have felt like?* I was confused about loving Kristen, Ethan, Kate, and Francesca.

Comparing my sexual and emotional experiences with Ethan,

Kate, Kristen, and let's just throw in Francesca, the trophy went to "Team Lesbian." I had truly loved Ethan with all my heart, but sexually, I wasn't in love with him. After Kristen and I got together in 1997, I came out to my parents. Their response was rather muted. Neither cared what my sexual orientation was. Frankly, they were just happy that I wasn't hospitalized and was holding down a job!

Kristen's parents, on the other hand, didn't take it as well. A year before it was legal for us to marry, Kristen officially came out to them. One day, we drove to her parents' quaint bedroom-community townhouse on the Cape, where her father enthusiastically met us in the driveway. Prior to this day, I'd had a wonderful relationship with Arthur and Lois. They thought Kristen and I were just good friends.

"Hey, girls! How are you today?" Arthur asked as he hugged and kissed us in greeting.

"We're great, Dad," Kristen said nervously. "We have something we wanted to talk with you and mom about."

"Come on in. She made your favorite cookies–the meringue ones you like so much."

Unlike my parents, who were very fashion-conscious, Studio 54 disco goers, Kristen's parents were more the calm, gentle, and sweet *Leave it to Beaver* types. I say this with absolutely no judgment. Her parents are wonderful, just very different from mine.

Kristen was so anxious about this conversation that as soon as we walked in, she just blurted it out, "Mom, Dad, I'm gay, and Alex is my partner."

She was met with dead silence. I didn't know where to look. Then, Lois sank down into her chair. Her only words were, "Arthur, get me a drink."

For many years, Kristen's fateful announcement drove a wedge between her and her family. Fortunately, that eventually lifted.

On May 17, 2004, four years after we had moved from our cramped Cambridge apartment to a tight-knit suburban neighborhood, same-sex marriage was legalized in Massachusetts. There was a big party at town hall. While it wasn't our intention to get married that day, Kristen and I got caught up in the hubbub and decided to marry that very hour on the town green. We ran back home, hollering to some of our neighbors, and I changed my clothes. After all, I was wearing worn shorts and a t-shirt. Following the ceremony, our friend Steve took our neighbors who had joined us to the town hall's dingy café, where he paid for everyone's lunch. "Look, I paid for the reception!" he exclaimed. We all laughed.

As the months passed, while the excitement of being married continued, it was clear that everything was not okay between us. Kristen persistently compensated for my autism symptoms, and I was barely getting by with just Valium and several high-dose supplements. I had long-since gone off of Lithium and Thorazine. Inside, I knew that something was wrong.

For some reason, my mood swings had been significantly quieter over the past few years. Instead of full-blown crazy, I was eccentric, yet functional. I even questioned if I had somehow shed my bipolar diagnosis. I was open about my autism diagnosis—I wore it proudly like a Girl Scout merit badge—but kept my bipolar diagnosis a secret, even to Kristen. I was petrified that she would reject me if she knew.

I had spent years learning how to conceal depression, suicidal feelings, hypomania, and hallucinations. I wasn't able to hide a full-blown manic/psychotic episode, but fortunately, I hadn't experienced one in years. Nevertheless, I honestly don't know what Kristen thought was wrong with me. She knew I had autism, but clearly, there was something more. I had been psychiatrically hospitalized three times since I first met her, and I *was* taking medication until a few years before we moved to the suburbs. Though she never probed about the reasons behind my hospitalizations and medications, I genuinely don't know if I would have been honest with her.

Despite my minor mood instability, we were now living in a lovely suburban community, and my next fixation was on having a baby. Getting pregnant while in a rocky relationship was like slowly sinking in quicksand. Theoretically, we were all set. We had a nice house in a good neighborhood, and Ravenwood was well established, yielding a steady source of income. Yet every time I uttered the word, "pregnancy," Kristen shut down the conversation. Thanks to my autism training, I knew that she didn't want to talk about this, but I was half of this relationship, and I did.

The topic oscillated without direction, and I despise ambiguity. Several months after I initially brought up my desire to have a baby, we were dining in downtown Boston when I'd finally had enough. I needed to let her know exactly where I stood on the matter. "Having a baby is a deal-breaker for me," I said with conviction.

"I have no interest in being pregnant," Kristen shot back.

"God, that's easy, then, because I very much want to be pregnant," I said, grinning with relief. Of course, I hadn't given any thought to how pregnancy would impact my mood.

Our table fell silent, which only seemed to amplify the chatter around us.

Somberly, Kristen said, "No. I don't want *you* to carry the baby. I don't want our child to have autism."

"Oh." Dejected, this was all I could muster. Her rationale had never even occurred to me. I was crushed. I moved the food around on my plate.

As we drove home, the tension was palpable.

Wrapped in my cocoon that night, I lay awake, thinking about how I could acquire a baby. I whispered to myself, "I'm a warrior! I've had to be! I can figure this out!" Then, lightning struck.

A few days later, I presented Kristen with my ideas. Reluctantly, she listened.

"We could adopt. My mother is adopted, and she turned out fine, but we wouldn't have control over prenatal care. Additionally, adoptions from other countries are often closed to gay and lesbian couples. Or…" I trailed off.

"I'm listening."

Brimming with excitement, I spoke quickly as I threw out my second idea: "Oh, this one is good! Okay, I have another option. It's a little out there. Creditable, but farfetched. If we were to have a baby the gay old fashioned way, we would need a sperm donor, right? What if we used *both* a sperm donor and an egg donor? Basically, the lab at Brigham and Women's Hospital mixes the two and creates the embryos. The embryos are then injected into my uterus, and bam! We have a baby! There is no chance of autism. Genetically, they're not mine. What do you think?"

Kristen didn't believe that this was actually possible, so I scheduled an appointment with Dr. Garcia from the fertility clinic at Brigham and Women's Hospital, who confirmed my hypothesis. We walked away confident that it would be improbable for our baby to have autism. We started the process.

In a frenzied state, I scoured the internet for egg and sperm donors. Sperm donors were plentiful, and there were even a few online banks that sold sperm cheap. Really cheap! We sifted through hundreds of donors' profiles, which included baby photos, personal history, attributes, hobbies, sound clips, and much, much more. We opted to pass on donors who might have autistic traits, such as those who preferred non-team activities, such as tennis, chess, or skiing, or those with highly intense careers, such as engineering or mathematicians. Of course, I know plenty of people who ski that are not autistic, but we were anxious about the whole process and simply thought we were being careful. Ironically, Kristen and I picked the same sperm donor: a cute guy with a clean social and medical history.

Finding the perfect egg donor, on the other hand, was an arduous task. Egg brokers were rare, and those we did find charged vast fees. Plus, we would have to go through an attorney.

Arriving at the attorney's office, we were ushered into a magnificent room with reflective gleaming hardwood floors, deep wainscoting, big plush leather chairs, and bright colossal windows, which looked freshly Windex-ed. It even smelled clean. Dan, the attorney, enthusiastically handed us two leather-bound books, each page containing the profile and an adult photograph of the anonymous donor. There were roughly fifty to choose from. The information provided was similar to what the sperm banks had offered. The main difference was that this was much easier to narrow down.

Some pictures had war-torn backdrops. Some women had unusual physical genetic mutations. Some just seemed, well, not upfront, such as the young woman who proclaimed, "I want to donate so I will be in good graces with God!" Amongst the rubble, we found our girl! She seemed entirely ordinary, was average-looking, and was majoring in finance. She ticked off all of our "doesn't have autism" boxes. Plus, her reason for wanting to donate was that she and her fiancé were both students at Brandeis University and needed the money. This felt honest. It would do.

Before Dr. Garcia could implant the embryos, we had to synchronize my hormones with the egg donor's. Going into this, I had no idea how these hormone manipulations would affect my body and my moods. I quickly discovered that the answer was "negatively." Both my bipolar and autism symptoms were amplified. Without the psychiatric medications I had long-since given up, I was an utter mess.

Each increased hormone injection and estradiol patch caused new symptoms to blossom. Some caused depression and despondency. Others perked up my mania, resulting in a lack of sleep and frenetic behavior. During one manic episode, I rewrote Ravenwood's human resource manual in one night, never even checking to see if my new policies were legal. I emailed it to my employees and expected them to follow the new policies immediately. I missed meetings due to excessive shopping, including setting up a lavish Pottery Barn boy's nursery when I wasn't even pregnant yet. Grand delusional ideas emerged. I love photography, and now, I was convinced that I was a famous photographer. As part of this delusion, I purchased an immense number of cameras, lenses, studio lighting, and equipment. This was the start of my draining our joint bank and retirement accounts.

Then, I fell from my mania, and depression crept in, usurping my world. I was encased in despair and spent days sitting on the couch crying about *nothing* for nine hours straight. I couldn't fathom why not brushing my teeth or showering and wearing the same clothes for days on end might indicate a problem. If it weren't for the fact that I owned Ravenwood and made my own schedule, I would have been fired.

Realizing what a toll this was taking on me, Kristen put a comforting hand on my shoulder one day and quietly said, "Al, it's okay if you want to stop."

Agitated, I exclaimed, "Not a chance!"

While my mind was cluttered and in disarray, this project was moving full steam ahead. "You can't," "You won't," "Not with your diagnoses" was not going to win.

I endured several cycles of various hormones and implantations. Every two months or so after an implantation, I broke out a pregnancy test, only to feel dispirited when it yielded negative results. After a year of trying, I finally saw the "+" sign that I had been longing for; I was pregnant. We were overjoyed.

On my birthday, our embryo was about five weeks old and due for its first ultrasound. The young technician squirted warm jelly on a wand and inserted it into me. At this age, the embryo is so small that it's impossible to see through the stomach. In a monotone voice, he explained where the tiny placenta and embryo were but noted that he could not hear or see a heartbeat, which should be present by now. "My condolences," he said matter-of-factly. I tried to hold back my tears but sobbed as my heart broke.

Then, an older gentleman with a thick graying mustache ushered in. "Do you mind if I take a look?" he asked. Again, there was the warm jelly and the wand. He saw the same thing the younger technician had.

As he was about to remove the wand, I looked at the ultrasound monitor to say goodbye when we all heard a noise. A swishing noise. Over and over. It didn't stop. Both technicians, Kristen, and I watched as the grain of rice on the screen started to pulsate. The embryo was alive! We literally saw the first moment my baby's heart started beating. It's a memory I will always treasure.

Once the baby was far enough along, we ended my fertility

medications. I was relieved that the psychiatric and inflated autism symptoms that had hitched a ride ended with them.

Sperm is cheap. Eggs are not! We purchased four extra cycles of sperm on the off chance that we would want more kids in the future. When we decided that we did, the egg donor graciously agreed to donate again. Kristen and I ended up with two stupendous children who are genetic siblings and exactly two years and two weeks apart.

Being pregnant was transformative. It was refreshing when compared to the horrible experience of being on fertility treatments. I felt exhilarated with my new identity; I was going to be a mom. I was looking forward to getting to know my baby's personality and preferences. There was so much that I didn't know, I didn't know, but I was excited to learn it all.

After reading countless books and talking with other pregnant people, I found that we shared the same feelings. For so long, I had just wanted to be normal. And now, I was. This was the first time in my entire life when I related to someone just because we shared a common situation. My life had always been complicated and centered around autism and bipolar disorder, which had pervaded my every experience. Being pregnant was different.

In attending prenatal classes and talking with folks in the ob-gyn's office, I was constantly surprised by the "I'm experiencing that, too" responses. We shared tips and tricks. Several of us in the expectant mother birthing class were still nauseated from heartburn, and Ellen, another expectant mother in the class, handed out saltines like combat rations. My unborn child was already loved, just like everyone else's in the room. I felt a connection, even if briefly, and I experienced what it was like to be normal. I just *knew* what to say and feel. There was no mystery. No translation manual required.

By the sixteen-week mark of my first pregnancy and with the remnants of a manic episode bubbling inside me, I was still convinced that my baby was a boy, as I had decorated the nursery in blue, green, and yellow tones with a full blue wardrobe before I was even pregnant. I was correct. I *had* to be correct. It wasn't because I had my tarot cards read, or I hung beads over my stomach, or I was carrying low, or the baby's heart rate was below 140 beats per minute, or I ate potato chips every day. It was simply because, as always, I had great tenacity and just thought I was right. I was simply confirming what I already knew by having a "waste of time" gender-reveal ultrasound. Kristen was more open-minded and thoughtful and brought two adorable outfits that she bought, one pink and one blue, to the ultrasound.

After a few quick measurements confirming that my son was healthy, the ultrasound technician noted with a smile, "Three lines. It's a girl."

"A girl? A girl?" I gasped in the direction of my stomach. "I thought you were a boy! How did that happen?" I was miffed about being wrong.

"See? You're not always right," Kristen teased. "And now, you have a new project: to redo the nursery and buy new clothes!"

"A girl?" I repeated in confusion. I couldn't believe that my son was actually a daughter. Kristen brought the pink outfit over to me, and as I hugged it, I smiled hugely. "A girl!" I was confused, but also thrilled, excited, and elated. I was having a girl. I grinned.

Walking to the parking lot, Kristen was bursting with excitement. Her words flew out at turbo-speed. I tried to be a good listener, but I couldn't focus. I was intimidated by the idea of having a "stereotypical girl," and images of dolls, tea parties, dress-up, and imaginative play danced through my brain. I could picture myself throwing a ball to my son or playing with Matchbox cars—things I was proficient with. But the kind of imaginative play that I had often observed girls being drawn to? That seemed like a bridge too far. Perhaps this is why I just assumed I was having a boy. *When my daughter wants to imagine that her pink stuffed bear is an astronaut, will I be able to play along? Will she reject my narrow slate of learned play skills?* Based on the work I had done with Kristen and the trio, I certainly had some imaginary play skills, but I was not engrossed by them. I hid my agony, not wanting to ruin Kristen's moment of excitement at the prospect of having a neurotypical daughter.

On the ride home, I thought I would vomit. My mind darted from one thought to another: *What if her social skills are better than mine? How am I going to help her? How will she help me? What will I do when she asks me to engage in imaginary play? What happens when she wants me to tell her a made-up story?* My great tenacity shriveled up as my glorified impressions of and confidence in motherhood collapsed. All of a sudden, I didn't feel so normal anymore. While I was now far from diagnosable with autism, there was still some residue of symptoms.

After a short stint in the dumps, I could hear my mother's voice insisting, "Put on your big girl panties. There's no time or room for wallowing in pity!" And so, that's exactly what I did. I had a new quest. How did I climb out of autism? I studied. With my daughter, I would need to study harder and learn to play better.

And there were indeed many tea parties in my future. I must confess that pretend play is still not my favorite activity, but I now have the skill under my belt.

After coming to terms with my shortfall(s), as the months passed, I grew completely attached to and smitten with the idea of having a daughter. And, I loved the new nursery!

CHAPTER 12

AWE

ON A CRISP, stunning, New England fall morning, Amelia was born weighing nine pounds and thirteen ounces. She had lush, dense black hair, deep brown eyes, and porcelain white skin. She was an amazing and unbelievably tranquil baby; she is a gift.

Before her birth, I researched numerous parenting styles and realized that each philosophy generally yielded the same results. Everyone needs a style and belief system that works for their family, and none is wrong. We chose attachment parenting, as that seemed most closely aligned with our values. The idea behind attachment parenting is that forming a close bond with their baby helps parents intuitively understand their child's needs. Baby and parents set the stage for healthy bonding, which develops over the course of the child's life. We picked the parts of attachment parenting that just felt right to us, such as co-sleeping, not letting the baby "cry it out," engaging in skin-to-skin contact, wearing the baby throughout the day, and breastfeeding on demand.

Amelia responded beautifully.

One raw, cold winter morning, Kristen and I headed out to do some errands. Amelia was three months old and bundled up in her thick light-pink infant snowsuit. We secured her into her bucket seat in the back of the car, and I sat beside her, just in case she needed anything, such as to nurse. (Perhaps I took this attachment parenting a tad too literally!) Kristen was driving down the road when, quite suddenly, Amelia began screaming uncontrollably. Her face turned chili red, which made my heart race.

"Pull over. Pull over now!" I demanded.

"What's wrong?" Kristen asked, her voice trembling.

"I don't know. Something's wrong with Amelia."

Kristen pulled over, and we undressed her. Her shade quickly returned to normal as she calmed.

This "redness" and screaming occurred occasionally over the next three years. Her symptoms were vague and didn't seem to alarm the pediatrician. Not knowing what to do, we often left her coat unzipped or at home, as that seemed to help.

Amelia exhibited other strange attributes as time passed, such as frequent dehydration, some requiring emergency department or inpatient visits with multiple IVs rushing fluids into her veins. During one emergency room visit, I lay beside her trying to count the drips, but they were too fast. Another time, when she was a toddler, I listened to every audible blip on the heart monitor. My exhaled breath echoed in my ears as I knew that for that one, single second, she was alright.

What's wrong? I always wondered.

Eventually, the doctors would release her, confirming that she was "back to normal." When we pressed for more answers, the doctors always simply replied, "There's no further need for treatment." We never got any answers.

But there were other concerns, too. Amelia's gross motor skills, such as crawling, standing, and walking, were delayed; she struggled with stamina; and she slept a lot. And I do mean, *a lot*. However, she was a lovely, happy, and engaged baby and toddler who literally started talking at four months!

Nevertheless, her symptoms troubled me. Presuming that something was wrong, we sought out expert opinions, all of which ended with, "She's just fine… You're overreacting… Babies get sick… Don't worry." Each time, I went on my way without ever learning the etiology. I'm not a pediatrician, and she was my first kid, so I wasn't going to doubt them. I started distrusting my own instincts. And all the while, her symptoms continued.

Focusing on Amelia, we turned our house into a kid's paradise and enjoyed every one of her waking minutes, even if they were sparse. I felt so fortunate to have sentence-long exchanges with my nine-month-old.

Ravenwood was my baby as well, so to nurture them both, I set up a nursery next to my office, which would house a nanny. Kelly was a bombshell-gorgeous twenty-something girl with straight blonde hair and a figure we were all jealous of. She *instantly* took to Amelia, and they were soon like two peas in a pod. Between acting as a "social re-inforcement" for the students to play with, Amelia's lengthy naps, and the adventures they went on to places such as the Children's Museum, the swimming pool, and playgrounds, they had a full schedule every day. Kelly stayed with us for several years, and she and Amelia got along swimmingly.

Kristen and I both wanted to have more children. When I was growing up, I didn't feel like I was missing out by not having siblings, cousins, or aunts and uncles, but as my parents got older, I realized that it would be nice to have a sister or brother.

Carson was born two years after Amelia following an unremark-able pregnancy and delivery. He had a gorgeous head of light-brown hair and chestnut eyes. Weighing in at nine pounds and nine ounces, he was plump and delicious, and from day one, we nicknamed him "the meatball." Amelia was ecstatic to have a sibling, and when she came to visit us in the hospital, she toddled down the hospital cor-ridors bellowing, "He my broad-der, Car-kon." I imagined the kids playing together, trick-or-treating, and, of course, having the occa-sional spat. We used the same parenting methods we had employed with Amelia, given their success.

Motherhood agreed with me. I experienced such a heartfelt bond with both of my children. I intuitively knew them, which is something my autism had never really permitted with others. Our connection was beyond my comprehension. When they nursed, my body relaxed and melted into theirs. We were one.

A few weeks after Carson's birth, lightning struck. This soft, quiet infant began emanating blood-curdling screams. Constantly. My life changed in twenty-four hours. Day after day, it was relentless. I felt helpless. Unlike Amelia, his screams didn't appear to be due to over-heating, so what was the cause?

Trying to take care of Amelia, Carson, and my company (while *not* manic) started pushing me over the edge. Kelly was great taking Amelia out to give her a break, but she couldn't be there all the time. I didn't know whom to attend to first. I didn't sleep or eat; I just held him. It was the only thing I knew to do. If I were manic, the lack of sleep wouldn't have affected me. But I wasn't. And it did. Taking him to the pediatrician (again) was useless. With his crimson-sealed Harvard diploma mounted on his wall, Dr. Elbert dismissively said, "It's just colic. Don't worry. It will pass."

The frenzied screeching continued for what felt like an eternity. I eventually grew impervious to the emotional waterfall. We persisted with visiting Dr. Elbert, who found multiple ear infections, rashes, etc. and gave us lots of prescriptions for creams and antibiotics. He always assured us that the screaming would soon stop. It never did. Unfortunately, life had to go on.

Out of groceries one day, I made a pilgrimage to Whole Foods with Carson, who was, as usual, wailing. In the international foods aisle, my shopping cart was overflowing with items, and I accidentally bumped into a heavyset middle-aged woman with curly fiery red hair, bright pink lipstick, and an excess skin tumbling out of her shirt. Her head slowly revolved around toward me, she gave me an appraising up-and-down glare, and then, she turned her attention toward Carson. Furrowing her brow, she wagged her finger at me and muttered, "Tisk tisk!"

I lost it.

I felt like Linda Blair in *The Exorcist*. A sleep deprived, nasty, vile scream came from the pit of my stomach. "Go to hell!" I shouted. "It's not my first kid, you know!" With that, I turned and ran out the doors, leaving my full cart behind. I hadn't lost my cool like that since being institutionalized, and while this was certainly justified, it scared me. What if my bipolar disorder were coming back?

I sat in my car, alternating between crying and hitting the steering wheel, for about half an hour before I regained my composure. Something was wrong, something no one had found yet. This could not be normal. I called the pediatrician again, and we drove right over.

I was pleasantly surprised to find that Dr. Elbert was not there and that we would be seeing someone else. After a thorough exam, this doctor determined that Carson was bleeding rectally, which was generally caused by food allergies. Fortunately, she connected us with a fantastic allergist who figured out Carson's allergy profile and created a strategic plan for what he—and I, since I was breastfeeding him—needed to remove from our diets. This included things like corn, soybeans, milk, peanuts, tree nuts, eggs, sesame, sunflower, tomatoes, oatmeal, rice, tuna, orange, chocolate, and many more! For months, it felt like I ate nothing. However, the effort was worth it; the screaming markedly decreased.

By the time he was a year old, while the screaming had diminished, it hadn't completely disappeared. And we were growing increasingly concerned about other things. Carson wasn't meeting any of his developmental milestones and, unlike Amelia, did not exhibit "normal" social behavior.

For example, one day, there was a committee meeting at Amelia's preschool to plan the fundraising bake sale. The three adults on the committee, Amy, Karen, and me, all brought along our younger children, who were about the same age. The meeting was often disrupted by these children trying to claim their mother's attention or expressing their needs. The other little boy, Nicholas, would frequently tumble into his mother's legs or raise his hands above his head and giggle while verbalizing, "Uh, uh," asking to be picked up. Carson, on the other hand, sat in the corner, flipped a plastic dump truck over, brought his eyes mere inches from the thick rubber wheels, and spun them for forty-five minutes straight. He was entranced, never exploring or looking elsewhere. The other mothers were impressed and remarked what a good boy he was. I smiled politely, but inside, I was frightened. I knew that the striking contrast between Carson's behavior and that of his peers meant something may be wrong. However, the pain of what this could be permitted me to only entertain flashes of these thoughts.

By twelve months, Carson didn't babble, had limited eye contact, didn't smile, didn't respond to his name, didn't show any interest in playing with toys or people, and didn't seem to know who I was, although I breastfed him *on-demand* twenty-four hours a day. I was a tad bit insulted by that last point. Our home vibrated with tension. Kristen and I never uttered the words aloud, but we knew what was wrong. I felt so deeply responsible for Carson's symptoms, as if I had control over them. *Was it that glass of wine I had during the Fourth of July BBQ?* I wondered. *Or when I tripped and fell in the park? Or was it the mercury from the tuna I craved and indulged in every day at lunch? Or, worst of all, had my genes somehow influenced him?* When we had Carson, the rules changed.

Kelly continued to "hang out" with Amelia when she wasn't in preschool, and I initially expected her to take care of Carson as well. But eventually, it became clear that this was too much for her. Kelly confided that she couldn't effectively nanny both children. After our somber conversation, I knew that I needed to find a workaround. For the time being, I would take Carson to work with me.

The first day I walked in with him in tow, he was screaming. One of our generally collected students peered into my office and yelled, "Can't you shut him the fuck up?" I sniveled in my office for hours. I wish I knew how.

Kristen and I discussed this problem that night and adjusted our finances. It wasn't feasible or fair to take care of only one child's needs, so we hired a second nanny to take care of Carson. Bernadette, or "Bernie," as she liked to be called, was about six feet tall and fifty years old. She looked like a drill sergeant in her combat boots and fatigues, and she sported broad shoulders and a military haircut. Upon meeting, she immediately took Carson from me and rocked him (pretty hard) while striking him on the back (also pretty hard). He immediately stopped crying and seemed happy for the first time in months. While I was skeptical of these methods, she had one up on me there. She was hired!

After working with Carson for just a few days, she apathetically commented one day, "It's weird that he doesn't seem to prefer you over a stranger." This, of course, made me feel like crap. However, she was right. In many ways, Carson was like a stranger to us.

One May afternoon, both kids were sitting in the living room. Carson, who just finished his twelfth course of antibiotics for ear infections, was spinning the propeller of a toy helicopter over and over again, and Amelia playing with musical instruments. Trying to engage her brother, my daughter came up behind him and blew a high-pitched, ear-piercing police whistle right in his ear. I cringed at the noise, even from across the room. Carson never even flinched. I told her to do it again. Same reaction. And again. Nothing. I ran into the kitchen, grabbed some pots and pans, and started banging them together behind his head as hard as I could. He never once responded to the noise.

Straightaway, we met with an otolaryngologist at Massachusetts Eye and Ear Hospital who tested Carson's hearing and recommended PE tubes, which would continuously drain the fluid buildup in his middle ear, helping him hear. It's a routine surgery, so we agreed. After the procedure, as we stepped outside the hospital's doors, he immediately oriented his gaze toward sounds such as honking horns, sirens, and a loud construction project across the street. Carson now *could* hear. Yet, as I nursed him later that evening, he still didn't gaze in my eyes.

My mother flew up for Carson's procedure and stayed to visit for a few days. While she was with us, I confessed my concerns: "Mom, I'm worried about Carson. He doesn't orient to faces, has no initiation of joint attention, and doesn't point."

Exasperated, she said in her thick New York accent, "I can't believe you two are in the field! He's autistic! Go have him evaluated!"

With great trepidation, Kristen and I scheduled an appointment. I thought, *My mother has to be wrong.* I was stewing in fear and guilt. Then, suddenly, I seemed to implode. I had promised Kristen that we wouldn't have an autistic child. Now, in addition to my fears about Carson's future, I was anxious about Kristen's reaction. Would she hate me for causing his autism? Regardless, I would have my answer soon.

At the neurologist's office, with my heart pounding, I calmly detailed Carson's symptoms and asked, "Please tell me I'm being neurotic. Are these due to his not being able to hear for so long? Will they go away as he gets used to hearing?"

"Children who are hearing-impaired actually gesture *more* as a way to guide someone's attention. They also don't display the type of social distance that Carson does. Look at him on the floor. He's whimpering, but instead of saying, 'Mama,' or looking at you or even gesturing to you, he's looking at the floor, rocking, and flicking his ears." The doctor confirmed her (and our) suspicions. Carson was autistic.

I'm not a religious person, but I talked with God all the way home. I wasn't sad. I was *angry.* Angry at God for causing so much tragedy in the world. Angry that we had selected donors so carefully, and yet, we still had a child who would experience similar misfortunes to mine. I always wanted my kids' lives to be better than mine. Now, Carson would face many of the same hurdles.

Two in the morning came and went, and sleep was still elusive for me. I finally got up and climbed out of my bedroom window and onto our scratchy black roof, which is where I did my best thinking. The night was quiet and calm with a cool breeze, and the only sounds were the cicada bugs. I felt such despair and guilt. I wondered if I had somehow done this to him in my womb. *Where do we go from here? How can I help?* I came up with many questions, but no answers. Memories of all the people who tried to "change" me over the years flickered through my mind. When I was a child, my nana was the only one who ever accepted me the way I was. Everyone else tried to force me to be like my peers, and I just couldn't. On the one hand, I wanted Carson to feel respected and loved for who he is. On the other, I'm his mother, and he's my baby boy, and I wanted him to be "fixed" so that he can have a "normal" life and not experience emotional pain. I could see both perspectives.

Kristen and I ultimately chose to focus on the latter goal. Unlike Kristen, I struggled with this. I felt like I was being asked to choose between my own perspective as someone with autism and my "mommy perspective."

There are elements of autism in myself and others that I celebrate and enjoy. I love my unique view of the world. I can appreciate why Carson was so fascinated with the truck tires at the preschool meeting—the ridges, the pattern, the way it spun. I get it. By having such a detail-oriented mind, I can become absorbed in almost anything and it feels orgasmic. I wanted Carson to be "normal," but I didn't want him to lose himself in the process. Perhaps I was just thinking about myself. I didn't want Carson to hate or resent me for trying to change him, which was a problem I encountered growing up. Furthermore, I loved him for him and dreaded any intervention that would change him. Regardless, I would be his champion.

Ravenwood provides the therapy that Carson required, and he immediately began twenty hours per week of play-based intervention and speech therapy, which is standard protocol. However, we noticed something peculiar: every skill that he gained, he lost within a week. This was extremely unusual. No one could explain it. We went back to every "-ologist" we could think of to gather their opinions. Everyone was stumped.

Like Sherlock Holmes, I devoured textbooks from Massachusetts's medical schools, searching for answers. I scoured the internet. Traditional medicine had become a dead end; they either told me that I was crazy or said with pity, "He's autistic. You have to accept the diagnosis."

Eventually, I found a "healer" a few towns over who claimed to have expertise in autism and allergies. Dr. Krause was a bona fide MD, but was *very* strange. She even looked like a mad scientist, with frizzy salt-and-pepper hair, round spectacles, and draped clothing. Her office was disheveled. Messy piles of paper were scattered everywhere. It was hard to find a place to sit. Out of desperation, I put Carson's fate into her hands.

Still, I needed to make sure that Dr. Krause wasn't a charlatan and, more importantly, wouldn't hurt Carson. She swabbed him and ran some labs, like most doctors would. But she also performed some strange tests that involved hooking him up to probes and analyzing his hair. Watching this, I thought, *Come on! You've got to be kidding.* My scientific mind was embarrassed by the very fact of this consultation. To add some semblance of scientific discipline to the meeting, I paid Dr. Krause to also test me (no genetic relationship, but also with autism) and Amelia (genetic sibling, but no autism) as controls.

When the results came in, she sat us down, placing all three results side-by-side. Carson's and my tests appeared to trend in one direction, while Amelia's seemed to indicate something very different. I couldn't tell what it was, but I knew something wasn't right.

I inhaled Dr. Krause's every word and finally felt like we had some direction. She recommend various supplements for Carson, which I agreed to, even as I wondered, *How the hell am I going to shove these down his throat?*

As our meeting was ending, Dr. Krause pointed to Amelia and muttered, "And get that one checked out. I'm more concerned about her."

"What, what? What did you say?" I shot back.

Not even looking up from her desk, she said in her deep, cracked voice, "Time's up. Schedule another appointment."

We followed Dr. Krause's recommendations, removing even more foods, such as gluten and casein, from Carson's diet and giving him a crapload of supplements, which would have been easier to give a squirrel. Surprisingly, within a month, he started retaining all taught skills. It was the first time in almost a year and a half that we saw any real progress. My heart melted the first time he looked at me and said, "Mama." We had done the right thing. Carson was now thriving.

Frustrated with never having gotten any answers about Amelia, I scheduled a follow-up appointment with Dr. Krause, and we conversed at length about Amelia's test results. In her witch-like voice, she assured me that Amelia's labs were different than Carson's and did not indicate autism. Instead, they were indicative of a child with metabolic dysfunction. At the end of our meeting, she slowly slinked out of her chair, gestured toward the door, and handed me a tattered business card, which read, "Adam Stratton, MD."

"You'll be in good hands with him," she said.

Honestly, I was impressed and grateful that Dr. Krause admitted that Amelia's case was over her head. This actually gave her more creditability in my eyes.

Appointments with Dr. Stratton were sparse, and there was a five-month waitlist. I never liked pulling favors, but in this case, I broke my self-imposed rule. A friend in the medical field landed us an appointment in three weeks.

In the meantime, I attempted to assemble all the pieces of the puzzle. Having observed other children Amelia's age at the park and in "mommy and me" classes, I could tell that she seemed "different." I just couldn't put my finger on how. I began to create a spider's web of what was different about Amelia, drawing one "symptom" for each strand of string. There was the occasional chili-red skin. Her motor skills were quite delayed. She was tired all the time and needed to be roused, even to be fed. A small cold could knock her down for weeks or, at times, months. She had several bouts of pneumonia. There were frequent emergency department visits and a few admissions for dehydration. And now, Dr. Krause had found that she had abnormal labs, including things I'd never heard of, such as lactic acid, carnitine, and pyruvate. Unfortunately, my web didn't end up with a clear center, but at least I now had a map of symptoms that a physician could hopefully use to diagnose and then help Amelia.

Amelia was about three and a half when we arrived at Floating

Hospital for Children to see Dr. Stratton. I could feel my ankles quiver as the elevator door opened. As I pushed Amelia's stroller over the threshold, I dropped her thick medical file, which I had brought along. A nice nurse smiled and silently helped me pick up Amelia's scattered records; I'm sure she could tell that I was anxious.

Dr. Stratton's waiting room had brightly decorated walls and plenty of toys, but my anxiety overpowered the décor. All I could focus on were the scary black letters on the door that read, "Genetics and Metabolism Center."

Dr. Stratton left his white lab coat in his office and greeted Amelia and me in the waiting room with a wide, alluring smile. He had a thick head of curly blond hair and a lively personality that soon made me forget about the label on the door indicating the seriousness of our visit. He played with Amelia while asking me general questions about her life.

"She was an easy baby," I said. "She rarely cried or fussed. She's so smart, connected, flexible, warm, and cuddly! I have millions of adjectives to describe her…" But I stopped. Dr. Stratton knew of me and of Ravenwood. He knew that I was familiar with children with disabilities such as autism, but he likely had no clue what my experiences were with neurotypical kids. I explained that I was an only child, as were both of my parents, so I have no cousins. Therefore, Amelia was my first exposure to infants and toddlers without disabilities. I was out of my league.

Dr. Stratton just shook his head, contorted his face, and shifted his jaw back and forth as he studied the lab results from Dr. Krause. He was also concerned about Amelia's labs and opted to rerun some tests and add a few additional ones. My heart was pounding with fear as we discussed the pros and cons of a muscle biopsy, a very invasive test for a toddler. The results are often inconclusive, so we decided against this.

We scheduled a follow-up appointment for the next week. I shook his hand and mumbled, "Thanks." Frankly, I don't know whether I was more anxious coming or going.

The following week, I took a Valium before meeting with him. When I walked in, Dr. Stratton was wearing that "I'm going to drop a bomb on you" face. In that moment, I wished that I had never learned how to take perspective. Amelia was asleep in her stroller, tucked in with a lightweight pleated pink blanket.

He gestured for me to sit down. "The tests came back inconclusive."

Okay, I was now breathing again.

He continued, "It's clear that something is seriously wrong, but our team can't pinpoint or label exactly what that something is."

Now, I wasn't breathing anymore.

"I'm sorry I can't be more informative, but my team is uncertain what your daughter specifically has. Her symptoms and lab results most closely resemble a carnitine deficiency falling under the umbrella of what's called a mitochondrial disorder. The mitochondria's job is to generate large quantities of energy to power the body's functions..."

My eye glazed over as he continued. I couldn't believe that something was actually wrong with my baby. Even worse, my lips were quivering like Jell-O, unable to articulate my questions. All I wanted to do was drive home, pick her up in her snuggly pink blanket, and rock her.

"We did find some unmistakably clear abnormalities. Amelia's ability to sweat is impaired, which is why she flushes and likely why she becomes so dehydrated. Dress her in loose clothing, even in the winter. Let her preschool know that it's okay for her to go without a coat. Make sure she drinks plenty of fluid, and it's fine if she drinks juice. She also has a carnitine deficiency, so I'm giving you a prescription for Levocarnitine. If she's sick or you suspect she's dehydrated, come to the emergency department right away and have me paged. The staff will take you right in. She can become very sick, very quickly, so please don't delay."

I finally managed to muster one question: "Will she get better?"

"No. She will likely get worse. I'm sorry."

Feeling woozy, I picked my heart up off the floor, and we went home. For hours, I rocked Amelia in her snuggly pink blanket. I thought I would never recover.

After that, I started treating her like a disease instead of my baby. I diligently cleaned her multiple times a day to wipe away the germs. If she fell ill, the entire house was scoured with Clorox. And, I held her tight, as if each day were her last.

As the years passed, my emotions eventually eased, and I began treating her like any other child again. But it did take time.

While Amelia still has… whatever we're calling it (we still don't have a formal, official diagnosis, and we eventually gave up trying to get one), thankfully, many of her symptoms abated over the years. While the doctors told us that her symptoms would progressively worsen, we found the opposite to be the case. Now, as a teenager, she no longer uses a wheelchair, she becomes ill less often, though she still doesn't rebound well. Her energy still remains a problem, but it has gotten considerably better. She also still overheats, but she doesn't truly wilt until the temperature rises above seventy-five or so. By preschool, Amelia also developed a progressive hearing loss and now wears a hearing aide. It's unclear whether this is due to the mitochondrial disorder.

Over the years, we've worked with amazing educational teams to provide appropriate accommodations for Amelia, such as air conditioning all of her classes, having half-days when necessary, partial home tutoring when she was younger, and using an amplification system in class for her hearing. They've been thoughtful enough to consider even such small details as what to do if a fire alarm goes off on a ninety-degree day. As with Carson, Amelia's educational teams have been a life raft.

Amelia is now in high school. She has an abundance of friends and is looking forward to college. She is highly involved in all aspects of theatre and continues to be a beautiful, remarkable, sensitive, and thoughtful young woman. And yes, she's still highly verbal.

While the ultimate outcome was the same, Carson took his own different, dark, and strange path. In addition to his autism label,

Carson was eventually diagnosed with a "mood disorder."

By eighteen months, Carson developed violent mood swings that erupted out of nowhere. They lasted anywhere from fifteen minutes to hours on end and happened multiple times a day, every day. This went on for years. He was a biter–the kind that breaks the skin—starting at age two, and this continued into elementary school. He bit everyone: his parents, his teachers, his sister, the nurse at the hospital who was just walking up the stairs, etc. He also jumped out of moving cars, flipped the principal's desk, tried to leap out of a two-story window, ran away in the middle of the night during the winter without socks or shoes, trashed rooms, stripped, and would say, "I want to die." He spent hours shaking long strands of Velcro, climbing into the dishwasher to spin the arm, and rolling Thomas the Train engines repeatedly in front of his eyes. Carson's problems were becoming increasingly significant, causing us to change course. While Carson had a plethora of interventions at this point, and we knew the knowledge was in there, he wasn't accessing the skills he was being taught. This was biological.

I felt helpless. Everything I knew about education and mental health was clearly wrong, as none of the interventions were working. I couldn't reach my son. After a behavioral outburst in the community, I would run home, put on a Thomas the Train video for him, and sob in the closet so that no one could hear. Looking out of control to others would only confirm my belief that I wasn't in control. Everywhere we went, Carson was just never happy and always aggressive or dangerous to himself or others. Again, I couldn't help but wonder if my biological makeup had influenced him.

Carson was about four when, one evening, he started screaming in his bedroom. I went to see what the commotion was about.

"Carson? You okay?" I asked from outside his door. I could hear him thrashing about. "I'm going to come in, babe."

As I turned the knob, I heard him quickly slide his huge bureau behind the door so that it wouldn't open. He was in another rage, which caused his strength to intensify. Trapped in the hallway, I heard crashing and thrashing, which went on for about two hours. Then, his room finally grew still. Pressing my ear to the door, I could just make out the sound of the bureau scratching the hardwood floors as he pushed it back into place.

Slowly, I opened his door. "Honey?"

"Mommy, will you sing John Denver to me?" he mumbled in a sweet voice.

"Of course."

After a few rounds of "Rocky Mountain High," Carson's face grew serious. "Mommy, there's bad people in my head that tell me to do bad things." He was *scared*.

It was then that I knew we were in trouble.

Kristen had previously begged me to put him on conventional medication, but I had refused. Now, after several conversations with her and even more with the universe, I reluctantly agreed. A trial of an antipsychotic medication called Risperdal, which is often used for autism and mood disorders, was instrumental in helping Carson and enabling him to access interventions. It was the right thing to do.

I initially refused to put him on medication because I couldn't grapple with my own emotions. If I gave Carson an antipsychotic and it worked, that meant he had a mood disorder. And if that were the case, had I given it to him? What would it mean for him long-term? I had so many questions and worries. I couldn't reconcile my own horrible experiences with what I needed to do to help him. In my worldview, until the day he ingested his first pill, all the hospitals and doctors who treated me had been wrong. And now, I was medicating my kid. Was I medicating him to keep peace around the house? Was this to make life easier for me? For him? For all of us? Did I really require medication, as Carson did?

For the first time, I considered my own experiences from the hospital staff's perspective. Perhaps they didn't have a choice, either. While my ongoing behavioral challenges back then were nowhere near as severe as my son's, they were present and needed to be addressed. In time, I was able to acknowledge that having medication on board was a necessary evil both for my son and myself. However, the treatment I endured was not. While I continued to be apprehensive about our decision to medicate Carson, ultimately, it seemed to make him calmer and inherently happier, which is what any parent would want.

With medication and appropriate interventions, Carson has continued to thrive. Many of his symptoms have since subsided. I don't know how or why, but I do feel incredibly fortunate for this fact, especially since this is not generally the case. As with Amelia, Carson's educational teams have worked wonders with him throughout the years. He has a full load of services ranging from speech and pragmatic therapy to one-on-one aides to help with behavior, social skills, and executive functioning skills. Eventually, we were able to switch him from an antipsychotic to an antidepressant, which continues to curb his anxiety and periodic depressions. Today, Carson is a strong, handsome adolescent who avidly participates in theatre, is a black belt in karate, and has some terrific friendships. And, of course, he loves videogames. I feel incredibly fortunate to have him in my life.

Once the kids were settled with their respective issues and teams by late elementary school and were making effective progress, I felt like I could breathe again. All throughout these harrowing years, I continued to have small, muffled mood swings. I thought I had finally out-thunk my mental illness. I was wrong.

CHAPTER 13

UNSTOPPABLE EXHILARATION

IN THE SUMMER of 2012, my parents, Kristen, the kids, and I went on a cruise from Montreal, Canada, to Boston, Massachusetts. Before embarking, I could sense tiny roars of hypomania. For the past several years, this feeling had ended up as nothing more than an acceptable high, so I wasn't worried about a full-blown manic episode. Many typical hypomanic signs appeared, but nothing that alarmed me.

We stayed in Montreal for a few days before embarking on our cruise. Each morning before dawn, I sprang out of the hotel's doors with my Nikon camera to take photographs of Montreal's homeless population, who appeared sculpture-like to me. I was fascinated. I wandered through the city, believing I was shooting for *National Geographic*. I must have taken more than six hundred photos. This should have been a clue that I was beginning to lose my edge. But nothing registered as out of the ordinary.

One morning, I became obsessed with a homeless man with long, stringy, graying hair who was lying on a wooden bench in the middle of a park. His painfully worn feet had black spots, and his tattered sneakers were stationed beside him. He made an excellent subject. Being hypomanic, I didn't take his emotions into account; only my needs mattered. As he slept, I captured him at various angles without flinching.

At one point, it was aesthetically crucial to me that I also photograph his flimsy, dirt-stained sneakers, but I didn't like their placement. So, I moved them. Noticing my movement, he sat up and barked, "Don't touch my stuff!" Dumbfounded, I just stood there staring as I weighed his needs against mine. If I weren't hypomanic and my autism antenna were up, I would have respected him and left. No, actually, I wouldn't have engaged in this escapade in the first place. But I stayed, took a few more shots, and then headed back to the hotel.

Other classic signs of impending mania were present as well. I stopped sleeping, but wasn't tired during the day. My artistic drawing skills were heightened. Lying in the hotel's mushy bed was almost painful, as the extra jolt of energy causes my thoughts to race. I was thirsty for knowledge; everything in my visual field seemed important. I was still lucid, though, so instead of mania-induced galivanting around at night, I simply read. This all seemed consistent with my other recent hypomanic episodes. Nothing to worry about.

A few days later, regardless of my budding mood, we embarked, and away we went.

Onboard, sleep continued to be elusive, and my mood grew even more effervescent. My eyes opened wider as my chest expanded to feel the sunshine that reigned from within my body. I was in the "feel good" place and not markedly impaired. Not yet. When hypomanic, my social skills thrive, and I make sense. Having extra vigor promotes friendships, especially since people like to be around jovial folks. This was enormously helpful when I sat at the ship's bar with my father, swapping stories and chatting with fellow cruisers. When I'm hypomanic, my thoughts just seem to stream right out of my mouth, regardless of appropriateness. I'm simply eccentric.

I can only speak from my own experiences, but for me, hypomania is intoxicating. It's analogous to cocaine. I simply feel great; nothing can drag me down or rain on my parade. I feel so deeply and see with immense clarity. My vision literally changes, and my creative juices ooze. And, being the master of my energy, I can produce good-quality work in a short period of time. I function, and I function successfully.

However, when the "feel good" place abruptly slips away and hypomania morphs into mania, my skill level decreases considerably. Whenever this happens, I feel ever-so-slightly scared, as I know this slope is slippery and steep. Reining in my residual autism symptoms becomes difficult. While I now have a plethora of coping strategies for autism, none of them is effective at staving off mania. My sensory system becomes overloaded by my internal sensations. Trying to control my numerous racing thoughts is like herding a colony of ants. During manic episodes, I grow increasingly oblivious to how others perceive me, and my autistic symptoms become worse. Reciprocal conversations feel impossible, as I cannot even consider the other person's agenda. My body's animation grows proportionally to my mood. I can't stop moving. Once, I walked for twelve hours straight and lost five pounds that week! When I'm in the thick of an episode, I *never* want to leave. The high is just too addictive.

Aboard the ship, as the days passed, my hypomania slowly crept closer and closer to an eruption. Loitering around my mood were pint-sized delusions and hallucinations. In a brief lucid moment, I realized that I was screwed. Sitting alone in our small cabin, I yearned to call Dr. Saar, but we were in the middle of the ocean, and I hadn't spoken with her in over a decade. As I rifled through my luggage, I decided to medicate myself by taking an abundance of Valium and heaps of vitamins that I brought with me. I didn't know if this would work, but I knew that I needed to do something. Fortunately, the Valium masked my symptoms enough that, for two days, Kristen, the kids, and my parents were blissfully ignorant.

Then, *it* happened.

Off the coast of Bar Harbor, Maine, our boat became encapsulated in a mammoth hurricane in the middle of the night. The giant ship began to list to one side at a frightening angle. I sprang out of bed.

Walking was onerous, as balancing was challenging. With each step, I was thrown into the walls. Thankfully, the kids were asleep in their beds, oblivious to the situation. Anxiety coursed through me, pushing me over the bipolar edge. I was scared. My mind grew congested, and I could feel myself catapulting into mania, with an accompanying psychosis. Yet, I was also invigorated; I knew that I could solve this ship's problem. My internal engine was running fast.

"Al, get back into bed," Kristen said as I headed for the door.

"I'm off to find the captain," I calmly announced as I stepped into the hallway.

"This isn't safe. Al, come on," Kristen begged as she chased after me.

A female ship's officer wearing a crisp white outfit, with straight, pulled-back, blonde hair and a polished British accent, was stationed in the corridor not far from our room. I marched up to her and demanded to see the captain. I thought I was the first officer and could right the ship. Kristen and the officer quickly flanked me like bookends, keeping me safe. I couldn't understand most of what they were saying; it all sounded like jibber-jabber. Occasionally, I caught a sentence or two.

After realizing I was trapped, I conceded and slid down the slick wall to sit on the floor. My attention was immediately hijacked by the wooden grains on the door. I thought the people who live in the wood grains were talking to me, like they had when I was fifteen. Although they hadn't visited for decades, they were now back. These "floor people," as I called them, either spoke to me directly or served as conduits through which I could communicate with others. I realize that the word "floor" suggests that they lived in the floors, but this term actually encompasses any wooden surface.

As I continued to audibly ramble in the direction of the wooden door, Kristen begged, "Alex! Al! Please get ahold of yourself."

"God, help me. I need to see the captain. I will save the ship, my Lord," I said aloud. The floor people were telling me that they had a message from God and that it was my responsibility to save the ship.

"Alex, you can't see the captain right now. He's not free," the officer said in her proper British accent.

Didn't they understand that I had a message from God? Surely, that trumped whatever insignificant activity the captain was currently doing.

"Al, you're scaring me," Kristen said. "Come on—"

Then, mania's verbal diarrhea hit at blistering speed. "I'll save the ship. I'm dancing now. Help me. Red. Red. Red. Please help me. I see all the nuns. What does this mean? Elephant. Give me a sign..." Every thought that entered my mind flew from my mouth, regardless of whether it made sense or not.

Kristen and the officer somehow managed to get me back to our cabin, and for the next two hours, Kristen did her best to keep me grounded in reality. She repeated, "The captain is not available," over and over again in a soft, gentle voice. Eventually, though reluctantly, I accepted defeat, climbed into bed, and slept through the entire night for the first time in weeks.

When I woke, the boat had returned to an upright position, but my psychosis did not subside with it. I wasn't lucid enough to ascertain what Kristen had experienced or thought of the previous night. We never discussed it.

Exhausted and, completely unrelatedly, physically ill with the norovirus, I stayed in our cabin while my mother, Kristen, and the kids went on a shore excursion to Bar Harbor, Maine; my father was off doing his own thing on the ship. Psychotic episodes are exhausting and disorienting because the auditory and visual stimuli seem so real. I had heard the floor people talking to me. They were as real to me as Kristen.

I was relieved to have some time to myself. Not knowing if Dr. Saar would even remember me, I tried to call her once we were in port. Unfortunately, no one picked up, and there was no answering machine or forwarding number. I was disappointed. I managed to open the balcony's heavy sliding door and sat outside, watching the ocean water swirl. I felt nauseous. *Where are my kids?* I suddenly thought. Looking around, I realized that they weren't anywhere to be found.

"You threw them overboard, and they drowned," a woman's creepy voice said from behind me.

Frightened, I asked, "What? What do you mean, 'I threw them overboard'? I don't remember that!"

"Well, you did it. Go find them, you stupid ass. Horrible mother..."

I frantically searched the ship, hoping to find them. I went to the pool, the "kids' lounge," the dining room, and the dessert section, all to no avail. I even enlisted the officers' help and had them paged throughout the ship. After several hours, I returned to bed. Coincidently, they walked through the cabin's door just moments later.

By now, my psychosis was in full swing. "Whoa, *they're* my kids?" I mumbled. Doubting what I saw, I choked on my words. Immediately, I had the perverse thought, *No, they're not my kids. These are duplicates.*

I kept my distance from them, but Kristen could understand and justify this because I was physically sick. Too embarrassed to tell Kristen that I had killed our children, I buttoned my lips. However, I was *not* going to parent these duplicates! For the remainder of the trip, I longingly watched for my real kids in the ocean, but they never appeared.

Not long after Bar Harbor, we disembarked in Boston. My parents headed off to Logan Airport to fly home to Florida. I was still not thinking clearly but managed to muster up enough sanity to say a proper goodbye to them. Then, Kristen, the kids, and I headed home, which was about twenty minutes away. In my head, I could hear each minute of the ride tick past. The drive felt like it lasted a lifetime.

At this point, my children were still duplicates, and I wanted nothing to do with them. My real children had perished. In retrospect, I realize that I was so psychotic, I was incapable of connecting with my children. That distance felt so deep, cavernous, and painful that I needed to come up with an explanation for *why* I couldn't connect with them.

Being contained for that twenty-minute ride home was unbearable. My autistic and manic body felt "giggly." I needed an exercise fix. The urge to scream was nearly uncontrollable. Parts of mania is comparable to the feeling of "ants in your pants," but on steroids. My mind and body need to wiggle. At such times, anything that can keep pace with my thoughts—bike riding, race walking, listening to loud music with an extremely fast tempo, etc.—is wonderful.

As we pulled up to our house, I jumped out of the car and started walking at blistering speed. My neighbor, Debra, was out on her front lawn and asked if she could tag along. With Debra as a captive audience, my verbal diarrhea began. I spewed the whole story of the floor people, throwing Carson and Amelia overboard, and how duplicates had replaced them. I begged her to take me back to Montreal and promised we would find the kids in the ocean. At first, she was laughing, as if I were making this all up. Then, she started to realize that I wasn't kidding. She suggested that we go see Kristen. We returned to my house, and privately they had a hurried, whispered conversation that I couldn't make out.

After this, my mania swelled with continued psychotic symptoms. My children remained duplicates. I avoided them.

I started spending money. Lots of money–close to $200,000 over a three-month period. Since I was in charge of our finances, Kristen questioned all of my purchases but didn't know the monumental total. When I'm manic, I have no concept of the value of money. It doesn't even occur to me how I will pay for the items I'm buying, let alone whether I actually need them. I see something and just purchase it. It isn't about the item itself, but rather, what my brain thinks I need in that moment. I can get as high shopping at Walgreens as I can at Tiffany & Co. I experience a quick rush, and when the high is over, I need to buy again to replenish it. Eventually, I emptied our checking and savings accounts, and Amazon packages piled up against our front door daily. At one point, I took out a home equity line of credit to pay for it all.

Wanting to redo our den, I hired a contractor. The more manic

I became, the more this project snowballed and the more I spent. I just kept pulling money from various retirement accounts and writing more checks. I ran around the house with a thick black Sharpie marker, indicating where walls should come down, where windows should be expanded, where new doors should be put in, and where new rooms should be built. I was out of control. By the year's end, there wasn't a room, wall, electrical outlet, or pipe left untouched. When it was done, we had a stunning new home that far exceeded our budget.

While we all enjoyed our remodeled home, some of my other purchases were bizarre. I ordered one hundred pairs of socks online, even though I don't like or even wear socks. Under the delusion that I was a horticulturist, I bought about thirty orchids. I'm not, and they died.

My psychotic symptoms continued to grow, expanding wider and faster than I could conceal. I have an experiential and professional understanding of psychosis, but to this day, my symptoms during this time seem freakish and bizarre. Sometimes, the hallucinations were auditory. Others were visual. Auditory hallucinations, which are more common for me, ranged from hearing a faint background sound, such as a radio playing, a human voice speaking to me or simple noises such as breaking glass to a female voice screaming derogatory comments about me. My visual hallucinations were more terrifying whereas it was harder to dismiss them. Because I could physically see the visual hallucinations they challenged my sense of reality. Whereas a voice *could* be real, watching a rhinoceros charge across the room was disorienting. Objects often seemed to appear out of nowhere. The context could be innocuous, such as a cat crawling along the ground. At other times, one object morphed into another, like in Michael Jackson's music video for "Black or White" or an M.C. Escher drawing. Not only were the hallucinations challenging, but the delusions took hold as well.

Every morning in my town, the numerous cars belonging to the Veteran's Taxi Company line up outside the train station to pick up commuters. Shortly after we returned home from the cruise, the floor people started giving me messages that Veteran's Taxi had stolen my occipital lobe, the part of the brain involved in vision. While all of the taxi drivers were informants, cab number 175 was the one that had swiped it and was holding my occipital lobe hostage. For weeks, I drove around, stalking the taxi drivers, until I finally found number 175.

One day, I was riding my bike past the train station when I spotted cab number 175. In an instant, I threw down my bike, sprinted over to the cab, opened the driver's-side door, and yelled, "Stop following me and give my occipital lobe back!" The driver responded in a foreign tongue, pushed me out of the way, slammed his door shut, and quickly drove off. I tried to follow on my bike, but couldn't keep up. I rode home, saddened that I had come so close to reclaiming my occipital lobe.

I had finally lost it. While this wasn't my first experience with mania and psychosis, it *was* the first time in many years that I had such a deep, disordered episode that it was evident to Kristen. I simply couldn't conceal this one.

One night, as we lay in bed, I experienced a pinhole of lucidity. "Kris, I'm scared," I said. "Scared of how far my mind has fallen. Scared I'll never dig back out. Scared that all the progress I've made with my autism is lost. I can't even find the room, let alone 'read it.' I want our kids back, not the duplicates."

Growing weary, but still supportive, she said, "You're going to see your therapist, Tracey, tomorrow. Remember our deal: you can't get out of bed until I get up in the morning. That way, I'll know you're safe."

"Okay." I was itching to see Tracey. I was getting worse. I was scared.

Morning broke. Knowing that I desperately needed her help, but highly embarrassed and unable to conceal or reflect on just how bad my illness was, I reluctantly arrived at Tracey's office. As much as I longed to see her, I also had an inkling of what a mess I was, and I didn't want to admit how far I had fallen.

Tracey was always incredibly caring and respectful and spoke to me like a person, not just a patient. Her voice was soothing, calm, and caring, as a therapist should be. Her thin frame and wavy, shoulder-length, silver-gray hair complimented her wardrobe that was filled with blues and smoky hues. She had been my therapist for several years now and had helped me cope with my life in general. However, I had never disclosed my bipolar disorder diagnosis to her; now, it felt too late. While my mood had, at times, been boisterous (hypomanic) or low (depressed) over the past decade, the impact was always fairly minuscule. When I became hypomanic, I simply scarfed down a few Valium so that I would be acceptably presentable for my forty-five-minute session with Tracey. When depressed, I labeled my emotions as "feeling overwhelmed." This was certainly true, and it could easily be attributable to stress from my children, company, and marriage.

I don't have many memories of my meeting with Tracey on this particular day, but here's what I do remember:

I couldn't stop talking. I talked endlessly. And rapidly. My filter was gone.

The floor people in Tracey's office kept sending me cryptic messages. People were staring at me through the windows of the apartment next door. They were keeping tabs on my whereabouts. They were informants. I was terrified.

Sitting was impossible. I started to jump up and down. I couldn't stop.

At one point, Tracey interrupted this boisterous display and asked if she could leave the room for a minute. When she returned, she informed me that she had spoken with Kristen, who was coming right over. I thought I was in trouble but couldn't stop my endless train of bizarre thoughts, actions, and words. I wished that Tracey would just throw her arms around me and squeeze tightly, indicating I would be alright, but I don't think I said this aloud. At the same time, I felt invincible. This combination of mania and psychosis was terrible; I felt exultant and haunted concurrently.

When Kristen walked in, it took me a second to peel my mind away from my own thoughts. When I was finally able to recognize her, I greeted her anxiously. "Hi, Kris,"

Quietly she said, "Hi Al. How ya doing?" With terror in her eyes, she asked, "Are the floor people still here?" She looked like she didn't really want to know the answer.

"Uh-huh." I felt like my response should have been longer, but seeing Kristen in Tracey's office sent my autistic antenna up; Kristen didn't belong there. When multiple aspects of my illnesses are in play at once, it's hard to predict which symptoms I will fail to manage.

Kristen and Tracey stepped outside for a few minutes to talk. *No good will come of this,* I thought. I resumed my jumping and cease-less chatter.

When they came back in, Tracey asked, "Does she do this at home?"

"Yep. She used to a long time ago, but hasn't in years. It's started up again since we got back from Canada," Kristen said. Not only was I psychotic, but also, I was completely overstimulated.

Tracey and Kristen had clearly concocted a plan in the hallway. Now, they presented me with several options, none of which I was amenable to. Their strongest recommendation was a brief psychiatric hospitalization, which was met with, "*No! No! No!* I will *not* go!"

Tracey and I had spent countless hours reframing my thoughts and identity away from that of "a mental patient." I had almost en-tirely stopped performing the ritual of checking my keys several times a day, as mental patients' keys are locked away. If I had keys, it meant I was discharged; feeling my keys was grounding. We were finally lift-ing the veil, enabling other, more appropriate and genuine storylines to flourish. This process took years. For so long, I had felt like I wore a scarlet stamp on my forehead that read "mental patient." It had finally started to fade. Now, with their suggestion, it was sizzling again.

I felt exhilarated and high as a kite. I didn't need to be hospitalized. However, Tracey and Kristen disagreed. They thought an intervention was necessary. Kristen made it clear that returning to the house was *not* an option. Tracey's expression contorted in a distressed or disturbed way; it was hard to tell which, but her eyes were noteworthy.

She pressed, "Alex, I can't help you right now. You're not able to access therapy. You need more care than I can provide. I really think a very short hospitalization would help. It can't feel good to be in your shoes. What do you think?"

I was shocked and suddenly had nothing to say. I felt betrayed, although, in a more lucid state, I likely would have agreed with her. I was angry, like a cantankerous, crusty old man being evicted from his favorite chair. I felt trapped.

I went down verbally swinging, but I eventually went down. It took a lot of convincing and trust for me to listen and agree to their recommendations. I was petrified that I would be restrained again. Tracey had a friend who worked in the psychiatric ward at St. Frances, and she assured me that restraining rarely happens anymore. From what she saw, I did not meet the criteria that would warrant restraints. And so, reluctantly, I agreed.

I needed to pack an overnight bag, so Kristen briefly took me back to the house. She kept telling me to kiss the kids goodbye, but my kids were in the ocean, not here. These were the duplicates. Kisses were not happening.

I was "calm-ish" during the drive to the hospital, but once we hit the emergency department, all hell broke loose. Like a bomb, my zealous, manic mind began spewing venom. My heart started racing. My body coursed with frantic energy. Old memories floated to the surface. I rescinded my promise to enter this hellhole. I was not putting on a gown and being admitted! As my energy increased, I started to jump and yell. All of my symptoms were scattered about, filling the room. The nurses dashed in and discussed restraints, but Kristen warned them that my behavior would be much, much worse with them. While disruptive, I wasn't hurting anyone, so they let me be. For now.

Soon after, two mountainous men escorted me to the psychiatric ward. The unit was old, dingy, painted Pepto-Bismol pink, and smelled like an armpit. As soon as we crossed the threshold, I heard a loud *thump*. It was the door closing and locking behind me. I peed a little in fear.

My room was right next to the nurses' station, where a Josephine also sat. Peering into my assigned chamber, I sank to my knees and sobbed uncontrollably. This room was different from the others on the ward. This was a quiet room. There was a thick door with a small window, a lock on the outside, and only a bed for furnishings. My body quaked with terror.

Whimpering, I whispered continuously, "I want to talk to Tracey. I want to talk to Tracey." Finally, someone handed me my cell phone, and Tracey and I spoke for a while. She again reassured me that I would not be restrained or tortured as before. I put great stock in her words, as she was always honest and we had known each other for years. Her magic appeased me, and, while still manic, I was less flustered.

Once Kristen was escorted off the ward, though, my anxiety grew exponentially and tears streamed down my face. I did not want to remain here alone. Within minutes, I made a b-line for the door, and the staff encircled me, triggering a combative response. Predicting what would come next, I forcefully got a grip on myself and calmed my body down, but I still announced in a raised voice, "I'm leaving, God damnit! I'm signing myself out. Let me go *now*!"

The staff did not respond to my demand.

Again, I clamored to be released.

And, they made no response.

After this happened a third time, I wondered if perhaps they couldn't hear me. In a calmer tone, I stated, "I'm going home now. Please let me out."

At that, a nurse ushered me over to a table and handed me a thin piece of pink paper in triplicate. She pointed to a few paragraphs. In essence, I had been committed for at least three days because I was unable to take care of myself. After the three days, if I still wanted to leave, but the doctors disagreed with this decision, there would be a hearing. Also, while committed, I couldn't refuse medication. I read these paragraphs a few times. Then, internally, I snapped. How could I possibly sleep in a quiet room?

Being manic, I spent the night pacing the hallway, despite the sedatives the nurses pumped into my system. I knew the drill: take my meds orally or have them shot in my ass. I swallowed the pills and my anger, which only energized me further. Unable to hold my tongue, and with so much to say, I verbally blared my thoughts all night long. But I wasn't wasting time. No, I was thinking.

By morning, I was convinced that I was a lawyer and needed advice from my "senior legal partners." While I knew that my legal arguments for discharge were solid, I required the Massachusetts general law statutes and case law to back them up. In short, I needed a lawyer. Even psychotic, I knew that I wouldn't be getting out of here in three days.

I spent all day by the community room's phone (my cell phone had been confiscated), vigorously dialing countless lawyers and government agencies to defend my cause. Several attorneys and agencies actually said they would take my case pro-bono and scheduled appointments. I kept the nurses apprised of my oppression and declarations that I would soon be free of this living hell.

While awaiting a call in the community room, I saw an older woman with a worn-out number-two pencil covered in bite marks and scraps of paper. She was trying to draw. I momentarily left my post and gave her my clean, new sketchbook and a set of fresh pencils. I didn't have patience for or interest in a non-Alex-related conversation, so I just said, "Keep it." She smiled.

On day three, the three people that comprised my treatment team—a psychologist, a psychiatrist, and a social worker—met with me for less than ten minutes. I barely let them get a word in edgewise as I pummeled them with legal facts, reminders of who was representing me, and my discharge argument.

Finally, they asked me to leave the room for a few minutes so they could discuss my case. I obliged. When I returned, they informed me that I could go home. I had won!

My discharge summary read, "Patient is leaving AMA" (Against Medical Advice). As for my diagnosis, they had scribbled, "Rule out schizophrenia." All this meant was that they didn't want to commit to a diagnosis yet or needed more information, since bipolar disorder with psychosis is often confused with a form of schizophrenia. In essence, there was no conclusive diagnosis. I examined this flimsy piece of paper and smirked at the staff who had met with me for a total of twenty minutes over three days. *How could they even know anything about me?* I wondered. As a staff member guided me to the front door, I ripped up the paper, threw it on the floor, jingled my keys, and walked off the unit. I was free!

Back home, nothing had changed, except now I was on two mood stabilizers and a hefty dose of an antipsychotic medication. Before unpacking, my first course of action was to dump the pills down my kitchen's noisy garbage disposal. I wanted my exultant mood to continue to bubble. All of my manic symptoms pervaded. I felt alive, deeply alive. I was profoundly connected to the universe. It was almost mystical.

I started spending massive amounts of money again. I bought Amelia a plethora of dress-up costumes and Carson, every train on the market.

Psychosis was also in the mix, as I thought there was an evil voice coming from Amelia's walls. One morning, I purchased a rose-colored paint and muffled the voices with my paintbrush.

Like many folks, we stored a lot of stuff in our garage. Whenever I have a major manic episode, I purge. This was no different. I wanted our garage to be cleaned out and looking "just so." When Kristen wasn't home, I called 1-800-Junk-Out, who hauled everything away in their truck. I never even considered how Kristen would feel about this, since much of what was stored in our garage was hers. Now, it was all gone.

Additionally, I started making poor business decisions, such as firing people and changing policies without just cause or providing employees time to adapt. All of these decisions seemed logical to me at the time. The next day, Kristen prevented me from going to work, as I could no longer hide the magnitude of my disability. I was on an indefinite leave of absence. And I was furious about it.

Kristen wanted to alert my parents about my current mental state, but I adamantly refused.

"I don't understand why we can't call your parents," Kristen said, annoyed. "They love you, and maybe they can help."

"I told you *no!*"

"But why, Al?"

Talking about my parents had briefly shocked me into reality. "If I call them, they're going to know something is wrong, and I don't want to worry them. I've worked for years to establish trust with them. They see mental illness as a weakness and are scared of it. This would crush them. I spent a good chunk of my life institutionalized, and I'm not going back to that place. Anyway, I'm fine. F-I-N-E, *fine!*" I shrieked as I walked away.

Kristen's voice got louder and more annoyed as I left the room. "For the record, you are *not* fine. You need H-E-L-P!"

Kristen, Tracey, and I needed to come up with a "Plan B." I don't think either of them imagined I would be discharged from the hospital, even *against medical advice,* and they quickly worked together to develop a new plan. They presented me with several options, such as trying a new hospital or a partial hospital program. The final option, which I did agree to, was hiring a private duty nurse to babysit me during the day while Kristen was at work.

This intervention, in theory, should have been effective. In reality, I was completely non-compliant. I frequently rode my bike away from home, dangerously crossing intersections because I thought I could fly. I spent hours shopping on the internet. I yelled and shouted whenever I saw fit. Having a nurse around all day gave me a captive audience with whom to share all my "big ideas." At this point, I did my best thinking when in motion. When my body was busy, my brain felt a fraction more organized. I paced and ranted all day. Nonetheless, a sea wall couldn't have stopped me from engaging in these behaviors. I still thought nothing wrong. This option wasn't working. Kristen and Tracey went back to the drawing board.

In July 2012, Tracey gently introduced me to the concept of a partial hospital program (PHP). This took place at a local hospital, where I would partake in various therapies throughout the day, but could return home in the late afternoon and stay home on evenings and weekends. This made Kristen's day *slightly* less stressful, as I was contained and the hospital's level of care was excellent. I would not be skipping out to ride my bike. Tracey was instrumental in benevolently encouraging me to accept this as the best option. She gently nudged me to try a hospital facility that housed a PHP program, but she didn't shove me into it. We talked at length about what this program would mean for my self-concept, and I reluctantly agreed to give it a try.

What's the appropriate attire for a PHP? I thought while staring in my mirror as I got dressed for my first morning of the PHP. Well, as Gilda Radner famously said, "I base most of my fashion taste on what doesn't itch," so I decided that cotton shorts and a t-shirt would be fine.

Tracey and Kristen trusted me to drive myself; in retrospect, I can't believe they did. I managed to arrive at Healthbridge Medical Center (HMC) safely and slightly early as I drove through all of the red lights. I shut off my car and sat pensively in the parking lot for about twenty minutes, digesting my anxious thoughts. The more I tried to slow my racing thoughts and simply breathe, the faster they moved. I was absolutely terrified to enter the hospital's sliding glass doors. I recognized that I had escaped long-term commitment by the skin of my teeth before, so I had better be compliant now. However, I wasn't sure if I could. More importantly, crossing the threshold meant that I was admitting I had a problem. It was akin to one's first twelve-step meeting for addiction. Finally, I mustered up my courage and went inside.

After filling out the usual demographic paperwork, I met Dr. Beth Keller, the director of the PHP and my assigned psychologist. Beth was an exceptionally tall, thin middle-aged woman with wild, curly graying hair. She had an accent that was hard to place; it was clearly not from the New England or the metropolitan New York/New Jersey areas. I felt an immediate bond with Beth and sighed in relief, hopeful that she would be sympathetic.

She was. Beth was kind, smart, and perceptive, but what I admired most about her was that she didn't judge me. I lay my cards on the table, disclosing my diagnoses and symptoms. She wanted to understand not only my bipolar disorder, but also how my psychosis and autism impacted one another. This was unusual. I suspect that because I'm so "high-functioning," no one in the past even considered how my autism symptoms affected my mental illness.

We talked for a long while in that first meeting. Beth was nothing but caring and professional. She and I worked together every day for many, many months over several stays and never once did she view or treat me like a "mental patient." I could tell by the nonjudgmental way she phrased her questions. She looked at *me* and not the diagnostic labels I bore. Her allegiance was always to "Team I Did and Will Continue To Succeed." Beth made me feel calm in the same way that Tracey did. I also continued to see Tracey while partaking in the PHP, and she and Beth proved to be a formidable team.

Beth was like Tracey and unlike other doctors I've worked with over the years; she wasn't uptight and clinical. She dove into my world first so that she could eventually drag me back into hers. My world was a mess, and I needed someone to wade through the muck with me. Beth did.

Before we started any therapy, we discussed topics that felt noninvasive, such as how fast my thoughts were sprinting. I explained that therapy and her self-help books didn't help quiet my thoughts, as I found the arrangement of the letters very stimulating. All I wanted to do was count the letters in each sentence, each word. "I love letters and numbers. I'm infatuated with them," I reported. This was a residual "autism thing," and Beth asked a few questions. Eventually, she moved on to deeper, sometimes provocative questions about other aspects of my illness.

Trusting Beth, I revealed to her—as I had to Tracey—that my "private thoughts" harassed me. The Veteran's Taxi conspiracy and the messages from the floor people were front and center, as were my missing kids and the duplicates who had replaced them. She asked me about the origin of the floor people, but it was now so long ago—they had first appeared when I was fifteen and in the hospital—that many of the specifics were muddled in my memory.

In subsequent sessions, we discussed my other symptoms. I explained that trying to complete tasks when manic was very hit or miss. For example, we were going to have spaghetti and meatballs for dinner the night before. Going to the grocery store for ingredients was confounding; when I walked in, I was immediately distracted by the colorful grocery items and the patterns of the produce and boxed foods. I left with sixteen peppers, three jars of tomato sauce, and a gallon of lemonade.

Beth and I discussed how while too many peppers, lemonade, and even the Veteran's Taxi incident were not detrimental, other behaviors were.

Without warning, my more private thoughts slipped from my mouth matter-of-factly: "Did you know I can fly? I'm invincible. On my way over, I went through every red light. I have no reason to oblige. If there was a car in my way, I'd just fly over it. If I got hit, well, it wouldn't matter because I'm indestructible." My babbling continued, "You know the hospital's four-story open-air garage? This morning, I drove up to the top, got out of my car, and straddled the ledge. I can fly! I came in because it was time for our therapy and—"

"Hold it!" Beth cut me off. Speaking very slowly and deliberately, she said, "Alex, you straddled the fourth-floor garage wall that's open to the ground? You could have been killed." I could tell she was… upset? Concerned? Worried? I wasn't sure what her face was saying, but I knew I had done something wrong. "Alex, we have to talk."

"Okay, fair enough," I said, but my thoughts continued to race.

"Your greatest fear is another inpatient admission, correct?"

"Yes." I was trying to attend to her words and answer her questions, but my thoughts were exploding.

"One of my primary jobs is to keep you *out* of the hospital, but these thoughts and actions are dangerous. There's something called 'inpatient thinking' and 'outpatient thinking.' Acting like you can fly, going through red lights, and straddling the fourth-floor garage wall are all examples of inpatient thinking. Merely *contemplating* these ideas is outpatient thinking. We can discuss them and process them, but you cannot *act* on them."

I could now tell that she was upset.

Beth and I shared many daily conversations over long walks in the PHP's hallway, as walking and talking is my preferred method of therapy. While enrolled in the PHP, I was unable to partake in many group therapies, as my constellation of symptoms interfered. I couldn't sit still. My thoughts sprinted away from me. I was hallucinating, and with autism in tow, I became obsessed with things like the number of letters on the hospital pamphlets that covered the walls. There were Wi-Fi router boxes hanging from multiple ceilings throughout the hospital, and each had a P-Touch label with a unique identification number affixed to it. I was obsessed with these. These router boxes were logical and consistent, and seeing them was as satisfying as eating ice cream. "I want to see 52TL1292," I would announce to Beth, who always indulged me.

I also saw Tracey regularly and shared similar information with her. With Tracey, I focused on defragmenting my psychosis in much the same way I had deconstructed my mind with autism. For the most part, mania feels like a gift, not a burden. It's not until later, when I'm able to resume my life, that I realize the extent of the hurricane's damage.

Psychosis is different from the start. It's like a terrorist in my mind, stalking me at every turn. The resulting hallucinations and delusions, which I used to call "daymares," are classified as a thought disorder. The neuropsychological evaluation I took before returning to college captured this well: "[T]he validity scales of the MMPI [personality test] indicated that her profile was probably valid and therefore interpretable. Scale 8 was moderately to markedly elevated (T=67). Persons with similar elevations may feel alienated and remote from their environment. They tend to think somewhat idiosyncratically and may be quite creative. However, some persons with similar scores may be schizoidal...[S]he exhibited a highly unusual and idiosyncratic experience of herself and her world..."

When psychosis sweeps in, I no longer see everything as a separate entity. Everything is connected in some bizarre way. For example, the day I finally encountered cab number 175, I saw a family of rabbits on my way home. I know these rabbits were real because I took a picture of them with my iPhone. I thought they were informants, letting cab number 175 know of my whereabouts. I also saw a woman walking down the street with headphones on; I thought the taxi driver was inside her headphones, broadcasting my thoughts. These three separate stimuli—cab number 175, the rabbits, and the women with the headphones—were now part of one single storyline, regardless of how disconnected they were. The longer the psychosis lingers, the more elaborate the storyline becomes because there are more experiences to fuel the fire.

Tracey was exceptionally gifted at compassionately asking pertinent and contemplative questions, which helped me convert my thoughts to words and, ultimately, dialogue. Together, we pulled apart each component of the story until they were once again separate storylines without any commonality. The Veteran's Taxi Company, the rabbits, and the woman with headphones had nothing to do with one another. This kind of intervention is generally successful before my psychosis spins out of control. However, once my psychosis highjacks my ability to think logically and rationally, it can be difficult to fight it.

Whenever I was in a more lucid state, Tracey would remind me that the problem was not my unconventional thoughts, but rather, that my mind reacted to these thoughts as if they were real, eventually blossoming into a delusion. She stressed that it was imperative to not label or judge these thoughts, as that was a source of endless frustration for me and contributed to my low self-esteem.

I could now articulate my thoughts and worries, but they continued to expand, and the medication the PHP put me back on was not effective. In August 2012, three weeks after I entered the PHP, Beth summoned me into her office. She was not her cheerful self. And the unit's psychiatrist was there. *She definitely doesn't belong here!* I thought. *This is bad!* My anxiety immediately revved up. I wanted to get out of there. I looked around for the commitment papers I was sure were lurking, but saw none. I wasn't accessing the program—I knew that—but now, Beth bluntly pointed out that my thoughts and actions had increasingly turned toward inpatient thinking. She informed me that she had secured an inpatient bed, and they wanted me to give it a try.

"Am I committed?" I asked in terror.

"Not now, but if you don't check yourself in voluntarily, we're going to need to. Alex, your behavior is dangerous, and we want to keep you safe." I had never seen Beth look grave before, but she did now. I could tell that this was hard for her and not her first choice. But I simply wasn't making good choices or effective progress.

"Can I at least go home to get my stuff?"

"It's not safe right now. Kristen will bring your stuff later."

I had a million questions for Beth, who was nothing but patient. Above all, I wanted to know if I was going to be restrained, what types of restraints they used, whether they had a "quiet room," and if Kristen could bring my computer. Most of these questions sprang from my fears from my old institutional days.

After about thirty minutes of incessant questioning, I finally responded in a shaky, hesitant voice, "Oh-okay. I'll go inpatient."

"Good choice, Alex," Beth said empathetically as she patted my shoulder.

While the proposition of being hospitalized again scared the hell out of me, I trusted Beth. She escorted me to the unit and stayed with me until my anxiety had somewhat calmed. All the while, she reassured me that I would be well taken care of. When she stood to leave, I lunged toward her and threw my arms around her. I was still frightened. But she needed to leave. I stared at her back as she walked away down the long corridor and out through the locked door.

About ten minutes later, once my anxiety had settled a little more, I looked around. The unit was clean and modern. The common room was a large space with a television, some matching couches, tables, games, and a Josephine right outside the nurses' station. The staff were interacting with groups of patients, and no one wore a hospital gown. Some staff members were even smiling and laughing. Weird.

After enduring the humiliating body search, weight, and vitals, I was asked to stay in Josephine until my intake was completed. However, it was impossible to quell my manic energy. Surmising that demanding I sit was a lost cause, the staff let me pace and talk.

HMC was unlike any hospital I had *ever* been in. My doctors, like Beth, wanted to understand me, not just my labels. And, they never made sweeping generalizations about me because of these labels. Autism and bipolar disorder mix and play off of each other in strange ways. Of utmost importance, I was considered part of the team, treated with dignity, and was given decision-making and veto rights. I felt respected.

The next morning, Kathy, my assigned nurse, tracked me down and presented a white ribbed cup filled with water and a baby cup containing a pill. I asked her what it was, and she responded with, "Zyprexa, an antipsychotic Dr. Samuals prescribed."

I protested like a sourly child, explaining that the medication was poisoned and that I couldn't take it. This was most likely due to my autistic mind remembering the Tylenol scare of 1982. Kathy's arguments failed to sway me. I refused to take my meds.

My treatment team realized that they needed a new plan and, a few hours later, fetched Beth, sending her in as the "heavy" to convince me that the medication was not poisoned. I saw Beth coming toward me with that grave "you're going to be hospitalized" expression. I knew this wouldn't end well. I didn't connect the dots and thought I was being committed. *Quick, I need to hide!* I thought. I darted into my room.

Knocking on the door, Beth asked, "Alex, can we talk?"

"I-I g-guess so. I'm not committed, am I?"

Beth stepped into my room. "No, you're not," she said gently. "This is about medication, but if we can't come to some kind of agreement, you will be. Alex, we all want you well. Please let me help you."

Beth tried multiple arguments to get me to see that medication was my best and most viable option. Still terrified, I told her about the Tylenol scare during my childhood, my previous experiences with believing medication was poisoned, and the horrible side effects of the antipsychotics I'd taken years earlier, such as Thorazine. Eventually, Beth convinced me to agree to a medication trial of a different antipsychotic and mood stabilizer. The medication prescribed by the PHP was not working anyway. The hospital did know of my previous kidney damage from Lithium, so that was off the table.

Within a few weeks, my mania died down, the psychotic symptoms vanished, and more importantly, my kids were no longer duplicates. I was no longer agitated. I became calm. Eerily calm.

As I came down from my manic high over a period of about a month, the hospital protected me from a harsh fall. Crashing out of mania by way of medication is akin to detoxing; a visceral storm of emotions and physical sensations sweeps in, knocking me on my rear.

HMC was genuinely different from any other hospital I had been in. Tracey and the HMC staff helped me understand my delusions and gently nudge me out of them. I was never once restrained at HMC; any exasperating behavior was met with comfort and understanding. They verbally coached me through my delusions, even when I was psychotic. Being inpatient actually felt very comfortable and familiar. It's not that I enjoyed the hospital per se, but having someone else "mind the store" and look out for my best interests helped me climb back down. The staff, Beth, and Tracey also let me borrow their sanity and stability while mine was being reconstructed.

About two weeks after I came down from my high, it was discharge day. Leaving HMC, I was tanked up on medication, which eliminated my psychosis and stifled my mania. I didn't recognize my-self. I was a flat, bland me who struggled to think. Taking Zyprexa is analogous to having the worse head cold ever; it's hard to think and focus on anything but tissues. Plus, I had gained forty pounds from my medications, and my clothes no longer fit. How was this a life worth living?

Back at home, I went through all the motions with my kids, work, and normal activities, such as grocery shopping with an actual list. But I never felt like myself. I tried to be happy, but I wasn't. I wasn't depressed. I was just expressionless and bland. It was like being in purgatory. I continued to gain weight rapidly. I hated my life. I didn't even glean joy from riding my bike anymore. Work was a disaster. I couldn't think and was making poor decisions.

By January of 2013, I couldn't stand feeling so medicated any-more. I craved mania, and I considered ditching the drugs, knowing that mania's high would return. And so, I did. Slowly, I soared.

At first, joyous feelings swooped in. Exuberant energy began to course through my body. I was back! With these orgasmic emotions swirling, excitable and impulsive behavior soon followed. Ignoring my children's pleas to go to bed, I would often drag them into the kitchen, crank up the music, and have dance parties. One night in February, I cooked a full Thanksgiving dinner at two in the morning.

The mania continued to soar out of control for about a month. However, when my kids started calling me "crazy mommy," things came to a screeching halt. That was the breakthrough moment when I realized that this wasn't just about me. My "medication holiday" was affecting them, too. Action was required.

I called Beth and was readmitted to the hospital in March 2013. The next six weeks of inpatient treatment and PHP ran much like the previous admission. Re-medicated, I spent a year or so feeling damp-ened, dull, and flat. Then, I once again deep-sixed my meds.

CHAPTER 14

HANGING BY A THIN THREAD

AFTER MY LAST admission to Healthbridge Medical Center in March 2013, I staggered in and out of work for a year or so, pretending to function. I was tanked up on psychiatric medications, which made me feel slow, unimaginative, flat, and blah. I wasn't me anymore. Not just the manic me, whom I loved, but also my regular old self was gone. My brain felt like glue. Instead of having a normal thought, every word I tried to process got caught in this paste. Like the adult characters in the *Charlie Brown* cartoons, everyone's voices sounded slow and garbled. Meetings were onerous. I hated these drugs and what they did to me, but given my state without them, my family and psychiatric team thought they were essential.

Between my hospital admissions and frequent truancy, my coworkers often wondered where I was. Even when I was "back to normal," my appearance at work was irregular. Kristen had left Ravenwood to work at a public school shortly after the school opened and had little contact with Ravenwood's staff. I don't think she told them anything at all. They were in the dark. The executive directors at Ravenwood Day School were my friends, and I was deeply worried that if I were honest about my whereabouts and bipolar diagnosis, our friendships would come to an end.

Not only was my work suffering, but my family was as well. Taking care of my children required far more planning, stamina, and vibrancy than I had in my current arsenal. I wasn't participating in my family life in any meaningful way anymore, and Kristen now had another child to take care of: me. Unlike when I was manic and had no introspection, I was now astutely aware of what I was incapable of. My inability to think quickly and socialize, even with my own children, was eerily reminiscent of my earlier autism symptoms when I struggled to engage in conversations with peers. This lack of engagement now seemed menacing. With autism, I didn't possess the skills; now, I possesses the skills but couldn't access them.

Loathing the medications' effects on my life, I felt profoundly morose and helpless. Every day, I sat on my velvety red couch and sobbed.

By June of 2014, I couldn't take it anymore; I simply needed to function. My mania addiction was rumbling. *Surely*, I thought, *just one more "hit" will get me through this rough patch.* Relinquishing control, I impulsively threw my pills down the garbage disposal and took another medication holiday, relying on my mania to fix it all. It's funny: in the moments when I crave manic energy, I only remember the positive aspects, not the consequences of my behavior or the toll it takes on my loved ones. Reflection only comes in hindsight, after the high crashes and the train derails.

Each morning, I woke up expecting to bask in mania only to be disappointed.

I waited. And waited. And waited. Nothing happened. In fact, I felt worse. Depressed. Dejected. Despondent. Days turned into weeks, and weeks turned into months. The mania never returned. All there was, was this horrendous enduring sorrow. Medication holidays had generally yielded mania in the past, and I could not comprehend what had gone wrong. I turned the blame on myself. My mind bubbled with insults: *You're stupid. You're a horrible mother. You can't even run your company. You're fat…* Uncomfortable in my own body, I squirmed about my house, moving from my bed to the couch like a sloth. I had no energy and very little interaction with my kids.

As time passed, I started to think that the depression would never end. I could no longer even imagine a better time. I was hollow, unable to feel. For months, I endured dark thoughts of suicide and even wrote compelling suicide notes to my family in my journal, listing reasons why they would be better off without me.

On August 25, 2014, I reached the end of my rope. I could no longer go on like this. I got online and looked up "lethal suicide methods." I didn't want to be in pain; I just wanted to die. Multiple options flashed before my eyes. Based on my research, I found that the best methods for a lethal, suicide involved gunshots to the head or hanging.

I didn't own a gun.

That afternoon, I was sitting morosely on the couch when Kristen entered the living room and sat down beside me. "Call Beth," she commanded in a firm tone. "Al, you need help. I can't watch you get worse and worse every day. We've tried all the outpatient interventions. They're not working. You need help." Her voice and eyes were full of concern.

Tears started streaming down my face. "I can't call Beth. She'll know I failed. I'm embarrassed. I can't be hospitalized again. I can't leave the kids."

"*Call. Beth!*" Kristen demanded.

"No!" I shot back, digging in my heels.

Kristen picked up the phone and dialed. "It's ringing," she said after a moment, shoving the phone toward me.

Beth answered. My voice trembling, I managed to whisper, "Hel-l-o, Beth Keller? It's Alex…"

Kristen wouldn't leave me alone for a second. Perhaps she stumbled upon my morbid internet browsing history. Perhaps she just knew what I was thinking. Either way, she drove me right to the hospital, where I was quickly committed.

Normally, I found the admission process embarrassing, but now, the requisite humiliating body search, weight check, and vitals seemed inconsequential. Once finished, Rosa, a mental health work-er, showed me to my room. It was down a long hallway. I seemed to move in slow motion. The walls appeared to breathe. Echoes of nega-tive thoughts—mostly about how I had screwed up my life, how my kids deserved better, how I couldn't escape this illness—reverberated through my mind. Rosa put my bag down on my bed and left.

The second she was gone, I looked around the room and tried to formulate a suicide plan. I immediately took the white bed sheet, strapped it over a tall wooden doorway within my room, and tied a knot strong enough to hold my weight. With the other end, I made a noose. I inserted my head, tightened it around my neck, and prepared to jump off the wooden dresser.

I had one foot in the air when a short mental health worker with curly black hair walked in. "What jah doing there, girl? Get down!" she said in a Caribbean accent.

Not expecting anyone would come in, I was a little frightened and profoundly distressed that I had been caught. This would make it even harder to attempt such a thing again. Still, I obeyed.

She made me take the noose off my neck and give it to her. Next, she took my wrist firmly and said, "Come with me right now." I was ordered to sit on Josephine.

Josephine was confining, yet familiar, and I sat curled up there, bawling uncontrollably, for hours. There were no options left. *I can't live*, I thought. *All I've ever wanted to do is die. I'll be at HMC forever. The world would be a better place without me. I'm such a failure, I can't even commit suicide right.*

While I sat on Josephine, the nurses came by regularly to check on me. They were comforting, not angry, as I had expected. Most asked why I tried to kill myself, but I couldn't summon up the strength to explain my thoughts. My lips were limp.

Kathy, my primary nurse, explained that I was now assigned a "one-to-one." In essence, someone would be with me constantly to ensure that I was safe. This reminded me of Stonyfield Psychiatric Hospital, and I initially panicked. At Stonyfield, having a "one-to-one" meant that I was not afforded even a modicum of privacy. The door had to be kept wide open while I used the lavatory, showered, and changed clothes. This treatment had been unnecessary and completely humiliating, especially for a teenage girl. HMC was different. My door was ajar for these activities of daily living, but the staff member didn't have to keep "eyes on" during them. This provided safety without indignity. A surprising benefit was that when a storm of tears erupted, there was always a shoulder to cry on, which was comforting. I knew they cared.

Despite this wrap-around treatment plan, which lasted for the duration of my three-month admission, my depression barely budged. I slept approximately twenty hours a day. Nothing evoked pleasure. The staff tried environmental interventions, such as swaying me gently, playing board games, eating, showering, brushing my teeth, and changing my clothes. Each task seemed insurmountable. About a month into my stay, I nuzzled my chin into my armpit one day and noticed that I smelled like the inside of a man's soccer cleats. This plan was not working.

The only other option was to change my medications. The doctors tried to find the magic bullet that would help me, but my body was belligerent. They tried literally every mood stabilizer on the market, with little success. The only drug that had ever worked for me was what Gabelman prescribed in college: Lithium.

In the end, the doctors ran out of new drugs to try. They had no choice. Despite my history of kidney damage, they put me back on Lithium and monitored my kidney function closely. They also added a chaser of Depakote, another mood stabilizer, and increased my Zyprexa, an antipsychotic, to its maximum dosage. As with the highs of mania, when I experienced the lows of depression, I hallucinated. The Zyprexa, which caused the "thought glue," eradicated these symptoms within days.

Once I agreed to try Lithium again, I expected to feel better fast. But I didn't. It took time. It was painful, but each day, I gradually inched toward shedding this depression.

Whether manic or depressed, I never fully believed that I needed medication. I always assumed that I could just "out-think" my illness. Using my thoughts meant that I was in control and could direct the illness's oscillating patterns—or just pretend that I didn't have bipolar disorder at all! If taking medicine begot stability, it meant that I had an illness and was not actually in control.

During this admission, accepting that I needed medication to remain lucid was hard and took lots of cajoling. Whenever I tried to label the bipolar disorder as a character flaw, Tracey helped me find a different, more accurate, term. Eventually, I was able to discuss my bipolar disorder as something that impacted me but did not encapsulate me; I was a person with a disability, not a disabled person. Ultimately, I fully accepted my bipolar diagnosis, which also required acknowledging that I needed to not only take, but also stay on medication for life. Unlike when I was younger, my medication holidays now affected other people: my family, my employees, and my students.

In addition to the medication change, everything was different during this admission. I spoke with Tracey over the phone, but it wasn't the same as seeing her in person. I missed her. Plus, Beth worked exclusively in the outpatient PHP department, so she rarely appeared on the inpatient unit. I treasured the times we spoke, even if it was only briefly. While my unit staff remained the same, the rest of the inpatient team had changed. My psychiatrist, psychologist, and social worker–the people with power–were all different. Unlike the previous supportive and caring teams who championed my effective coping strategies, these new people did not strive to see how autism and mental illness collided. Never once did they visit my world.

Reminiscent of Stonyfield Psychiatric Hospital, I was only permitted to stay in the community room with my one-to-one. Listening to music and journaling on my computer was impossible, as I was not permitted access to electronics. When I experience mood instability, having a way to express my thoughts, no matter how unhinged, stabilizes me and enables me to tolerate them. With no other choice,

I wrote by hand, which was laborious and not nearly as effective. Mostly, I jotted down my ghastly despair, how my depression felt like a failure, and how I longed to see my children and parents.

My parents were not privy to my two prior admissions at HMC, though they had been suspicious about my long absences. Their storyline for my life was, "Our daughter is happily married and has two lovely children, a thriving school, and a beautiful home with a white picket fence." Yes, my house literally had a white picket fence! This idyllic portrait, while true, lived alongside my illness. The more ill I became, the more I clung to this half-truth version of my life. Afraid that my illness would hurt my parents and remind them of previous mental hospital incarcerations, I elected not to share.

Selfishly, I was also concerned that their involvement would diminish the success of my treatment. For years, Tracey and I had struggled to integrate my identity and get me to accept both that I had a mental illness and that I was a successful, whole person. My parents had always been so invested in my being "normal" that I couldn't risk destabilizing my concept of self for their sake. I needed to keep them in the dark.

Kristen, however, was overwhelmed and frustrated by the situation. During this admission, she contacted my parents, informed them of what was going on, and sent them a copy of my journal from the past two years, which included all of my manic, psychotic, and depressing thoughts. Recent entries included suicide notes, psychotic detailed plans, and concerns that I had injured my daughter—which was absolutely not true. My parents took the next flight up from Florida.

"Alex, your parents are here," Raymond, a tall mental health worker, announced one day in his deep voice.

It was impossible to camouflage my unkempt state. I was unrecognizable, having gained over one hundred pounds. My hair was knotted, resembling Rastafarian dreadlocks. My eyes were small slits due to a mix of crying and a medication hangover.

When the unit doors opened, I saw my parents in their serious tailored business clothes, and my heart sank.

My mother later confessed, "You looked like the walking dead. Just awful. As if you took ten thousand tranquilizers. It was obvious that you were in a bad place."

Feeling a sense of both shame and relief, I hugged them, never wanting to let go. "Hi, Mom. Hi, Dad," was all I could muster. I began to whimper.

"How are you doing?" my mother asked.

"Okay, I guess." Wiping snot from my nose with my sleeve, I asked, "How long are you going to stay for?"

"We're here to help, so however long that takes," she replied in a supportive, but also serious and somber tone.

Initially, I refused to let my parents talk with my treatment team. I was worried that my incremental acceptance of being ill would be overshadowed by my parents' need for me to be "normal." Plus, they always encouraged me to never feel sorry for myself. I can still picture my mother saying to me as a child, "I cried because I had no shoes until I saw the man who had no feet." This time, though, it was me without feet. Eventually, I realized that I needed their help and agreed to sign the release-of-information form.

This was probably one of the best decisions I made during this admission. Not only did they help with my eventual discharge planning, but they also stabilized Ravenwood. By this point, the directors of Ravenwood were furious with me. They had no idea where I was. In the fall of 2014, while I was still hospitalized, both directors quit on the same day, and Ravenwood was left with no one at the helm. Fortunately, we were able to promote Lara Quinn, a rock star employee, to an interim Chief Executive Officer position. She worked with my parents and our consultants to create a new infrastructure that got Ravenwood back on track.

Kristen was generally involved in my treatment, but during this admission, she was strangely distant. During my manic admissions, I grew accustomed to semi-weekly visits with the kids who brought commodities from the outside world, such as pizza, for the entire unit. Just like in elementary school, pizza earns one social credit in a psych ward. However, this time, I was so gravely depressed and heavily medicated that the nurses instructed Kristen to keep the kids at bay for their own wellbeing. During this eleven-week admission, I only saw them once every two weeks. I never wanted to say goodbye, and it broke my heart each time they had to leave. Kristen would pull them off me crying. I wanted to bust through the locked ward door and scoop them up. But, of course, this never happened. I didn't have the energy. Other than these scant visits, Kristen was mysteriously absent from my treatment. I often wondered why there was a change, but even before all of this, Kristen and I never talked about our emotions. Now, it felt too late to start.

A week before my scheduled discharge, Kristen requested a meeting with my team and me. She kept it short and simple: she wanted a divorce, and she had filed a restraining order to keep me away from her and the children. My heart sank. Honestly, I was fine with the divorce. We had been together for seventeen years, but our marriage had fizzled over a decade ago. The thought of not hugging my children, however, caused me a great deal of anguish.

My kids are what I live and breathe for. I love everything about them. The thought of not hearing their laughter, the sound of Carson's videogames, them bellowing from the dining room, "Mom, can you help me with my homework?" or "What's for dinner?" stabbed at my heart. I had missed these little things for the past three months. Hugging their photos gave me a reason to remain alive. And now, they were being taken from me.

After the news of the restraining order and three boxes of tissues, I put my emotions in a vessel and slept, alternating with whimpering, for days. I cried so much while holding their photographs that the pictures were covered with watermarks and ruined.

Despite Kristen's announcement, my treatment team still felt I could be discharged within the week. Perhaps my insurance had run out and they simply couldn't continue to treat me. I'll never know, though, since the reason for my discharge wasn't in my records. I was still deemed so unsafe that until the week before I required a one-to-one, I was heavily medicated, and my depression hadn't abated much. Tanked up on Lithium, Zyprexa, Valium, and Depakote, I was being discharged, ready or not.

A few days prior to my discharge, I met with Olivia, my social worker. She was matchstick-thin with an elongated neck and sported tight, curly, shoulder-length brown hair, which bounced when she walked. She looked like a five-foot-five Pez dispenser. Whenever she was on the unit, she avoided eye contact, and she always treated me like a "marginalized mental patient." Olivia would often say, "We're going to have a conversation," when she actually meant, "I'm going to talk *at* you." I hated her.

At this meeting, as soon as I walked into her office, she handed me a scrap of yellow paper with some writing on it. "Here's the name of a worker with the Department of Mental Health," she said. "We arranged a call for eleven a.m. on Tuesday. She has information about shelters—"

I interrupted her: "What? A shelter? Oh, you're mistaken. I have an excellent job and a lovely house that I just had remodeled. I'm not going to live in a shelter!"

Irritated, she shot back, "Alex, you can't go back to your house. Kristen has taken out a restraining order. You have nowhere to go."

My thinking was still fuzzy, and the ramifications of a restraining order still hadn't permeated my mind. Now, reality sank in. All I could muster was, "Oh. Yeah. Right."

There were no other options, so my parents took matters into their own hands and requested a meeting with the treatment team, which was held that afternoon. They used their hotel's computer to research long-term treatment facilities in Massachusetts. My mother found a residential facility, Exler Institute, which specialized in people with bipolar disorder. It was swanky, but unfortunately quite costly at about thirty thousand dollars a month and didn't take insurance. My parents graciously offered to pay for it. To expedite the process, my mother dropped off my psychiatric records to the admitting department and received a call the next day.

Initially, they refused to take me, claiming that my illness was just too severe. However, my mother had a hard time taking "No" for an answer, and she pressed for an in-person meeting, which they granted. At this meeting, my mother used her infinite wisdom and lawyer-esque demeanor to plead her case. She was successful. I was on the waiting list!

Unfortunately, this waiting list was long: two months long, in fact. I was being discharged in two days, with no place to go. My parents amiably offered to let me stay with them in Florida until the Exler Institute had an opening. I accepted.

Leaving for Florida was painful, but at least Kristen permitted me to say goodbye to our children. The restraining order had already expired, having been in place for just a few days. I kissed and held them tight, whispering in their ears, "We're going to be all right." Then, I said farewell for an undetermined amount of time. I wept on the plane for the entire four-and-a-half-hour trip. At one point, my mother whispered softly in my ear, "We'll fly up every three weeks and see them. I promise." I was relieved. I couldn't possibly do another long stint without seeing my babies. I didn't know how.

My stinging tears ended as I crossed the threshold of my parents' apartment and inhaled the ocean air. My parents had retired to Florida several years ago and purchased a spacious condo on the eighth floor of a building overlooking the ocean in Boca Raton. My body sank into the cushions of the couch on their terrace. I felt a calming presence as I chatted with the universe.

While there, I occasionally considered throwing myself off the balcony, as this option seemed just as lethal as a gunshot or hanging. But I knew that was "inpatient thinking," and I didn't want that. My heart hurt. Everything in my life was in chaos, and I was too medicated and didn't have the stamina to find a way out of this dark, dingy cavern. I didn't even have a map.

However, parking my ass on the terrace and drinking orange juice all day was not curative. So, my parents graciously let me borrow their friends, including Meri, who had also retired there. Together, they lent a plethora of support. I also needed a comprehensive therapeutic plan. My mother took the lead and assigned tasks to others. Through this "divide and conquer" methodology, we came up with a plan:

- "Aunt" Meri found a partial hospital program that used group dialectical behavior therapy (DBT), the same methodology as HMC. Although not originally designed for bipolar disorder, DBT is now the gold standard for the condition's treatment. I also partook in individual therapy several times a week there.
- My dad found an amazing psychiatrist, Dr. Heidi Erikson, with whom I met with weekly.
- I made arrangements to speak with Tracey once a week by phone.
- My mother ensured that I completed my daily living tasks every day, such as showering and brushing my hair.
- It was expected by all that I would eat dinner with my family every night, which imparted structure to my evenings.
- Finally, since I had gained over one hundred pounds from HMC's medication regimen, my mother outfitted me with a new wardrobe.

Dr. Erickson reminded me of Dr. Gabelman in that she was warm, kind, and caring. She struck me as very down-to-earth. She smiled a lot and had a great personality. Dr. Erickson was tall, broad-shouldered, and had light, flowing hair. Above all, I was in awe of her intelligence. To this day, I've never met a smarter psychiatrist. She had an encyclopedic knowledge of medicine and a savant-like ability to practice. During our first encounter, not only did she ask me the same psychiatric questions I had answered at HMC, but she also asked me numerous medical questions pertaining to parts of my body that I wasn't even aware existed, such as my parathyroid. Her labs were all-encompassing, confirming how one drug affected the others or other parts of my body.

Almost immediately, Dr. Erickson began to delicately lower the dosages of my medications. I slowly emerged. I started to be able to think again. Within two months, the "dopey and dazed" feeling began to slip away, as did some of the excess weight. While I voted to say *adios* to all the meds, this was not part of her agenda. We both knew the answer to my request. She did, however, recommend some alternative treatments, such as fish oil, extra Vitamin B and D, an additional alternative form of Lithium, progesterone, and other things I'd never heard of. She also cleaned out my diet and, having seen the effects this had on Carson, I was eager to try.

While I abhorred medication, Dr. Erickson's recommendations enabled the depression to slowly lift. As in the past, the Lithium prevented my mania from rushing in to take its place and annihilated my psychosis. And while I'd had kidney damage in the past, it would take another three years of being back on Lithium for it to reemerge. At that point, Lithium was a good option.

In truth, it's not medication itself that I hate; it's the insidious side effects. Everyone has different experiences with medications, but for me, Lithium causes excessive thirst and diarrhea; Depakote causes hair loss and an embarrassing tremor; and Zyprexa causes "paste-thinking," memory fog, exhaustion, weight gain, and metabolic syndrome.

Being so far away from Tracey was torturous. Back home in Massachusetts, whatever damning thoughts I had were immediately hushed when I walked into her soothing office. But now, there was no office. While phone therapy was not the same, Tracey continued to play a crucial part in my treatment, and I learned to make the most out of our teletherapy. When we did speak, just the sound of her soothing voice and her wise words of wisdom put my mind at ease. Given her consistently insightful and profound astuteness, I took her advice to heart. When I couldn't imagine that life would ever be any different, she reminded me of the other mood states I experienced and that "this too shall end."

Tracey was also paramount in enforcing coping strategies as I climbed out the cavernous depression. Over the phone, we began unwinding the taut strings of my faulty logic. Every string represented a false belief I held about myself, such as "I'm a mental patient," "I'm unlovable," and "I'm unhealable." We explored these messages' origins and what it meant to have them tacked onto me. Through it all, Tracey worked in conjunction with my treatment team, whose focus was stabilization, a return to Massachusetts, and reinstatement to my job.

While my parents and I have an exceptionally close relationship today, this was not always the case. As a child, reaching out to them was sometimes met with belittlement. Expressing deep feelings was considered a sign of weakness in my family—or at least it felt that way. For example, at my nana's funeral, I was a wreck. I was unable to cope, and tears rushed down my face. But all I can recall from that day is my father swatting my leg, saying, "Stop it! Pull yourself together!" That, coupled with my experience at Stonyfield Psychiatric Hospital, conveyed the message that I should never extend myself to ask for help or display any emotion. This resulted in me shutting off my emotions and slowly becoming incapable of asking for what I required. In the end, I had been surrounded with support from people like Kristen, Tracey, and Beth, yet I didn't feel worthy of help and therefore couldn't access it. Even now, with Tracey, I rarely voiced "need." Most of our conversations during my time in Florida were about my suicidal feelings and attempt.

My exploding manic and depressive episodes over the past few years had permitted Tracey and me to grow closer as I revealed my emotional distress with more and more honesty. This enabled us to discuss effective coping strategies that I could employ when feeling distressed. One of my all-time favorites is how Tracey taught me not to fear my thoughts, but to instead accept them. "Don't judge the thought," she said. "It's only a thought. Let the emotion ride in the backseat." I now know that reacting to my anxiety and emotions is a choice. Putting them in the backseat permits me to access them, if necessary, but they don't get to usurp the ride. For example, I was afraid of thoughts such as wanting to jump off my parents' terrace. I was worried that I'd impulsively do it. Then, I became terrified of my thoughts and did everything I could to avoid what I was fearful of. I moved inside, getting as far away from the balcony as possible. This kind of response continued until Tracey taught me her "back-seat" trick. Avoiding the stimuli only reinforces the anxiety. Therefore, I needed to put the anxiety in the "backseat" of my car and ride with it. After that, I intentionally sat on the terrace and experienced the anxiety until it subsided. It wasn't fun, but it worked.

In addition to Tracey and Dr. Erickson, I also attended a PHP. Florida's PHP was much like HMC's. There was group therapy mul-tiple times per day focusing on different skills and activities, such as cognitive behavior therapy (CBT), dialectical behavior therapy (DBT), and art therapy. CBT holds that our thoughts, feelings, beliefs, and behaviors affect each other. Therefore, identifying and changing our thoughts influences our emotions and moods. I learned that our thoughts are influenced by our core beliefs, which are like mental filters or sunglasses that dictate how we will perceive and respond to a situation. For example, my core belief might be, "I'm unlikeable." While my social skills are better now, I still often think of myself as the awkward elementary school kid I once was. If I see a friend walking down the street and she doesn't say hello, I might think, *She doesn't like me* (thought). I might feel hurt and sad (emotions). And I might avoid her in the future (behavior). The goal of CBT is to identify the distorted core belief and automatic thoughts that spring from it and then replace these with more objective and realistic thoughts such as, *She has earbuds in. Perhaps she didn't hear me.* With a more objective stance, emotions shift in a positive direction.

DBT is based upon the biosocial theory of mental illness and is a specific form of cognitive behavior therapy. DBT focuses with greater depth on helping people regulate their emotions, stabilize their inter-personal relationships, and mindfully accept their current situations. The goal is to help people accept their problems and experiences—in other words, ceasing to fight reality and simply acknowledging reality as it is—while simultaneously eliciting change in the opposite direction. Learning DBT skills is done through organized modules based on specific themes, such as mindfulness, distress tolerance, emotional regulation, and interpersonal effectiveness, all of which I learned at HMC, Florida's PHP, and later with another therapist, Dr. Rebecca Cadden. The best way I can describe DBT is through the old phrase, "You can't keep a bird from landing on your head, but you can stop it from building a nest." While I can't stop a manic episode from occurring, I can certainly not engage in behaviors that fuel it, ultimately making it worse.

When I was initially in HMC's PHP program, I was sky-high with mania and unable to access therapy. Now, however, my mind was decelerated with depression. I was primed and ready to engage.

My therapist at Florida's PHP was Dr. Melissa Ross, a gorgeous, perky forty-something who arrived at work each day with freshly styled hair, full makeup, form-fitting clothes, and high high heels, which clicked when she walked. I always knew where she was based on the sound. Her personality was boisterous; she was a breath of fresh air and a pleasure to be around. She and I worked extensively on my concept of self in relation to my disabilities. I knew what autism felt like. I knew what mania felt like. I knew what depression felt like. And I knew what being heavily medicated felt like. The great conundrum lay in how to integrate them and live authentically. Both Tracey and Melissa felt that it was degrading when I referred to myself as a "mental patient," and Melissa immediately banned this utterance from her office.

As the dosages of my medications decreased, my mood lightened just a bit. As I started feeling better, I occasionally teased Melissa, using the phrase "mental patient" over and over again just to playfully get a rise out of her. For the most part, I was just kidding, but on some deep level, I did feel like a "mental patient" again.

One day, Melissa got frustrated with me and asked, "What evidence do you have for being a mental patient?"

I started to rapidly ramble: "I'm psychotic. I hallucinate. I have delusions. I don't have keys. My social skills suck. I follow a schedule that's not my choice each day. I can't choose what I watch on TV. The couches are itchy. I'm required to take medication. I've spent years in mental hospitals."

When I paused to take a breath, Melissa jumped in and asked, "Are any of these true right now?"

I thought for a moment. "Hmm... Well, I guess not."

"Some of the things you mentioned are not even in the present. For example, you *do* have keys. And you can control what you watch on TV. Alex, you're not a mental patient anymore. You can choose to stay in that mindset, but there's a whole, wide world out there, and we'd like you to join us in it. This is an exciting time in your life. You get to recreate yourself by keeping aspects that you like, discarding the ones that aren't healthy, and accepting your illness for what it is."

Tracey and Melissa worked as a team toward the same goal. They reminded me of my capability, tenacity, and fortitude. I often heard phrases like, "What evidence do you have for such-and-such?" or "Do you think your perception is a little distorted? And in what way?" They reframed my thoughts and helped me create more rational and accurate statements that I held on to between sessions.

My emotional roots run deep. I have been dealing with autism my whole life and mental illness nearly as long. When I was younger, emotional displays generally resulted in being restrained or disbelieved at Stonyfield Psychiatric Hospital. Both responses hurt. Now, as an adult, I was terrified of letting even an ounce of emotion out for fear that I wouldn't be able to rein it back in.

About a month into my treatment, Melissa became frustrated with my lack of emoting. She jumped onto the couch next to me and metaphorically took me by the collar, declaring, "It's time to let your emotions flow."

"Yeah, right," I muttered. "They're tucked so far down, I can't even find them." In reality, I was afraid that if I experienced my emotions fully, they would never stop, and I would drown in them. Melissa tried some traditional talk therapy to get me to open up, but I refused to go down that path. "Nope. Nope. Nope," I said.

However, Melissa was persistent and wouldn't take "No" for an answer.

The next day, I was in the lobby when I heard her clicking shoes coming toward me down the hallway. She playfully grabbed my arm and tugged me into her office, where there were two cartons of eggs on her desk. "Are we cooking?" I asked, confused.

"No, we're not cooking, silly. We're getting at your anger in a different way. This is what we're going to do…" Her eyes opened wide as she explained, "I emptied the eggs and filled them with various colored paints. You and I are going to the parking lot. You're going to yell—yes, yell—what you're angry about at the top of your lungs and throw the eggs at a large canvas. The eggs will break, and you'll be left with an enormous abstract collage… and less anger!"

I thought this whole plan was ridiculous and tried to leave the room, but Melissa stopped me. After a little more convincing, I begrudgingly agreed and followed her to the parking lot.

My first throw was weak. The egg barely hit the canvas, and my "yell" was more of a controlled whisper.

Melissa rallied, cupping her hand to her ear and encouraging me, "I can't hear you. You can do better than that. Come on, Alex. You can do this!"

Each muscle in my body slowly began to tense. I felt angry. I picked up another egg. And another. With each throw, my yell grew louder and deeper until I roared.

"I hate you!" Medium blue splat…

"I hate this fucking illness!" Larger green splat…

"I hate what you've taken from me! Damn it! Damn it! Damn it!" Exploding red splat…

"I'm tired! Tired of being broken!" Colossal yellow splat…

"And I miss my kids. What did I do to them? Oh my God, what did I do to them? I damaged them. They have a crazy mother. I hurt them. I never wanted to hurt them. I love them so much. I can't live without them..." I fell to my knees, cracking the rest of the eggs by my feet, and cried. I was emotionally exhausted.

This exercise chiseled away my impenetrable fortress of emotions, enabling a few cracks of daylight to get in. I was primed to feel. Once the canvas had dried, I hung it in my closet as a reminder that I can feel anger without perverse consequences.

The wrap-around support I received in Florida was yielding positive results, as evidenced by less frequent and less intense mood cycling. The psychosis was gone. I was no longer a prisoner of my own mind.

Just as this therapeutic support started clicking into place, Exler Institute called. They had an opening. Initially, my ears perked up, but after discussing my options with my parents, I declined their offer. Their program was more intense than my piecemeal program in Florida, but what I had was working stupendously, and I was a welcome guest in my parents' home.

After six months, Dr. Erickson's medication regiment stabilized me, so I only experienced minor mood shifts. I was in good shape. I felt therapeutically intact and ready to move on with the next steps in my journey: returning home, spending time with my children, and resuming my position at Ravenwood.

CHAPTER 15

NEXT TO NORMAL

AFTER SIX MONTHS of living in a highly therapeutic environment, it was time to leave Florida and head back to Massachusetts. As I was still tanked up on medication and a little foggy, my mother accompanied me on this new journey.

From the start, she did what she does best: take the reins, organize things, and be painfully blunt. Glancing at me on the airplane, she said in a calm but firm voice, "You're going to either sink or swim. It's your choice!"

I was a little frightened. *What if I drown?* I thought.

In the course of a single weekend, my mom found a delightful apartment for me with fancy amenities. She attractively furnished it, hung pleasing pictures on the walls, stocked my fridge, and set up an office area with a desk to remind me that the goal was to return to Ravenwood Day School in some capacity. Functioning as a "real person" was the eventual expectation.

At the end of this frenzied weekend, I hugged my mother good-bye and longingly stared at her shiny black taxi as she drove off to the airport. Aloud, I whispered, "Swim, Alex. Swim..."

It wasn't easy at first.

In Florida, for twenty-six hours a week, my existence had consisted of intense, engaged, therapeutic interventions. I had been fully padded with support. Now, back in Massachusetts, the sheer number of therapeutic hours plummeted. I continued my weekly work with Tracey for forty-five minutes at a time, saw my new Massachusetts psychiatrist each week, and periodically connected with Dr. Erickson, but without the aid of the PHP and my family's reinforcement, my functioning dwindled. I was isolated. Mostly, I watched television and the ticking clock.

Judge Abber, our assigned divorce judge, felt that I was stable enough to visit with Amelia and Carson twice a week. Before every visit, I spent hours fixing myself and my apartment up, making sure everything was just so. I was afraid that if I had a hair out of place, Kristen would suspect that my mental health was wobbly and report back to the judge. I also thought that if I looked well, I would be projecting the message to my children that I was their capable mother again and that they could count on me. I wanted my newfound stability to shine through.

At this point, Carson and Amelia were in middle-to-upper elementary school. During our first few visits, they were kind of distant. While they hugged me in greeting, it felt forced and reserved. I couldn't blame them. They were cautious, as they didn't know what to expect. From my initial hospitalization at HMC to my time in Florida, I had missed almost three years of their lives, leaving them with inconsistency and bizarre memories during that period. My illness had impacted them greatly. They were old enough to know that something was wrong, but not old enough to fit the pieces together. As I reintegrated into their lives, what they needed most was time to get to know the new, appropriately medicated me.

During this period, Tracey and I addressed how my relationship with the kids would not go back to the way it was before. Instead, it would eventually blend with new memories and feelings to become something new and different.

Not only did Amelia and Carson need to experience me now, but they also needed to understand why their prior encounters with me had seen so strange. They already knew about my autism, so this would involve disclosing and explaining my bipolar disorder. I was coming clean.

About four months after I returned to Massachusetts, Amelia and Carson were visiting me when I called them into the dining room. "I want to talk to you for a few minutes," I said. My palms were sweating, and my heart was racing. "I have something important that I hoped we could discuss."

"What, Mom?" Amelia asked.

"I wanted to tell you about why I was in the hospital and in Florida. Why I acted strange sometimes, and why I'm doing so much better now." I started with a question because I didn't want to give them more information than they could appropriately handle: "Can you tell me what seems different about me? Different than other moms you know?"

Amelia hesitantly replied, "Umm... Well, they're not in the hospital all the time. Their house always stays the same. Our changes a lot." She paused for a moment, then added, "Can I tell you something else? It was really embarrassing at the summer party when you were dancing like a crazy person and made my friends move. And then, there was the time you kept telling me that I wasn't your daughter. You called us 'the duplicates.' I still don't understand that."

Carson chimed in, "And Mommy, it's kind of fun to have dance parties in the kitchen, but then, I get tired and want to go to sleep, but you won't let me. And when you pick me up from school, the music in your car is so loud, I don't want to get in. Oh yeah, and remember when I was in Ms. Wilson's class and you were walking me to class, and Ben pushed me hard into my locker, and you grabbed his shirt, and you yelled at him in front of everyone? I was really upset. All the kids teased me."

I paused to fully absorb their words and digest my emotions. After all, this was for and about them, not me. "I'm sorry that I put you in these awkward predicaments," I said. "I hope you know this was never my intention. I'm genuinely sorry, guys. Really sorry. I know I can't change the past, but I sincerely want to make it up to you. I'm going to be your stable mom from this day forward." I was holding back my tears, but proud that my kids could be honest. "I understand that I could be really fun, but it went too far. I also understand that sometimes you felt like you had to take care of me. I can assure you that you don't have to do that anymore."

I took a deep breath and continued, "I have something wrong with my brain. It's not contagious. It's not dangerous. I'm not going to die. And it's not an excuse. But if it's not treated, it makes me do weird or scary things. It's called bipolar disorder, which means that sometimes I'm really happy and others, I'm really sad. There's nothing you can do to fix it or help me. No one caused this. It's not anyone's fault. I was born this way. The only thing that works is medication. The medication makes me feel yucky, which is why I stopped taking it a few times. But if I'm going to be the best mom I can, I need to stay on the medication, and because I want to be the best mom and someone you can be proud of, I've made a commitment to do so."

Carson sweetly followed up with, "Mommy, do you like Florida or Massachusetts better?"

"I *love* Massachusetts *much* better because that's where you guys are!"

That seemed to be good enough for them.

As the months passed, I regained joint legal custody of my children and requested more visitation time. While Kristen was not initially amenable to this, we eventually came up with an arrangement that resembled a more typical divorced family. Before enacting it, though, we needed to memorialize the document in court. A week before our scheduled court date, I received word that Judge Abber died, making our agreed-upon visitation schedule null and void.

After fighting with a new, surly judge for years, I now finally have additional hours each week with my children, but it's far from a 50/50 physical custody agreement. While I love my kids, like most parents of teenagers, I'm sandwiched between friends and after-school activities. This is the way it should be, but I'm sad that I missed and continue to miss so much.

It took quite some time to rebuild my relationship with my

children, but today, I have a strong, robust bond with my kids built upon honesty, trust, stability, and diminished symptoms.

After several months of gaining confidence through successfully parenting my children and learning self-worth with Tracey, I started to dabble with the idea of going back to work. Of course, it helped that my mother kept hinting and pushing me in that direction.

One beautiful August morning, I took the plunge. Sitting in Ravenwood's parking lot, I killed the ignition and grabbed hold of my ears as my brain reverberated with, "You can't," "You won't," "Not with your diagnoses."

Taking a deep breath, I opened the car door. The summer's heat was oppressive, so I scurried across the blistering pavement. No one was expecting me. I felt like a kid on her first day of kindergarten. I had expected this to be easy. It wasn't. Having gained over one hundred pounds from the medications, I was also embarrassed to be seen. Passing reception, I flanked the long corridor's walls and made my way to my office. I encountered many staff members who greeted me pleasantly. Thankfully, no one asked about my whereabouts. I was relieved.

When I arrived at my office, I glanced at the nameplate on my door, which read "Alexandra West, Chief Executive Officer." I knew that this wasn't my title anymore, but I was going to give Ravenwood a shot anyway. Inhaling deeply, I crossed the threshold and stationed myself behind my oversized glass desk. I could feel my body calming as I stood there, rubbing my hands back and forth across the cool surface. I smiled. I was back!

Making a meaningful contribution to the students and the organization was still of paramount importance to me. However, the medication continued to interfere with my ability to think, and this, coupled with losing my hypomanic self, meant that I was not nearly as productive as I had once been. Even though I was physically back, I was uncomfortable in my own skin. I felt lost, unprepared, and ill-equipped to function at work.

Before returning, I made the decision to be open about my bipolar diagnosis. "Openness" would be part of my new normal.

On my first day, I met with Lara Quinn, the interim chief executive officer who was appointed during my absence. She ran Ravenwood brilliantly and, honestly, much better than I ever had. The staff was happier, rules were consistent, and overall satisfaction from the parents was higher. The company I built had good bones, but Lara came in and remodeled it through a business lens. She took the staff's perspectives into account and did things like adding a human resources department and other managerial positions to help the organization as a whole.

After a few weeks of hard thinking, I asked Lara to permanently retain the chief executive officer's position, as this was best for the students and staff.

Fortunately, she accepted.

As with many things in life, I was now left with more questions than answers. If Lara was the chief executive officer, then what the hell did that make me? This felt like a hugely important question.

Over many meetings, Lara and I eventually decided who would be responsible for which aspects of the company. The division of labor felt appropriate and matched our skill sets. The educational aspects of the school were running smoothly and would be handled by the principal. Lara would handle the financial and business side of things as well as overseeing the staff. I would continue to be the organization's visionary and work on various side projects, making important contributions to Ravenwood's staff and students. Ultimately, I ended up being attached to the clinicians and administration, which is where I felt I could contribute the most. The title that most suited my job was chief operating officer. This was fine with me, and I liked my new job.

In time, this stable, medicated me became the new normal and was much preferred at work and with my children. I'm now much more consistent and predictable, and people appreciate that.

Still, I was slightly uncomfortable with taking on this new role. I often thought of Beth and Melissa, who would say, "Alex, this is an opportunity to reinvent yourself."

The process of reinventing myself began with focusing on areas of strength while downplaying areas of diminished capacity. I pondered how my mental illness and autism could fit into this reinvented self, since I could no longer deny my bipolar disorder nor simply stamp a derogatory label on it. I now understood that this was not productive. These labels were a part of me. This proved to be a monumental project. Making demeaning comments is easy; labeling them neutrally somehow makes them seem more real and a part of me. But they are real, and they are a part of me.

Tracey continually reminded me that living an integrated and authentic life, neither judging nor denying my mental illness or autism, was ultimately a change for the better. I've accepted that, from time to time, I still need to lasso some bipolar symptoms that escape from the barn. And while I appear "normal" to most people, I still possess some fragments of autism. At Ravenwood, I squirm at large school-wide events, as I become overstimulated and struggle with striking up conversations. I've aced small group interactions in quiet environments, but crowds still present a challenge.

I have always accepted my autism. It feels natural, and I can live with the remnants that I have not been able to work past. Hypomania was also easy to integrate into my new self-concept. However, like a raging tiger, I fought the very idea of accepting and integrating my depression, mania, and psychosis. The trio had destroyed my life multiple times over the years, hurt my children, and nearly shattered my business. Integrating my bipolar diagnosis as a whole was challenging, because mania and psychosis are a part of that diagnosis. Accepting them also meant being vulnerable and reliant on my therapy team, as I tend to be blissfully unaware of how extreme my moods are when they strike.

To function, I needed to set up protective systems that would enable my therapy team to serve as a barometer, reflecting how I was doing. For example, it's hard for me to accurately connect the "feeling good" place of hypomania with something that may become problematic. I simply feel amazing! When I'm manic or psychotic, I never believe that the episode has become bad or overwhelming. By having my therapy team in place to help me reflect on my current mood state, interventions can take place right away, instead of when it's too late. This also helped me integrate mania and psychosis into my new normal.

Soon, I started to wonder if there were others who had mastered this challenge. The $64,000 question was, "How does someone function post-psychosis, post-mania, post-severe depression, and post-suicide attempt? How can I integrate all of this pain?"

And so, this new journey began.

Years ago, there wasn't a guide to help me find my way out of autism. So, with the help of Kristen and the trio, I created one. Bipolar disorder and autism, although very different disabilities, yielded the same process. My therapy team provided some excellent tips and suggestions for identifying different mood states, such as listing all the early warning signs—going to bed later and waking up earlier, having a hard time sitting still, having endless "brilliant" ideas, becoming irritable quickly, etc.—on chart. They also helped me emotionally process the past few years' dysfunctional memories. And yet, none of them have "lived" a bipolar life. I needed a whole-package deal, which I couldn't find. My psychiatrist recommended I turn to books.

I became a private eye, researching academic, scholarly, and mainstream internet sites, journals, and books. While the academic and scholarly knowledge was marginally useful, my psychiatrist recommended some memoirs that hit a home run. I read both Elyn Saks's *The Center Cannot Hold*, which is about a woman with schizophrenia, and Kay Redfield Jamison's *An Unquiet Mind*, which is about a woman with bipolar disorder. I could relate to both, as our experiences were quite similar. This proved to be a comfort, as I often felt alone and weird. They both inspired me to reveal my disorders publicly. *If they could without repercussions*, I thought, *why couldn't I?* Both women are highly accomplished professionals who, regardless of the illnesses that inhabit them, have succeeded. They were people I could look up to. While I was still practicing walking, these women ran. In awe, I watched their TED talks on YouTube to gain even more insight into how they did it. I felt inspired and encouraged. And, I saw that I was on the right track.

What I really sought for my bipolar disorder was an encyclopedia of interventions, like the one I had created for autism. My current arsenal was wafer-thin. The bipolar disorder strategies I had learned focused on mindfulness and coping skills for emotional regulation and distress tolerance. While these were beneficial, they weren't as useful during a psychotic flair. Not finding any such encyclopedic reference, I went ahead and created one with my therapy team's assistance. Some interventions, I learned from others; some, I invented myself. I'll detail a few of my favorite interventions below, in the hope that they might help others with bipolar disorder.

For me, the most useful intervention was not a particular skill, but rather, how I was treated by others. When I was regarded as an equal and respected member of my treatment team, therapy went well. This isn't to say that I always liked or agreed with my treatment team's plan. But, establishing a baseline of trust is essential for effective treatment.

For example, when I'm manic, I'm a lousy driver. I drive too fast, don't obey the rules of the road, and sometimes believe that my car can fly. Beth, Rebecca, and Dr. Erickson set strict boundaries, saying that I was not allowed to drive until this episode ended. They reinforced this with reminders like Post-It notes throughout my house and on my keys. This is enormously helpful when I've lost objectivity. I can usually identify when my driving skills are "off" in some way, but I sometimes struggle to see a problem with that. However, there is enough fundamental trust built into our relationship that I know they are just trying to keep me safe and out of the hospital, so I comply.

Aside from trust, the second most valuable intervention is digging deep and not shying away from hard conversations. During one major depressive episode, Rebecca and I had an in-depth conversation about my suicidality. This extended far beyond the typical questions of "Are you suicidal?" and "Do you have a plan?" No, she used a backhoe to dig into my psyche. Most psychiatric professionals would try to talk me out of my desire to commit suicide by reminding me of all the reasons I have to live. Rebecca didn't. She wasn't afraid of or uncomfortable with the topic. This may sound bizarre, but her calmness was comforting; she met me where I was. Rebecca also told me how my committing suicide would personally impact her, which profoundly affected me. I had never considered her perspective before.

Rebecca used a DBT technique called a "pros/cons list." She had me list several reasons why committing suicide was a bad idea—such as, it would have a negative lasting impact on my kids—as well as a good idea—such as, it's an easy way out. I felt heard. Rebecca then helped me see that these few positive consequences were just short-term solutions and that there were better options. Of course, we also worked together to create a safety plan that made me feel secure until the depression lifted. Asking probing questions might seem invasive, but for me, I feel safer knowing that these thoughts are outside my head and shared. Especially when I'm suicidal, the worst thing is to tiptoe around the subject. Avoiding or skimming over the topic doesn't make the emotions or desire disappear.

The same notion applies to being psychotic. Ask questions! Many questions! Most professionals whom I've encountered attempted to deny my reality ("No, Veteran's Taxi hasn't stolen your occipital lobe"), effectively ending the conversation. This just makes me feel isolated and alone. A better option is using cognitive behavior therapy methods to validate my current state by asking guided questions. This, in turn, can open the door to other, alternative realities. For example:

Therapist: "Is Veteran's Taxi stealing just your occipital lobe or other parts of you as well?"

Me: "Just my occipital lobe."

Therapist: "Can you explain more? Why would they want to take just your occipital lobe?"

Me: "Because my vision is special, and they want to steal it and harness its powers."

Therapist: "What kind of powers does your occipital lobe have?"

Me: "It makes colors brighter and edges sharper."

Therapist: "Why else might colors be brighter and sharper? When else have you noticed these sensations?"

Me: "When I'm having a manic episode. It's the only time I'm very artistic."

Therapist: "How is this impacting you?"

Me: "I'm scared all the time because Veteran's is after me…"

The perceptual distortion of colors appearing brighter and edges sharper when I'm manic is exciting and distressing, much like what I imagine an acid trip would be like. Unable to explain this rationally, I assumed that something was wrong with my occipital lobe, like it had been stolen. Through continued questioning, my therapist was able to help me see that this delusion was a way to make sense of an unusual situation.

Once I understood this, I was able to use CBT's cognitive restructuring techniques to determine what evidence supported my belief and what evidence did not support it. This opened the door to another possible reality (I'm manic, and my vision changes when I'm manic). Without another possible reality, the only one that can exist is mine. When asking these guided questions, it's vital to not collude, invalidate, or argue. Take the middle ground. When I'm psychotic and someone denies my reality, my already emotionally fragile state collapses, birthing another delusion, such as, "All the people around me are cyborgs with a collective conscious," since everyone was saying the same thing, and that thing conflicted with my reality.

Beyond these general principles, there are several specific interventions that have helped me:

Having others take perspective for me: My ability to take perspective when manic is severely compromised. Therefore, it's useful if people, such as a therapist, psychiatrist, coworker, or good friend, speak freely of their observations of me. Being abrupt, blunt, and jarring is effective. One psychiatrist I worked with never held back. Once, when I barged into her office during a manic episode, she said, "You look like a crazy person!" This bluntness was jarring, and it made me realize that I was up shit's creek.

Avoiding "inpatient thinking": I still carry Beth's stern, yet caring, voice in my head all the time. Her question, "Alex, is this inpatient or outpatient thinking?" has helped guide me over the years. Once I determine that a behavior is "inpatient thinking" (such as not paying attention to traffic rules), I can figure out if the thought requires an immediate intervention. I keep a list of both what is inpatient and outpatient thinking as well as what does and does not require intervention, so that I don't need to recreate the wheel every time I have an episode. Additionally, a list serves as a tangible reminder of what's not okay and what might lead to a hospitalization, which is a great motivator to abstain from engaging in the behavior.

Not making the problem worse or letting the symptoms fester: Once mania is unleashed, I'm like a cocaine addict savoring the high. The last thing I want to do is discuss it, as I know interventions will commence and an unpleasant crash will follow. However, in my new normal, full disclosure is expected, regardless of how uncomfortable I am. I've learned that, like cancer, if an episode lingers, it metastasizes and becomes difficult to rein in. I keep a checklist of symptoms, rate myself every day, and review this checklist in therapy each week. At the first sign of a symptom, such as decreased need for sleep, increased spending, difficulty sitting still, racing thoughts, fleeting suicidal thoughts, etc., my therapist helps me initiate interventions. Rebecca also taught me to not make the problem worse by engaging in behaviors that encourage it. She calls this "practicing mania." For example, my spending is now somewhat under control, but I can get as "high" from researching items to purchase as I do from making the purchase itself. Even "window shopping" online fuels my mania.

Not spending excessively: I managed to curb my spending by being held accountable to others, including Rebecca and my parents. Of course, this hasn't eliminated the urge to buy things, but it has cut down on the action of buying. My parents have access to my bank account and credit cards, and they monitor them regularly, noting excessive spending. I have also limited the number of credit cards I possess and lowered the maximum balance that I can spend. I try to immediately delete credit card offers that come via email, but if I'm manic and see a "Fifteen percent off when you sign up for a JJill credit card today" email, I'm not always successful. However, I immediately close the account once the episode ends. At work, large purchases must be approved by our CFO and CEO, so I'm not skirting around the system and getting "high" at work. Tracey taught me to freeze my credit cards in water when I'm manic. That way, if I want to use them, I must first wait for the ice to thaw, which buys me some time to rethink my impulsive decision. She also encouraged me to remove stored credit card numbers from online retailers. Finally, my parents have put my inheritance in a trust, so that I have enough money to live comfortably, but not spend excessively.

Curbing excessive talking: When I'm manic, telling me to stop talking is ineffective. Every racing thought needs to be verbally discharged. *Now*. Depending upon how far my mania has grown, setting agendas and boundaries can be useful. Often, setting limits, such as, "Set your timer. You have five minutes to talk, and then, it will be my turn," helps organize my brain. If I interrupt when it's not my turn to talk, reminding me of the rule is useful. Taking notes and summarizing what the other person said is also somewhat effectual. Even if I miss half of what the speaker is saying, I've attended to them and processed at least some information. The speaker also then knows what needs to be repeated.

Giving in to excessive movement: Being manic feels like I've overdosed on caffeine. My body and mind are revved up, and I can't stop moving. Please don't ask me to! I need to walk, ride my bike, go to the gym, jiggle my body, or play loud music and dance. Anything physical to discharge some of my pent-up energy is useful. It's literally painful to sit still as my body convulses.

Being creative: I can't explain why, but when I'm manic, I see and connect with the universe in a pleasant, albeit different, way. It's a deep, profound, visceral association, which I only experience in this state. I have a passion for creating a physical manifestation of this connection through art. I set myself free with sketchpads, watercolors, charcoal, markers, colored pencils, clay, chalk on the sidewalk or driveway, collage, or, my ultimate passion, photography. When I'm manic, the quality of what I produce is significantly different than when I am in a "normal" state or depressed.

Engaging with, but not acting on "big ideas": When I'm manic, I have "big ideas." Dr. Erickson always encourages me to design as many companies/products as I want on paper, even going so far as to create a business plan for them. *But,* I cannot act on them until I'm no longer manic. Then, I can reevaluate the idea. Like spending, there's something about discussing these ideas that fuels my mania; simply verbalizing them makes them feel actionable. In contrast, when I write my "big ideas" down, I discharge them from my brain, which is relaxing. I've also learned to set a limit on how many projects I can start at one time. After the mania crashes, it's helpful to have fewer pieces to pick up.

Taking action when depression descends: When depressed, the hopelessness is in the driver's seat and I feel like doing nothing. Despite many hours of sleep, I'm mentally and physically exhausted. Melissa introduced me to a DBT concept called "opposite action," which calls for doing the exact opposite of what you are feeling. For example, if I'm depressed, I need to get out of bed, take a shower, and put on clean clothes, even if I don't feel like it. Rebecca took this one step further suggesting if I'm manic, I need to stay in bed all night, even if I'm not tired. Opposite action requires trust in the process and knowing that engaging in more useful patterns of behavior will bring me closer to an emotional balance.

When depressed, I also have goal-oriented tasks set up like a checklist of what I need to accomplish that day. Simply seeing the list with items checked off gives me a sense of pride, which is good for my self-image. Sometimes, I even hang it on the wall with a gold star.

I try to get outside each day, despite wanting to crawl under the covers. This "airing," as my nana used to call it, is good for the soul. Most of the time, I show up at work, even if I don't accomplish anything there. Simply having a destination is important.

I also have lists of activities that can distract me. Some of my favorites are looking at vacation photos and pictures of my kids, reading notes that I wrote to myself to remind me that "this too shall end," and reading nice notes from students and families thanking me for the work I've done, which helps me remember why I should carry on. It's also a good idea to have a plethora of self-soothing techniques, such as snuggling under a weighted blanket, listening to music, taking hot showers, binging on Netflix, or reading a good book.

If I'm particularly stressed, one DBT technique I find extremely useful is to ask myself, "Can I solve this problem right now?" If I can't, I put it away. This helps decrease any perseveration I may have on the issue. Of course, I also repeat my positive mantra, "I can, I did, and even with my diagnoses, I'll continue to succeed."

Finally, if I'm feeling suicidal and need help, I have a great supportive therapy team to call.

Determining whether hallucinations are real: If I don't get caught up in my mania and instead work with my treatment team on medication interventions right away, I don't experience psychotic symptoms because the episode doesn't progress. However, if I let the episode fester and psychosis enters the picture, there are still successful interventions to fend off hallucinations.

For auditory hallucinations, using competing stimuli to block the sounds such as earplugs, humming, listening to music, or turning on white noise (for example, an app on my phone, a fan, or the air conditioner) can detract from the stimuli. If I think I've heard or seen something, I look around. Are other people orienting their attention to the same stimuli? If not, it's likely a hallucination. I can also ask a trusted friend or therapist if they heard or saw the stimuli, too. If I'm alone, I use my iPhone to take a picture or video of what I think I'm seeing or hearing. If the image or sound doesn't show up on the camera, I can say with conviction that it was likely a hallucination. Also, becoming familiar with my hallucinations is invaluable to identifying an episode, as they frequently reappear. For example, when I hear things like soft music, an old muffled radio show, or a familiar man's voice making derogatory comments, it's a good sign that I am experiencing a hallucination.

If all the evidence points to me hallucinating, I call my treatment team immediately. My psychiatrist can tweak my medications, which decreases the duration of the episode, and I can also receive emotional support.

Fending off delusions: For me, delusions are the most difficult symptom to treat because I trust what my mind is telling me more than I trust other people in my life. When I believe that I can control electricity, it's a deep conviction, and I become angry or frustrated when people try to convince me otherwise. Instead, it's more effective to have those around me ask questions. Lots of questions! This helps me organize my thoughts and come up with evidence both for and against my delusion. This type of intervention also has the benefit of being nonthreatening.

If the delusion is minor and inconsequential, such as feeling boisterous and making plans in my head to sell Ravenwood so that I can own the largest Whole Foods Market or quit my job and work for *National Geographic*, I ignore it. However, if I start to act on the delusion, it is a bigger problem that needs to be addressed.

I have also found it helpful for others to be incredibly blunt about my lofty self-image and ideas because, in this state, I'm fairly self-absorbed. For example, when I was talking about being a *National Geographic* photographer, Dr. Erickson, who knows that I'm not terribly outdoorsy, reminded me that I would need to carry my own heavy equipment and camp. Instead of acting on these delusions, she instructed me to keep a "fantasy/wish journal," detailing my importance.

Finally, when I was in a non-psychotic state, I wrote a list detailing my reality: "I'm divorced. I have two kids. I have one car. I work full-time at Ravenwood…" When delusional, I can compare my list to the list in my head and see that I don't, for example, have ten cars and don't work for *National Geographic*.

Now that I had a plethora of effective interventions and a relatively stable mood, I couldn't retreat to a covert life. It wasn't possible. I also had a strong desire to expand my social network. As I accepted my bipolar disorder as a part of me, it felt disingenuous to not disclose this aspect of myself to my close friends as well. However, this was harder than it seemed. First of all, how does one even disclose such a thing? How much was I willing to share? How close of a friend does one need to be to hear this information? I was stumped.

With my autism diagnosis, disclosure was easy. My first meeting with the autism support group had, over the years, spun off into other requested talks where I blabbered about my life. Soon, I was well known as an adult with autism. Additionally, when I first began working at the Little Red Schoolhouse, my whole world was consumed by people who had a connection to autism. Disclosure seemed natural. And, nowadays, due to the high prevalence, almost everyone knows someone with autism.

Disclosing my bipolar disorder, however, was considerably harder. I made index cards of all the categories of acquaintances, such as friends, parents, colleagues, random strangers, etc. On the back, I listed the benefits of disclosing my diagnosis to this category of people, what their potential reactions might be, and what the consequences might be. This is where my Theory of Mind shone!

Yet something still didn't feel quite right. The words "bipolar disorder" fell off my tongue, but explaining the scope of my symptoms, especially my psychosis, my suicide attempts, and the extent of my mania, made me recoil from the project. However, after speaking with Tracey, I realized that it wasn't necessary to unveil the extent of my disabilities. Not every symptom needed to be publicized. What I chose to tell others was my choice.

Like being gay, having both a developmental disability and a mental illness is just part of who I am. Tired of hiding and making excuses,

I practiced "coming out" with bipolar disorder on myself. Standing in front of my mirror, I recited the "canned line" I had prepared. After a few rounds, it felt innate. I decided that I would disclose to anyone with whom I had regular interactions or who had an important impact on my life.

The first person I told whom I didn't know well was my new hairdresser. I knew the protocol of social interactions in the hair solon: after discussing your hair, talk about your life. Well, my life involved bipolar disorder. This stylist seemed nice enough and a good, low-risk person. Still, my heart was pounding in my chest, so I decided to start with a less provocative topic. When it was time to talk, I started the conversation with "my ex-wife." My gayness was now on the scene. She didn't miss a beat. She asked a few follow-up questions and used the pronouns "her" and "she" when referring to my ex-wife, so I thought I was okay.

I soon decided to move on to my next topic. I casually threw out there, "My psychiatrist is changing my meds, and I'm feeling a little funky. I have bipolar disorder, and it's hard to treat."

With her gorgeous thin frame, blonde bombshell hair, and effervescent personality, she continued working on my hair as she quickly jumped in, "Bipolar disorder? Oh, I totally understand. I have depression and anxiety. I'm on three medications. My sister has bipolar, too. We all think my uncle on my father's side had bipolar. He killed himself. What a shame." She turned me around to face the mirror and said, "Well, how do you like it?"

"Fabulous!" Honestly, I wasn't sure whether I was referring to my hair or the conversation. Either way, I was relieved at how easy it had been, certainly easier than I had anticipated. Plus, I was surprised to realize that others outside of mental institutions struggled with mental health challenges and still functioned.

It's not that I minded people knowing I was graced with bipolar disorder, per se. I was just afraid that they would judge me. I had put too much effort into creating my new normal to risk it toppling. However, after a great deal of contemplation, I decided that keeping this detail a secret would only do me harm. So, I ripped off the Band-Aid.

When disclosing my diagnosis, I often appeared to be calm and collected, but inside, I was quaking and thinking, *Please don't flinch. Please don't flinch…*

When I first started telling my colleagues, I would abruptly say things like, "It's good to be back from the hospital, where I dealt with my bipolar disorder…" For the most part, I was pleasantly surprised by the lack of reaction. Some people asked follow-up questions, whereas others glossed over it or averted their gaze. Both felt unsettling. However, a close colleague confided that she, too, had bipolar disorder. We were Lithium cousins! As with my hairdresser, I was relieved to know that people outside of a hospital setting struggled with mental health issues, too. Overall, it was remarkable how much the school staff cared.

Having opportunities to practice, disclosing my bipolar disorder grew easier with time. Disclosing my diagnosis made it real and something that I couldn't retract. This has been beneficial to my continued wellbeing, as broadcasting my disabilities thickens and supports the storyline that I am well and thriving, despite my disabilities.

Within two years of my starting back at work, I knew that it was time to branch out even further. My divorce was now many years in the past, and I had integrated my new normal into my self-concept. Lara was thriving as Ravenwood's CEO, and I had a purpose. Occasionally interacting with my friends and attending a bipolar support group on a semi-regular basis provided some social interaction. I was ready for the next step: dating. This was challenging. I would clearly be bringing my new normal to the table, but I didn't have an index card for a first date.

Dating is extraordinarily difficult under the best of circumstances and without a disability, but I opted to put my best new self out there anyway. I just woke up one day and decided that I didn't want to be alone for the rest of my life.

Fortunately, Match.com has a reputable LGBTQ+ section. After some time, I connected with a woman about my age named Katie, who also had two children. She was slender, with beautiful auburn hair cut in a bob. We went to dinner at my favorite Italian restaurant, but the chitchat was sparse. My hands were noticeably trembling from the Depakote and Lithium, and I kept spilling fettuccini and red sauce on my crisp white button-down shirt. She probably thought I was exceptionally nervous. It was clear that she was uncomfortable, as she kept averting her gaze and glancing at her watch. I raised the white flag and asked for the check. Later, I asked her on a second date, but she declined.

A few weeks later, I landed a date with another woman, Charlotte, who carried the same girth as me, so I wasn't too self-conscious about my looks. Her personality was boisterous and robust, just like my ex-wife's. She took charge of the conversation with pleasure, so I immediately thought that this might go well. I also wore a dark-gray turtleneck and jeans to hide any accidental spills and knew not to order a meal with red sauce. Charlotte had no children of her own, but told me about her fantastic relationship with her loving family back in Iowa. It sounded utopic.

"So, tell me about *your* family," she eventually said.

"Well, I have two amazing kids," I began. Suddenly, I froze. My mind was stuck. I started panicking about possibly needing to disclose *why* I was divorced, which would lead to my bipolar diagnosis and I knew this was not first date material!

She didn't seem to notice my nerve. "Do you and your ex-wife share physical custody?"

I started squirming. I knew where this was going. *Fuck,* I thought. *How do I answer this? I need more index cards…* Aloud, I said quietly, "No, she has full physical custody." I mentally cheered myself on and reminded myself to smile. "But I get to see them for eleven hours a week."

"Eleven hours? Wow. How did you get such a lousy deal?"

My brow was sweating. *Pull up! Pull up! How do I answer this?* The full, honest answer was that I had been out of my ever-loving mind and thought the floor people were hurting them. But I couldn't possibly say that. There was an awkward silence, and I quickly scrambled for a "normal" answer. "I had a lousy divorce attorney," I sighed, making a disappointed face.

Next came the questions about growing up. I was starting to feel like this date would never end. Charlotte's family lived about fifty miles outside of Des Moines on a farm. Hearing her stories of racing her three brothers on her family's trackers and having some kind of competitions involving hay, my attention started to fade. She and her mother made cookies from scratch every Friday for their entire extended family. Her dad was home by five p.m. every night for dinner. *You've got to be kidding me,* I thought. While it sounded idyllic, this New York City girl simply doesn't know anything about farm life. And frankly, farm odors offend my autism. They're too pungent. My cookies came from the frozen section of the grocery store. My mother and I sliced and baked about half of them, then ate the rest of the cold cookie dough. This was considered "homemade" in our house!

"You must have had a million friends growing up in New York," Charlotte continued.

What's with all these questions? And what the hell do I say? That I had autism and my peers hated me? That my first hallucinations started at age ten? I managed to cobble together an answer: "I was kind of busy. I always had a project, and I was on my own a lot. New York City had its advantages and disadvantages." *Keep it vague, Alex, and change the subject!* "So, what do you like to do in your free time?"

"I *love* sunbathing at the beach," Charlotte enthused.

Gross. I hate the feeling of wet sand between my toes.

"Hanging out with friends," she added.

I can only tolerate so much of even my dearest friends.

"And drinking beer at local taverns," she finished.

Yuck. Bars were too overstimulating.

"What about you?" she asked.

"Oh, mostly seeing my kids, photography, and art museums."

We both soon realized that we were not a good match, we

finished our meal, and the date finally came to an end.

I had a few other dates after that, but I eventually decided to take a break from dating. I wasn't giving up, but I needed to step back for a while to shore up my "new normal" so that questions like Charlotte's wouldn't faze me so much.

Thickening the storyline of my "new normal" life involved reinventing myself. With each member of my therapeutic team, whom I came to dub the "Coast Guard," I sat on their couches and worked through who I was and who I could be. Just like with this book, I could choose what storylines to put in the foreground and what I could leave to hover behind the scenes.

I started with a blank slate, strengthened the storylines that were true, and discarded what I could do without. I threw away thoughts such as, "I'm crazy, a mental patient, intellectually impaired, and will never amount to anything." Obviously, "You can't," "You won't," and "Not with your diagnosis" went in the trash can. I wanted to toss out my depression as well, but Tracey reminded me that it was a piece of who I was, so I kept it...albeit reluctantly. I had no problem keeping my mania, but Beth reminded me that I only had a small suitcase; there was only room for *slight* hypomania. I so desperately wanted to ditch the psychosis, but Tracey helped reframe it so that, while psychosis was a part of my history, there was no need to thicken that storyline. It happened. Period. Now, in my "new normal," psychosis is more gentle, subdued, kinder, and forgiving. Finally, Tracey taught me that my thoughts are just that: thoughts, not truths. Just because I think it doesn't mean I need to believe it.

These talented therapists helped me organize my information into three categories: what I like and want to keep; factual, but not judgmental, characteristics of my illnesses; and things I'd like to discard. When I had completed this work, I had a "new normal." It wasn't what I wanted, but I could live with it. We decided that I was an achiever, ambitious, entrepreneurial, balanced (new), compassionate, consistent (new), even-keeled (new), imaginative, introspective, experienced mood swings, consistently patient, pleasant (now consistent), quirky, and self-reliant. The new normal that emerged was pretty okay!

Today, I have wonderful, caring parents, amazing kids, a dynamic therapy team, a few great friends, stupendous colleagues, and fond memories of working with Beth and Melissa. I'm incredibly fortunate, as I'm acutely aware that this might not have been the outcome. I live in my "new normal" with my feet on the ground and my baby toe in the air. While I miss the mania, I kind of like it here! Going forward, I know that nothing's off the table.

For years, I thought that if I hid my mental illness, people would respect me. On the contrary, what I found is that people respect me more when I'm real. As Jane Wagner once said, "See, the human mind is kind of like...a piñata. When it breaks open, there's a lot of surprises inside. Once you get the piñata's perspective, you see that losing your mind can be a peak experience."

I have found acceptance.

Lightning Source UK Ltd.
Milton Keynes UK
UKHW050319060822
406904UK00006B/205

9 781977 230775